MALE VOICES ON WOMEN'S RIGHTS

Manchester University Press

Male voices on women's rights

An anthology of nineteenth-century British texts

Edited by
Martine Monacelli

Manchester University Press

Editorial matter copyright © Martine Monacelli 2017
All other matter copyright © as acknowledged

The right of Martine Monacelli to be identified as the author of this work has been asserted by her in accordance with the Copyright, Designs and Patents Act 1988.

Published by Manchester University Press
Altrincham Street, Manchester M1 7JA
www.manchesteruniversitypress.co.uk

British Library Cataloguing-in-Publication Data
A catalogue record for this book is available from the British Library

ISBN 978 1 7849 9277 4 *paperback*

First published 2017

The publisher has no responsibility for the persistence or accuracy of URLs for any external or third-party internet websites referred to in this book, and does not guarantee that any content on such websites is, or will remain, accurate or appropriate.

Typeset in Baskerville by
Koinonia, Manchester
Printed and Bound in Great Britain by
TJ International Ltd, Padstow

To Germain,
for his invaluable support of my endeavours

Contents

List of figures	*page* ix
Preface	xi
Acknowledgements	xvii
Introduction	1

I Comrades in struggle — 44
1. 'Arouse! Awake! Rescue your sex' (William Thompson, 1825) — 44
2. 'Throw off the degrading yoke' (R. J. Richardson, 1840) — 48
3. The root causes of women's subjection (J. S. Mill, 1869) — 52
4. Against the sexual double standard (W. T. Stead, 1885) — 55
5. 'A thousand-times-told tale' (Edward Aveling and Eleanor Marx Aveling, 1886) — 60
6. The time is come to act (George Holyoake, 1892) — 64
7. 'Woman ... cast aside the chains' (R. P. Downes, 1900) — 69
8. Banding together in the fight for human liberty (Dr W. Moore Ede, 1912) — 74
9. What is feminism? (W. L. George, 1913) — 77

II Provisions to be made for the education of women — 83
1. The cultivation of a woman's understanding (The Rev. Sydney Smith, 1809) — 83
2. What is learnt from teaching girls (The Rev. F. D. Maurice, 1865) — 88
3. 'The highest aim of any true system of education' (W. Cooke Taylor, 1868) — 92
4. A system of public education for girls (Charles Kingsley, 1869) — 96
5. 'They will not be unsexed by education' (Alexander Grant, 1872) — 100

6	Admission of women to university degrees (William Forsyth, 1875)	104
7	Progress in the cause of women's higher education (The Rev. J. L. Davies, 1879)	107
8	Are women's brains inferior to men's? (D. G. Ritchie, 1889)	111
9	'The moral benefits of co-education' (The Rev. Cecil Grant, 1908)	115

III The vindication of women's civil rights — 119

1	A proposal to make marriage a civil contract (W. B. Adams, 1833)	119
2	'Talents merely to fold in a napkin?' (W. J. Fox, 1833)	122
3	A law to protect married women's property (Lord Brougham, 1857)	126
4	'The remnant of an old barbarous law' (Arthur Hobhouse, 1870)	130
5	A question of justice (Henry Fawcett, 1873)	135
6	A eugenicist point of view on the marriage question (Karl Pearson, 1885)	138
7	'A sanatorium with female attendants' (Henry W. Nevinson, 1909)	143
8	'Why I went to prison' (Victor D. Duval, 1910)	147
9	Women's share in the Co-operative movement (Joseph Clayton, 1912)	150

IV Towards a new sexual culture — 155

1	'The most important discovery made upon mankind' (Richard Carlile, 1826)	155
2	A man's devotion to his children (William Cobbett, 1829)	160
3	United only by nature's laws (Robert Owen, 1844)	165
4	'The return of powerful sexual feelings' (G. R. Drysdale, 1855)	169
5	A father's role in the education of his children (J. R. Seeley, 1870)	173
6	A Malthusian view of married life (Montague Cookson, 1872)	177
7	'A new code of manners between the sexes' (Edward Carpenter, 1896)	181
8	A new age about to commence (The Rev. Frederick A. M. Spencer, 1912)	185
9	'A new avatar of love' (Havelock Ellis, 1912)	189

References	194
Index	198

List of figures

1 George Jacob Holyoake after A. E. Praill, photogravure, 1903, given by Mrs Holyoake-Marsh, 1928, Photographs Collection, NPG x18573 © National Portrait Gallery, London *page* 65
2 Walter Lionel George by Henry Walter ('H. Walter') Barnett, vintage bromide print, 1910–1920, NPG x45280 © National Portrait Gallery, London 78
3 Sydney Smith by Samuel Freeman, published by T. Cadell & W. Davies, after John Wright, stipple engraving, published 4 February 1817, given by the daughter of compiler William Fleming MD, Mary Elizabeth Stopford (née Fleming), 1931, Reference Collection, NPG D7661 © National Portrait Gallery, London 84
4 Arthur Hobhouse, Baron Hobhouse by Fradelle & Young, platinum print, circa 1885, given by Lady Clay, 1957, Photographs Collection, NPG x15579 © National Portrait Gallery, London 131
5 Richard Carlile after unknown artist, lithograph, 1825 or after, purchased with help from the Friends of the National Libraries and the Pilgrim Trust, 1966, Reference Collection, NPG D8083 © National Portrait Gallery, London 156

All images reproduced under CC BY-NC-ND 3.0.

Preface

Over the years feminist scholarly studies have increasingly moved beyond women's history *per se*, but comparatively few, since Sylvia Strauss's groundbreaking work (1982), have focused on men's activism in the emancipation movement.[1] Kathryn Gleadle's seminal analysis of Unitarian milieux (1995) marked a turn in the historiography when she brought to light an early feminist tradition grown 'out of the male world of radical politics' (Gleadle, 1995: 174). But following John and Eustance's appraisal of male support for women's suffrage (1997), and perhaps because of its adverse evaluation,[2] critical interest in the subject abated again. It was revived in 2010 by two monographs, one uncovering the rich intellectual contributions of eighteenth-century radicals to the making of modern feminism (Chernock, 2010), the other investigating the lives and campaigns of ten nineteenth-century pioneers of women's rights (Monacelli and Prum, eds, 2010). Laura Schwartz's uncovering of Freethought as a fundamental feminist current in 2013, and Ben Griffin's exposure of the roots of women's movement in liberal political culture in 2014, have made further demonstration that it is difficult 'to establish clear boundaries between a distinctive tradition of "feminism" and other political traditions' (Griffin, 2014: 318). This collection of writings provides fresh historical evidence that the engagement of both sexes in the struggle for emancipation was far more fundamentally collaborative than generally acknowledged, and is therefore a contribution to the ongoing reconsideration of British men's roles in the architecture of feminism.

1 Perhaps because of the danger that studies of men and masculinities might subsume women within a dominant male frame of reference (John and Eustance, eds, 1997: 2).
2 Male support was judged ancillary, embarrassing, even of questionable value, as suggested by John and Eustance's title *The Men's Share?*

In the feminist Pantheon John Stuart Mill and William Thompson have always featured high, somewhat screening the constellation of progressive literati, scholars, men of thought, letters and action, gravitating around overlapping and intertwined political circles (Owenites, Christian Socialists, Freethinkers, etc.), who also promoted – in some cases pioneered – women's rights. Their pronouncements, publicized in Parliamentary debates, lectures, autobiographies, newspapers, essays, sermons, pamphlets, and seminal books, amalgamated into a lively public forum for interrogating anew, or discussing novel, gender relations. It is the purpose of this book to allow the voices of other 'champions of the fair sex' to be heard again, thanks to a selection of their writings.[3]

My primary concern has been to offer a wide array of meaningful, self-contained passages, developing a clear argument. All extracts are therefore unabridged, and no two are written by the same author. The brief presentation of each writer is intended to make the text easily exploitable by all, but also to whet the reader's appetite for the man's oeuvre. The texts have been classified into thematic and chronologically progressive chapters, dealing with major aspects of women's rights, and containing, for the sake of balance, nine authors each. Chapter I presents a cross-section of male activists who took up arms with women against their subjection. Chapter II charts educational reformers who prized the female intellect and supported its development. Chapter III looks at a range of exponents of women's civil rights and at the rationale behind their arguments. Chapter IV highlights a variety of advanced intellectuals[4] whose challenge of gender roles paved the way for modern sexual culture. Whether visionaries of a new age, mouthpieces of a major movement, or more obscure figures, all these men were progressivists, but they were divided by individual commitments, professions, beliefs and multiple confessional identities; the chorus of voices is therefore neither uniform nor unanimous. The justification for linking together such a motley crowd of individuals comes from their common concern with, and perspectives on, the social position of women. Personal differences in viewpoints, paradoxically, fade into insignificance compared to the consistent spectrum of ideals (even if sometimes more abstract than practical) that emerges from their writings, and points to a collective force at play in the nineteenth-century redefinition of gender norms.

---

3 First editions have been traced, original spellings and punctuation kept.
4 The word 'intellectual' is used here in its modern sense; it was not widespread in Victorian England.

Besides being recuperative, giving scholars and general readers access to some rare, neglected, or forgotten documents, this text collection is designed to provide a platform for revising common assumptions, or misconceptions, regarding the nature, depth, and extent of men's support for women's rights. It allows the exploration of the 'complex web of intertwined male identities' (Griffin, 2014: 163) which shaped a movement ultimately 'concerned with describing, explaining and changing the behavior of men' (*Ibid.*: 8). From Thompson's *Appeal* to Ellis's *Task of Social Hygiene*, radical and conservative stances co-exist, sometimes conflicting within the same opus, and 'feminist' commitments remained limited by deep-seated anxieties, and/or a desire to retain male authority.⁵ The emotional tensions created by shifting gender norms are particularly visible in the writings of ambivalent or controversial 'feminists'. Positioning oneself as a 'feminist' (a word originally coined by doctors to designate the presence of feminine characteristics in males) was problematic for both sexes,⁶ and men who did were unsurprisingly lambasted for their lack of virility and worth.⁷ Prior to 1894, the term 'feminism' itself is of course anachronistic. The existence of an ideology promoting the same rights and opportunities for both sexes however justifies its use, as does the fact that men who had a cogent awareness of women's vassalage to men, and a desire to put paid to it, often *dared* to describe themselves as such.⁸ The playwright Laurence

5 On narratives of manhood and fatherhood in the nineteenth century see Stefan Collini (1991), John Tosh (2005), Matthew McCormack (2007), T. L. Broughton and Helen Rogers (2007), or Julie-Marie Strange (2015).
6 It was not uncommon for female activists in the 1880s to reject the appellation, particularly after 1903, in order to dissociate themselves from the suffragettes.
7 The anti-suffragist Eliza Lynn Linton for instance depicted them as 'effeminate worshippers who wrap themselves round in the trailing skirts of the idol and shout for her rights, because they are not virile enough to respect their own', 'The Wild Women as Politicians', *Nineteenth Century*, 30 (1891), 83. The libel pushed some men to pose as Antis (Griffin, 2014: chap. 6), and should alert the historian to (possible) differences between public rhetoric and private motivations (Skinner, 1969). Similarly, the display of male emotion, praised a century before as a sign of enlightened manliness (Chernock, 2010), was no longer congruent in the nineteenth century with the rigorous standards of male conduct. See Cobbett's concern about signs of effeminacy [IV, 2]. Bracketed numbers refer to documents in the anthology.
8 In contradiction with their biological sex – if one subscribes to the argument that this makes it impossible for men to be called feminists (Kimmel and Murphy, 2004).

Housman prided himself on having 'become a feminist and a suffragist long before the day of battle actually arrived'.[9] Yet, neither men nor women ever formed a monolithic block for or against women, and the fact that the term was used indiscriminately to cover several distinct (or narrow) aspirations (suffrage, education, marriage laws, custody rights, labour rights, etc.)[10] renders the concept inadequate for analysing gender politics in the nineteenth century. Scholars have thus warned historians against 'overprivileging this particular identity merely because it has tended to be cast as a powerful, overarching political commitment by late-twentieth-century historians. "Feminist" writers, then, might have used a variety of different perspectives to understand cultural and political questions of gender because "feminism" was largely a "black box term", a placeholder for a space in which all sorts of discourses might operate to give content' (Delap, 2005: 384). Fluctuating national discourses,[11] dictated by social, economic, and political imperatives, necessarily inflected and complicated ideological attitudes. Very few individuals were champions of women's emancipation through and through, and many changed their minds in the course of their careers (the suffrage case is an example). Respectable middle-class people,[12] restricted by rigid Evangelical standards,[13] were little inclined to overturn the structure of the family,[14] reject the sexual division of labour, or

9 Housman, *The Unexpected Years* (London: Jonathan Cape, 1937), p. 141. Housman was a prominent women's rights activist (*Articles of Faith in the Freedom of Women*, 1911).
10 As pointed out by Walter Lionel George, also a self-styled feminist [I, 9].
11 In the eighteenth century, for instance, 'the public endorsement of female suffrage served as the ultimate marker of enlightened "manliness"' (Chernock, 2010: 127). Claudia Nelson (1995: 15) contends that the Mother Question was the Victorians' primary concern.
12 The middle class should be understood as a heterogeneous social group comprising professionals, industrialists, shopkeepers, farmers, clerks, independent craftsmen, even 'artisans' belonging to the aristocracy of labour.
13 'The Evangelicals had made social disapproval a force which the boldest sinner might fear' (G. M. Young, *Victorian England, Portrait of an Age* (Oxford: Oxford University Press, 1936), p. 4. The Evangelical tradition regarded homes as havens to be guarded, which explains attitudinal contradictions to women's claims. Male authority was highly dependent on marital unity – a determining factor in the opposition to married women's votes. Paradoxically, however, the movement provided a valuable training ground for several female champions of emancipation, see Introduction n. 22).
14 Christians of all denominations shared the same view of the home as

subvert the dominant concepts of femininity – except in socialist circles where a complete transformation of society was called for. Although they recognized women as individuals in their own rights, or hankered after a better balance of power between the sexes, they continued to celebrate the 'feminine ideal' of the Victorian angel in the house. They might have been prepared to push the boundaries of propriety to their limits, but they remained trapped in a 'double-bind' (Dyhouse, 1981: 59),[15] torn between two sets of standards. It would therefore be unhistorical to fault male 'feminism' on such grounds since very few women activists themselves were prepared to contravene acceptable codes of female conduct, and continued to regard the home as sacred, and motherhood as their role *par excellence*.[16] Home, besides, was not systematically antithetical to political space.[17] On the contrary, in many cases, it was a locus of intense intellectual discussion, particularly in Dissenting families who played a crucial role in the emergence of radical culture.[18] What the writings of this collection demonstrate is that sex equality in the nineteenth century was rarely an end in itself. It was advocated by an iconoclastic vanguard of social reformers of both sexes,[19] inhabited by the vision of a more egalitarian order (which they attempted to translate into national practices) much more than by a gendered outlook, or by the concept of

---

    the basis for the moral order of society. Chartist periodicals propagated a working-class version of female domesticity similar to the middle-class concept. Female activists themselves frequently lapsed into eulogies of the 'domestic ideal'. Allowing women to work without restrictions was therefore considered as immoral.

15 Beatrice Potter (Webb) experienced this frustration as having a 'duplex personality'. More examples of women's inner tensions 'between the public path' and 'private duties' in Davidoff and Hall (2002: 138–9, 184).

16 Similarly Chernock warns that characterizing men's promotion of women's rights as systematic propaganda for the male cause is a failure to read it in context (2010: 124).

17 The concept of 'separate spheres' has also undergone significant re-evaluation as an acceptable explanatory framework for exploring gender relations: see Shoemaker (1998) or Delap et al. (2009).

18 Kathryn Gleadle, 'British Women and Radical Politics in the Late Nonconformist Enlightenment, c.1750–1830' (Vickery. ed., 2001).

19 'Sceptics in religion, democrats in politics, reformers, visionaries, romantics – these men and women represented a style of social dissidence bold in its assumptions, universalist in its claims' (Taylor, 1983: 2). That is why neither men nor women can be celebrated simply as isolated 'heroes' or 'champions' of emancipation.

women's rights *per se*.[20] The empowering of female 'agents' was an integral feature of a wider agenda for social regeneration or, for some, of a social revolution in the making. The interaction of these (far from mutually exclusive) groups in the struggle for human freedom and progress considerably modifies the stereotypical narrative of feminism, and 'alerts us to the importance of perceiving feminist discussions as part of a dialogic process' (Gleadle, 2002: 13).

Rather than setting up males in the place of the female activists in feminism, this book attempts to complement feminism's intellectual history. It has no intention to lessen in any way women's *fundamental* roles in the definition of their rights or in the emancipation process itself. But let it be said once more that the contributions of the male players have been too long in eclipse.

---

20 Josephine Butler led her purity crusade 'in defence of citizen rights, not women's rights' (Goldman, 2004: 141). Schwarzkopf underlines that 'class issues predominated over those of gender in the political motivation of female Chartists' (1991: 216). Gleadle significantly distinguishes between two tendencies in feminism: 'A cerebral and intellectual phenomenon', in the 1830s, which combined 'with the excitement of a visionary new age', and 'a more narrow more uniquely feminist perspective', which 'crystallized into practical schemes to advance women's position' from the 1850s (2002: 173–5).

Acknowledgements

I am glad to acknowledge my indebtedness to the people who have helped make this publication possible. I want to thank Angela V. John and Lucy Delap for their friendship and encouragement with the idea of the book, as well as the three anonymous scholars who refereed my proposal so positively. Thanks are also due to the staff of the Interlibrary Loan at the University of Nice Sophia-Antipolis, and to the LIRCES, for their material and financial assistance. Finally I want to pay tribute to Professor Gilbert Bonifas whose knowledge and expertise of the Victorian world never ceased to inspire me.

Introduction

In the late 1850s, ostentatious campaigns, spearheaded by iconic female figures and focused on specific causes (such as the promotion of education, the abolition of the double standard, the protection of married women's property, suffrage, etc.), marked the beginning of what is known as the women's movement. The significant changes in women's politics that subsequently unfolded in Britain have often been misconstrued by later generations as the result of triumphant (sole) female combats against males anxious to defend their privileges. In recent years historical accounts of emancipation have become less celebratory of women's achievements and more inclusive of the intellectual heritage on which they were built. They demonstrate that the struggle for women's rights, rather than a sex war, has been an unsteady march, rooted in a long tradition of male (and female) political engagement, with alternating phases of quiescence and effervescence[1] – sometimes benefiting from the most paradoxical factors.[2]

In the mid-nineteenth century, a remarkable florescence of ideologies concerning gender and the role of women brought the debates on the Woman Question to a head.[3] Gleadle argued that in the early 1850s a

1 A pace which historians have compared to the syncopated rhythm of jazz (Brown: 1991).
2 See Bush (2007) on the positive legacy of the women's anti-suffragist movement.
3 Reflected by a report on the front page of *Eliza Cook's Journal* (14 December 1850): 'The subject of female improvement has been a very popular one of late; and hosts of books have been written and published on the subject. The "Daughters," "Wives," and "Mothers" of England, have been lectured in turns, as to what they ought, and what they ought not, to be. "Woman's rights and duties" have been enforced at great length; many a "Plea for Woman" has been put forth; the subject has formed the theme of novels, prize essays, poems, treatises, and articles in Quarterly Reviews, until the public mind

sense of impatience had grown amongst female activists: 'Many were beginning to feel that the intellectual argument had been won – the time for action had come' (2002: 173).[4] As explained by Lilian Faithfull, who was to become one of the first female magistrates in England, the movement emerged as a product of the age, 'a time when every institution, every convention, every tradition, was being subject to criticism', when women 'could take part in the flow of the new life and thought and constructive energy'.[5] Women's grievances were fertilized by a maelstrom of heterodox ideas whose strength was sustained by the spread of radicalism.[6] All the female leaders of the emancipation movement, without exception, frequented at least one of the radical milieux which agitated for reform in Britain throughout the nineteenth century.[7] Most of these women were born into the ranks of the new industrial

---

seems pretty well saturated on the subject.' 'Men and Women. – Education of the Sexes', *Eliza Cook's Journal* (London, vol. 4, April 1851), p. 96.

4 In 1869, the appointment of the Endowed Schools Commission inflamed women's claims. Elisabeth Wolstenholme rejoiced: 'It will be the fault of women themselves, if they do not use it as the most powerful lever ever yet applied to raise the education of women', 'The Education of Girls: Its Present and Its Future', in J. Butler (ed.), *Woman's Work and Woman's Culture* (London: Macmillan, 1869), p. 314. In a favourable intellectual climate the results could be quite spectacular: that year single women gained the municipal franchise, and wives the right to keep their earnings.

5 Lilian M. Faithfull, *In The House of My Pilgrimage* (London: Chatto and Windus, 1924), p. 7. Bessie Rayner Parkes also reported: 'Except for the material need which exerted a constant pressure over a large and educated class, the "women's movement" could never have become in England a subject of popular comment, and to a certain extent of popular sympathy', *Essays on Woman's Work* (London: Strahan, 1866), p. 55. Ray Strachey acknowledged that 'the Radicals of the fifties and sixties or the philanthropists … quickened the Women's movement to life', *The Cause: A Short History of the Woman's Movement in Great-Britain* (New York: Kennikat Press, 1928), p. 64.

6 The term radicalism covers a number of different and often combined philosophies, reflecting a moral rebellion against privileges, waste and abuse of power, and deriving spiritual nourishment from a Christian conception of man's duty on Earth. It alluded less to a programme than to a state of mind, to a social and intellectual stance rather than a doctrine.

7 Female political writers in the 1790s (such as A. L. Barbauld, E. Heyrick, Rachel Lee, or Ann Jebb, Mary Wollstonecraft) had all been intimate with radical milieux.

middle class or in clergymen's households:[8] they had been educated by benevolent fathers or shared their brothers' tutors; all benefited from the (often financial) backing of male relatives or friends. This collection invites the reader to (re)discover a few of the numerous male figures of radicalism who not only endorsed the women's movement but whose practical support proved crucial to its progress. In spite of the amount of prejudice that broke loose, and of the implacable (but in the end ineffectual) opposition that rose against female emancipation (including from women themselves), the importance of this factor cannot be minimised without seriously distorting the history of feminism.

In the rapidly expanding radical press,[9] in Parliament, from pulpits and hustings,[10] at public halls,[11] at Mechanics' Institutes,[12] in radical clubs,[13] at soirées and salons,[14] and of course through a considerable number

8 The rest came from Owenite co-operative circles. The aristocrats Sophia Chichester and her sister Georgiana Fletcher Welch are exceptions; they nevertheless supported Owen and Carlile.
9 Thanks to the free press campaigns, the stamp duty on newspapers was reduced to a penny in 1836, and finally removed in 1855. Improvements in printing made hundreds of thousands of copies of daily newspapers available, including the verbatim speeches of political leaders. Radical papers in particular, some of them with a large circulation, were all vehicles for the discussion of women's rights.
10 The debating societies such as the Literary and Philosophical Societies were mixed-sex venues. The Dissenters' highly politicized sermons were also for women attenders a source of engagement with current affairs.
11 In the 1840s, the Owenite Halls of Science, the Chartist People's Halls, or the Unitarian Athenaeums had a policy of admission to women. From the 1850s some of these halls were turned into popular freethought venues, such as the City Road Hall of Science, the John Street Institute in London, or the Secular Hall in Leicester.
12 Initiated in 1820s by Unitarians, they admitted women in the 1830s. The most popular were Manchester, Liverpool, and Leeds. Before a national system was set up, educational opportunities were provided by informal adult night classes, and elementary Sunday schools for working-class children (Royle, 1980).
13 Such as the Cosmopolitan, the Century, the Political Economy and the New, the Radical Club, or *Ad Eundem*.
14 The fermenting world of London radicalism met at the fashionable soirées of the Pankhursts, the Chapmans, the Brays' Rosehill circle, etc. The Chartists depended on countless tea and dinner parties, picnics, and soirées (Schwarzkopf, 1991). The Secularists relied on the organization of bazaars, teas, musical evenings, until the fivefold increase of coffee houses provided

of publications, women's role and status were challenged throughout Britain by an intricate nexus of radical circles. Their members may have been divided by religion, class, and intellectual legacy, but their common denominator was a faith in scientific methods, a belief in perfectibility and progress through reason derived from the deistic ideas of the Enlightenment, and a strong commitment to liberty[15] and quality.[16] Too idealistic or independent to accept the party Whip or discipline, they were mostly non-party men, or ahead of their parties on a number of issues; they hardly spoke in one voice but echoed one another in many ways. Often related, they influenced, critiqued, or responded to one another.[17] All were social reformers anxious to grapple with the 'condition of England' question,[18] and all drew on a rich tradition of ideas, largely inherited from the eighteenth century,[19] which provided an intellectual base for women's claims. The recognition of women's civic rights, the development of their education (without which there could have been no emancipation), the progressive extension of their sphere, was therefore indissociable from wider reform campaigns which acted as a stimulus for female reformers to start their own, and offered them opportunities as well as male support and patronage.[20]

---

them with new venues for their gatherings. Annie Besant, Charles Bray, and Sara Hennell met at the publisher Thomas Scott's salon.

15 John Stuart Mill's *On Liberty* (1859), a plea for a secular, pluralistic, open society, ranks among the most influential works of radical Liberalism.

16 Thomas Paine stands as the fountainhead of political and religious freethought. His *Rights of Man* (1791–1792) established the natural equality of all men and their equal claim to political rights. *The Age of Reason* (1794) denounced the Bible as spurious.

17 Thompson's *Appeal* [I, 1] was written as a response to James Mill's stance against women's suffrage; Malthus's *Essay on Population* replied both to Godwin's egalitarian social propositions and Condorcet's advocacy of contraception; Richard Carlile's and George Drysdale's books echoed each other [IV, 1 and 4].

18 The expression was coined by Thomas Carlyle to refer to the (miserable) condition of the working classes as a result of the Industrial Revolution. Between 1832 and 1850, *Sartor Resartus*, *Chartism*, *Past and Present*, and *Latter Day Pamphlets* inveighed against the disastrous effects of the mechanical age and the dismal science of economics.

19 Chernock (2010) has demonstrated that the late British Enlightenment was a launching point of feminist discussion.

20 Maria Grey recognized her debt to Lord Lyttelton in the promotion of girls' education: 'A younger generation … may forget what they owe to him, but we, whom he helped through the heat and burden of the day, can never

Woman's place, woman's mission

The role that women came to play in the public sphere resulted largely from the coalescing of interweaving visions regarding their (divine) mission on Earth.[21] The Evangelicals, a revival movement spearheaded by Lord Ashley and William Wilberforce into the 1840s [I, 8],[22] were passionately determined to ward off a social revolution by addressing the moral needs of their nation. At the core of the movement lay a recognition of women's natural ability to bring about spiritual reformation, which at heart bore a contradiction. The Evangelicals viewed women's primarily domestic roles as central to the stability of society (a belief influential in the concept of 'the Angel in the house', and responsible for the sentimentalization of home as 'the nursery of virtue'), but their faith in women's 'higher nature' and superior powers led Evangelicals to enrol women in the perfecting of society at large. Shepherded into active public duties, and thrust forward into new responsibilities,[23] the women who worked for the improvement of prison conditions, in temperance movements, in the fight against prostitution, or for the abolition

---

forget' (Fletcher, 1980: 131). In 1903, Emily Davies was equally grateful to Sir Joshua Fitch. She rectified his obituary in *The Times* which had neglected to mention him as leader of the movement to admit women to universities.

21 The (Evangelical) Sarah Lewis's best seller *Woman's Mission* (1839) was one of the most powerful exaltations of women as the instruments of God for the regeneration of the world. The development of a freethinking version by Sara Hennell (*Present Religion as a Faith Owning Fellowship with Thought*, 1889) testifies to the pervasiveness of the rhetoric.

22 Originally started with Methodism and Wesley in the 1730s, the Evangelical faith crossed denominational lines; it found a home in Nonconformist as well as Anglican churches. Female activists (known as 'Tory feminists') took a salient role in spreading the gospel and enforcing its ethics. The movement produced several fine theologians, such as Mary Astell; it not only gave women opportunities for self-expression but also increased their visibility (Andrews, 2015: 56–66).

23 This factor is crucial to 'understand these women and their cause ... for it was the dimension in which their lives had validity or reality, and in which the age *wished* to articulate its experiences and aspirations' (Bryant, 1979: 73). Lilian Faithfull explained: 'The change that occurred in the attitude of women towards life was more significant than any change in their circumstances. They took a new view of their duties, their capacities and other functions of the State', *In The House of My Pilgrimage*, p. 9. Emily Davies or Josephine Butler were two of the most celebrated examples.

of slavery were given a sense of self-worth, a spiritual motivation, and an ideological justification for expanding their activities outside the domestic sphere. Woman's mission became woman's power. Benevolent action 'elevated motherhood and the moral power of women to a point that was inconsistent their total subordination' (Hammerton 1992: 71).[24] Additionally, the Evangelicals' emphasis on the imperious necessity to perfect the art of wifehood and motherhood made for the public acceptance of female education (even if initially along strictly moral lines).[25]

Owen's small Socialist movement,[26] which preceded, and partly overlapped with Chartism, was the first and only working-class organization of the early nineteenth century to make equality of the sexes an integral part of its campaigns. The campaign against sexual oppression and the ideal of domesticity was particularly powerful in the writings of two of its most eccentric disciples, the communitarians John Goodwyn Barmby and his wife Catherine.[27] Significantly they shared a faith in the morally purifying character of women, and regarded femininity as a spiritual lever to elevate society. Socialist millenarians however transformed the Evangelical idea of women as a moral vanguard into a more mystical one, that of the 'Woman Saviour'. In the 'Doctrine of the Woman',[28] the Rev. James Elishama Smith prophesied a revolution in gender rela-

24 A point confirmed by Lady Bowring, who declared that philanthropy was 'ultimately associated with the attainment of the social advancement and proper position of woman, and ... [her] absolute political equality with those of the other sex' (Goldman, 2004: 139).

25 Cultivating the female intellect while preserving feminine characteristics was at the heart of the enterprise. The objective was best illustrated by Hannah More's *Strictures on the Modern System of Female Education* (1799). William Carus-Wilson's Clergy Daughters' School (1823) at Cowan Bridge, or the College for Ladies and Young Children (1854) in Cheltenham exemplify the early efforts of the Evangelical clergy to that end.

26 Owen's Association of All Classes and All Nations (1835) became the Rational Society in 1842. It counted sixty-five branches, and dozens of newspapers with an estimated readership of four hundred thousand.

27 Goodwyn Barmby pleaded for a more 'equilibriated' power between the sexes, 'The Man-Power, the Woman-Power and the Woman-Man Power', *New Moral World*, 9:18 (1 May 1841), 268–9. Both hoped ultimately that sex differences would give way to a divine androgynous personality transcending and combining male and female qualities (the reunion of Adam and Eve).

28 Published in his paper, the *Shepherd*, 15 August 1835. Smith became a highly popular milleniarist preacher. A friend of Anna Wheeler's, he contributed to Owen's periodicals and to Eliza Sharples's *Isis*, and lectured at the Rotunda.

tions, the advent of the New Jerusalem – a strictly egalitarian era, in which the best elements of both sexes would unite into a new race of men and women thanks to the Coming of a female Messiah.[29] Anna Wheeler, Anne Knight, and Emma Martin conceived woman's mission in the new social order as redemptive and regenerative.[30] The Owenites' insistance on female education in the 1840s, whether for egalitarian or utilitarian objectives, provided scores of women actively involved in the development of the new science of society with opportunities for self-improvement.[31] Owen may have rejected the sacredness of the family, and demanded its abolition,[32] but his reliance on 'Social Missionaries'[33] to usher in his New Moral World [IV, 3] chimed in with the feminized moral agenda of the Evangelicals.

Similarly, the presence of working-class women in Chartism had an indirect impact on gender rights. The notorious emphasis of the movement on women's maternal duties and responsibilities,[34] a subject on which its male and its female members were in nearly total agreement, should preclude any recognition of its role in the emancipation of women, particularly as female suffrage was never included in the People's

29 Faith in a female Messiah, also embraced by the Saint Simonians (*La Femme libre, La mère*), originated in a late eighteenth-century breakaway Quaker group, the Shakers. Joanna Southcott was the most famous female heretic of this coterie. Smith amalgamated Southcottianism, Owenism, and the teachings of the Saint Simonians into his 'Doctrine of the Woman'.
30 See Taylor (1983: 148, 177, and chap. 8) on the place of women in the communities.
31 Dispensed in the halls of science or the schools and libraries of the Rational Society. The scientist George A. Fleming was one of the few to recommend women be 'educated equal' to men.
32 In common with William Godwin, one of the theorists of British Jacobinism (*Enquiry Concerning Political Justice*, 1793), Owen did not believe that married couples could remain emotionally and physically satisfied with one another until death [IV, 3].
33 Some of these were formidable female preachers: Emma Martin, Margaret Chappellsmith, Frances Morrison were officially employed as lecturers. Frances Wright, Anna Wheeler, Eliza Macauley, Catherine Barmby were Owen converts. Mary Leman Grimstone and Harriet Taylor also took a keen interest in Owenite feminism.
34 Although *Labour's Wrongs and Labour's Remedy* (1839) by the Owenite and Chartist John Francis Bray was a moderate attempt at releasing women from domestic and economic tyranny.

Charter.[35] However, not only did a number of Chartists like Gerald Massey,[36] Charles H. Neesom,[37] the publicists John Watkins and John LaMont, 'Ipswich Chartist' William Garrard, or Goodwyn Barmby[38] support women's votes, but Chartism found in Richardson its theorist on women's rights [I, 2]. Lovett's National Chartist Association (open to women) contained staunch Unitarian suffragists like Collet Dobson Collet and W. H Ashurst.[39] The articles of James Haughton in *The People's Paper*, or John H. Parry in the *National Association Gazette*, sustained the notion of women's franchise. In Sheffield, the Owenite Isaac Ironside, secretary of the Hall of Science, pushed the Quaker Anne Knight to present a petition for the vote,[40] which the radical MP J. A. Roebuck presented in Parliament in 1851. The Birmingham leader T. C. Salt's convening of a large public meeting of twelve thousand women in 1838 was at the origin of the Female Chartist Associations. Even if conceived primarily as auxiliaries to the movement, these associations subsequently snowballed throughout the country. Consequently women may have enrolled in Chartism as militant wives and mothers (a way for male Chartists to buttress their authority), they also made housewifely duties politically significant; they legitimated the bettering of their working conditions in factories by publicly denouncing them as detrimental to the home. The entrance of domestic concerns in the public arena enhanced the social value of working-class women. It gave them a feeling of pride, a degree of autonomy, and emboldened them to speak and lecture (Schwarzkopf,

35 The Republican W. J. Linton and Unitarian William Biggs protested against female exclusion from the Charter respectively in the *National* and *Leicestershire Mercury*, two important forums for feminist debates. The *National Association Gazette* and the *Republican* aired Linton's views on suffrage, finally gathered in *The English Republic* (1851). Several radical members of Lovett's Association became key figures in the women's rights movement.
36 He embraced woman franchise and sex equality in 1895, once turned Christian Socialist (B. O. Flower, *Gerald Massey: Poet, Prophet and Mystic*, 1895).
37 With his Chartist wife he founded the London Female Democratic Federation.
38 In 1841, he co-issued (with Catherine) a *Declaration of Electoral Reform* asking Chartism to become 'unisexual'.
39 The lawyer William H. Ashurst, a member of the South Place chapel group, turned the *Spirit of the Age* into an arena for women's rights discussion. He organized the campaign in protest of women's exclusion from the World Anti-Slavery Convention. The Ashurst clan was actively engaged in the repeal of the Contagious Diseases Acts.
40 Few women Chartists affirmed their right to vote. Exceptions are Susanna Inge, Anne Knight, or Marion Reid in 'A Plea for Woman' (1843).

1991: 242). Viewing Chartist women as mere adjuncts to their male counterparts would not do justice to the scale of the movement. If one adds the opportunities offered by the creation of Chartist schools,[41] and the benefits women derived from the political advice of their male companions, to the large numbers of female associations, militants and contributors to the Chartist press, the movement can indeed be viewed as 'a period of political apprenticeship' for women (Schwarzkopf, 1991: 254).[42] Besides, women's domestic place was not justified by invoking intellectual inferiority; on the contrary, William Lovett (an early Owenite) viewed their educational role as pivotal for the progress of humanity.[43] Whether in 'Woman's Mission' (1842) or in *Social and Political Morality* (1853), which denounced the double standard and recommended teaching children 'physical and moral laws', he stimulated female Chartists to seek knowledge – even if, admittedly, the recognition of this right served gender-specific purposes serviceable to the community.

The role of the Unitarians – a small congregation of rational Dissenters but paradoxically the most influential on the cultural life of the country in the 1830s and 1840s – was crucial in lifting the barriers against women's emancipation.[44] Their rejection of Original Sin, their belief in human perfectibility and in the shaping by their environment of the individual (who must therefore be educated), their concern for individual liberty and fraternity were central to the endorsement of woman's right to equality.[45] Attachment to domesticated womanhood, a point on which W. J. Fox or

---

41 Schwarzkopf described Chartism as 'a great educational venture' (1991: 196). Female Chartist Associations were actively involved in the anti-Poor Law and anti-Corn Law agitation.
42 Women's central role in the struggle for the Charter was regularly extolled by Henry Vincent in the *Western Vindicator* (1839).
43 See William Lovett and John Collins, *Chartism: A New Organization of the People, Embracing a Plan for the Education and Improvement of the People, Politically and Socially* (1840).
44 Unitarianism was the first laboratory for feminist thinking (Gleadle, 1995). Taking their cue from Locke and Hartley, and mostly following the recommendations of Joseph Priestley, Unitarians had been at the forefront of women's education since the eighteenth century. Priestley inspired Bentham's theory of the happiness of the greatest number. The divine and philosopher James Martineau had a large following in the nineteenth century, and made a huge impact on British theology.
45 On their creeds see for instance J. Estlin Carpenter, *Unitarianism, An Historic Survey* (1922)

W. B. Adams [II, 2], both fiercely anti-clerical, differed from mainstream Unitarians, did not preclude a concern for personal fulfilment. Women's intellect and judgements were respected within their ranks. The (often) excellent liberal education they enjoyed[46] was the logical consequence of the Unitarians' aspiration to a self-improving society, promoted by educationalists like John Aitkin,[47] John Morell (*Reasons for the Classical Education of Both Sexes*, 1815), R. Lant Carpenter,[48] Thomas Southwood Smith,[49] and William Frend (*A Plan of Universal Education*, 1832). Samuel Wilderspin's and J. H. Pestalozzi's childrearing ideas posited a sophisticated interaction between mothers and children, sowing the seeds of a more dynamic model of womanhood in their ranks. Even though the Unitarians aimed at the advance of the needs of society rather than the specific needs of women, their quest for fairer modes of social organization led to seek the removal of legal injustices against women.[50] The egalitarian preacher George Dawson and W. J. Linton, a regular member of W. J. Fox's coterie, were amongst the first agitators for the rights of married women.[51] The lawyer Matthew Davenport Hill, and publicist James Silk Buckingham in 1832 started a groundswell of suffrage agitation, carried on by Linton,

46 On early educational ventures, such as George Holt's Liverpool Girls High School, the schools run by the Hills in Birmingham, the Carpenters and J. P. Estlin in Bristol, or the Shaens in Essex, see Watts (1998: 121–39). The lectures of the Dissenting academies were public. Several male promoters of female education and high-calibre women like Jane Marcet or Harriet Martineau came from Unitarian backgrounds.

47 Aitkin denied the existence of '*sexual* qualities'. See *Letters to a Young Lady on a Course of English Poetry* (1807), or *Letter from a Father to His Son on Various Topics Relative to Literature and the Conduct of Life* (1793). T. D. Hincks and Jeremiah Joyce also commended education for both sexes. John Relly Beard supported women's education for its own sake (*Self-Culture*, 1859).

48 See the Revs William Shepherd, J. Joyce and Lant Carpenter, *Systematic Education* (1817), or Frederic Hill, *National Education* (1836).

49 His implicit denial of the maternal instinct in *The Philosophy of Health* (1834) provoked heated discussion.

50 The lawyers W. H. Ashurst, William Case, Sidney Hawkes, W. Shaen, J. H. Parry, James Stansfeld, and MPs William Smith and Thomas Talfourd were all involved in the early debates on prostitution, marriage and custody rights (Gleadle, 1995: 124–30).

51 See Linton, 'Love and Marriage', published in the *Reasoner* (1: 7, 15 July 1846); Dawson, 'On Social Reformation', *People's and Howitt's Journal* (2: 5, 1847), and 'Relations of Great Men and Women', *Shakespeare and Other Lectures*, George St Clair (ed.) (1888). Dawson's lectures attracted a wide following all over Britain.

Samuel Bailey, and John Forster in the Unitarian press (Gleadle, 1995: 71–4). The Unitarian conception of marriage as a democratic union where force played no part blurred the delineations between the public and the private spheres. To the image of the family as either static (Evangelical) or despotic (Owen), they opposed a more liberal, caring, and egalitarian vision, warmed to Owen's collectivised schemes, and adopted associated housing [III, 1].[52] The opening of the Mechanics' Institutes to women (as early as the 1830s) was prompted by the conviction that female education was beneficial to marital relationships. As to the Whittington Club and Metropolitan Athenaeum (1846), which accepted women as equal members, it was their ambition 'to inaugurate a new cultural and educational dawn for women'.[53] Unitarians were confident that the development of the female intellect would have a beatifying effect on society as a whole. In her memories of the Whittington Club, Eliza Lee Follen could not have made the point clearer: 'Every well-informed woman is a missionary sent out into the world' (Gleadle, 1995: 166), an opinion shared by the writer Eliza Meteyard who added: 'In the better unity of her characteristics with that of man, seems to lie the real secret of the question as to woman as a moral and social agent' (Gleadle, 1995: 156). This unique experiment in adult education entailed the development of a new code of social manners between the sexes as a result of mixing. It was hailed by the Freethinker William Shaen as 'one of the most important social movements of the day' (Gleadle, 1995: 152). Amongst those, and equally significant in the challenging of the dominant constructions of womanhood, Secularism provided a most powerful intellectual tool.

Freethought or the empire of reason

After the decline of Chartism, and until the rise of Socialism in the 1880s, a loose network of heterogeneous atheistic and rationalistic groups[54] served as a new outlet for anti-clericalism and working-class radicalism.

52 On Owen's collectivized model of social organization see Taylor (1983: 48–54).
53 It carried out an extensive feminist propaganda with the help of sister institutions created in Birmingham and Liverpool (Gleadle, 1995: chap. 5). W. Shaen, D. Jerrold, W. Ashurst, the Howitts, Southwood Smith, and the Stansfelds were involved in the experiment.
54 Ranging from the free press champions, the Owenite Rational Religionists, former Chartists and Unitarians to Holyoake's respectable Secularists and Bradlaugh's hard-liners.

Emerging from the Enlightened tradition of the rights of man as much as from Owen's utopian socialist tradition,[55] they formed what is known as the Secularist or Freethought movement,[56] divided by various forms of religious scepticism, but cemented by a fierce rejection of the moral and cultural authority of the Church, and a commitment to science and reason.[57] From the 1850s, the Freethinkers fought to rid society of false and repressive beliefs, reviled all existing religions and sacred books, and particularly targeted traditional Christianity as the primary cause of women's oppression. As demonstrated by Schwartz, 'Secularism and the women's movement developed in tandem' (2013: 156). The sustained critique of organized religion and of the 'truths' of the Bible, the refutation of the God-given notions of *natural* sexual difference, offered a most fertile terrain for the rethinking of sexual norms and conduct.

The movement called Secularism[58] was first launched by a former Owenite social missionary, G. J. Holyoake [I, 6] – and later on taken over by Charles Bradlaugh, the charismatic leader of a more assertively atheist current which revived the infidel spirit of the 1840s.[59] Its mission was 'to promote personal morality' and 'to root out the tares that blight the growth of humanity, and to sow the seeds of progress' (Schwartz, 2013: 156). Anxious to make a clean break with the old label of atheism and infidelity, Holyoake attempted to give freethought a more respectable touch by making it as morally upstanding as Christianity.[60] Secularists were far less libertarian in their critique of traditional sexual morality

---

55 On the close links between Owenism and Secularism see Royle (1974).
56 In the 1850s there were over forty Secular societies in Britain, mainly concentrated in the manufacturing towns, representing an estimated number of a hundred thousand educated males and females, most of them Chartist and Owenite sympathizers. Laura Schwartz makes a distinction between the organized movement, supporting the separation of Church and State, and the freethinkers, 'individuals who held unorthodox religious views', but did not identify with the movement (2013: 6).
57 'From the cradle to the grave man should be guided by reason and regulated by science', Holyoake, *Rationalism: A Treatise for the Times* (London: Watson, 1845), p. 31.
58 The first Central Secular Society (1851) was organized by Holyoake.
59 From 1866, Bradlaugh's views caused a split in the movement. Holyoake subsequently founded the British Secular Union in 1877.
60 Dogmatic Christianity was rejected, but not Christian morality, which continued to shape the Secularist code of conduct.

than 'infidel' feminists (Schwartz, 2013: 136 and 194).[61] But their trust in a forceful female intellect called forth the enlisting of women in the movement as preachers of truth. The multiplicity of lecture halls,[62] Sunday meetings, and newspapers created a community of free and equal male and female speakers.[63] Women were included in educational pastimes with men, and their roles as auxiliary fundraisers and recreational organizers were valued and politicized.[64] In practical terms the experience was stimulating and empowering, for not only did the movement open a democratic arena of participation for them but it distilled an intoxicating craving for rational inquiry in a small (but dynamic) group of women.[65] In their agitating for a scheme of rights – 'the right to think for oneself, the right to differ, the right to assert difference of opinion, the right to debate all vital opinion' (Royle, 1974: 292) – the movement gave them the freedom to challenge sexual stereotypes, at which a most prolific press kept firing deadly ammunition. Charles Southwell's *Oracle of Reason*,[66] Bradlaugh's *National Reformer* (which popularized theories of evolution),[67]

61 Though they remained marginal, in the 1830s and 1840s feminist 'infidels' like Emma Martin, Eliza Sharples, Margaret Chappellsmith, and Eliza Macauley, whether or not formally employed as social missionaries, lectured on the evils of Christianity.
62 Edward Aveling [I, 6] deserves a special credit for setting up the Hall of Science school (1879) which ran formal classes for young men and women; its scientific programme was ambitious and its success made the scheme infectious. Several of the figures of this book were involved either as pupils or teachers (Royle, 1980: 317–24).
63 The anarchist Agnes Henry was renowned for her Wednesday lectures at the Hall of Science in 1893.
64 The Secular societies' committees did not discriminate against female members: Harriet Law and Annie Besant were allowed to become presidents of the Freethought League. Laura Schwartz argued that the movement provided women with a gender neutral role which inspired a whole generation of female activists (2013: 119).
65 They represented just over twenty per cent between 1885 and 1900 (Royle, 1980: 130). All were prominent propagandists: Matilda Roalfe, Sophia Dobson Collet, Sara Hennell, Frances Power Cobbe, Harriet Martineau, Florence Fenwick Miller, Mona Caird, Annie Besant, Kate Watts, Hypatia Bradlaugh Bonner, Mary Sowden, Edith Vance, Miss Thornton Smith, Harriet Law.
66 See also his defiant *Essay on Marriage, Addressed to the Lord Bishop of Exeter* (1840).
67 It also promoted woman suffrage (with supporters such as the writers Christopher Charles Cattell and J. M. Robertson or the lecturer H. V. Mayer), legal changes relating to married women, and equal educational opportunities.

Holyoake's *Reasoner* (in which he first denounced women's subordination) and *Secular Review*,[68] G. W. Foote's *Freethinker*,[69] Charles Bray's *Coventry Herald*, Redalls's *Secular Chronicle*,[70] or Charles Voysey's sermons (*The Sling and the Stone*)[71] disseminated a range of iconoclastic views on the question of education, prostitution, suffrage, marriage, and birth control.[72] *The Elements of Social Science* [IV, 4], a pure product of freethought, was Drysdale's bold attempt at legitimizing a more positive attitude to sexual relations. Guy Alfred Aldred's *The Religion and Economics of Sex Oppression* (1907), revised into *Socialism and Marriage* (1914), or the poet Benjamin William Elmy's *Woman Free* (1893)[73] exemplified the gender dynamics of freethought culture. The egalitarian manifesto of the Ethical movement proved equally attractive to women. Similar in spirit to Secularism, it offered a variety of social activities and educational lectures (given by several of the luminaries of this book) which propagandized women's political, legal, and economic rights.[74]

Secularists were also influenced by Auguste Comte's Positivism.[75]

68 W. S. Ross (incidentally the only anti-suffragist Secularist) co-edited the review in 1882 with Charles Watts, and ran a series of articles (1887–1888) against the priesthood (republished under the title *Woman: Her Glory, Her Shame and Her God*, 1890). The intrepid war correspondent Florence Dixie was a contributor to the journal (which became the *Agnostic* in 1888).
69 Foote's significance as Freethinking leader has been underestimated. See *Flowers of Freethought*, 2 vols, 1893–1894.
70 In 1876 it boasted a 'Ladies' Page'.
71 A friend of Frances Power Cobbe and Annie Besant.
72 J. M. Robertson's *National Reformer*, Foote's *Freethinker* and J. W. Gott's *Truth Seeker* advertised contraceptive methods (Royle, 1980: 258–9).
73 He was vice-president of the National Secular Society in 1875. His sex education manual, written with his wife Elisabeth Wolstenholme Elmy, supported birth control (*The Human Flower*, 1894).
74 The Ethical Society was created in 1886. Led from 1887 to 1892 by Stanton Coit, the new dynamic (and suffragist) minister of the South Place Religious Society, it counted seventy-five societies in 1915. See Zona Vallance, *The Ethical Movement and Women* (1905), or G. Spiller, *The Ethical Movement in Great Britain* (1934).
75 His philosophy offered a new model of 'scientifically and historically' justified social organization, promising to reconcile order and progress, based on one (lower) class governed by elites. Comte's Religion of Humanity was to be brought about by his Priests, the intellectuals of the Positivist society. The Oxford don Richard Congreve headed the English movement, mostly made up of Oxford university radicals, and founded the 'Church of Humanity' in Bloomsbury in 1870. Llewelyn Davies [II, 7] was on intimate terms with the

In spite of its narrow views on women's sphere, Comte valued the 'feminine element' as essential to the ordering of his new society. His veneration of women as the vehicles of morality, his appeal for 'the restoration of the love element', attracted female devotees like Beatrice Potter (Webb), Harriet Martineau,[76] George Eliot, or Emma Paterson.[77] Comtist wives (like Francis Pattison, Emily Beesly, Mary Alice Bridges, or Ethel Harrison, whose marriages were exemplars of successful partnerships) were clever, educated women forming a remarkable group of political (Comtist) activists. By 1859, in spite of its modest membership, Secularism had acquired a (subversive) notoriety which forced public discussion: 'There is scarcely a pulpit, metropolitan or provincial, in which discourses have not been delivered against its doctrines, and the attention of the public directed to its errors' (Royle, 1974: 287). That year, an atheist, James Stansfeld, was returned to Westminster. In the 1860s Holyoake had become a respected figure (Royle, 1974: 289). The gradual shift of Secularism towards political mainstream, attested by the appearance of a wide range of freethinking views in reputable reviews, was accentuated by major attitudinal changes in the Anglican Church regarding the temporal role of its clergy.

The Broad Church movement

The enlargement of women's role in society was also 'a by-product of the clergy's attempt to increase their power over their congregations' (Davidoff and Hall, 2002: 108),[78] both in order to ward off the threat of

---

leading Positivists. Comtism also aroused the interest of Broad Churchmen (Kent, 1978).
76 She made him familiar to English readers (*The Positive Philosophy of Auguste Comte, Freely Translated and Condensed by Harriet Martineau*, 1853).
77 Emma married one of the founders of the Working Men's Club and Institute Union, Thomas Paterson, who introduced her to Secularism and Positivism.
78 This objective became crystal-clear during the Church's pro-suffrage campaigns. See for instance the Rev. William Temple's article 'How the Woman's Movement May Help the Cause of Religion' (*The Religious Aspects of the Woman's Movement*, 1912), or the pages of the Church League for Women's Suffrage's *Monthly Paper*: the Rev. D. S. Margoliouth for instance regarded 'the equalization of the sexes in all rights and duties' as a means of restoring 'the place of the Church in the State as the authorized advocate of right and justice', *Monthly Paper* (October 1913), p. 291.

Disestablishment and to thwart the advance of Socialism. In reaction to the succession of reform acts from 1828 which they analyzed as the beginning of the end of their historic Church – all the more so as it had become the target of radical activists who attacked it as a bastion of corruption and privilege, and of the Freethinkers who rejected the authority of orthodox religion – a number of anxious churchmen, occupied by quixotic social concerns, set out to connect piety and activism. Known as Liberal Anglicans,[79] they saw themselves less as saviours of souls and more as social redeemers. They were concerned with working-class men and women's needs for spiritual and moral education, and convinced that 'the province of religion was much more national and political, much less personal than is commonly supposed'.[80] They fought for an extension of the role of the Church to social activity, in greater co-operation with the State. The movement took its cue from a variety of sources, notably S. T. Coleridge's *The Constitution of Church and State* (1830),[81] and Thomas Arnold's *Principles of Church Reform* (1833), which developed the idea of an organic society with a spiritual state guided, unified, and humanized by the Church.[82]

For Broad Churchmen, the service and training of religious women in Church life and activities was regarded as essential to the success

79 The term applied to a wide group of Whig politicians and like-minded theologians in the universities, whose policies and doctrines tended to dominate Liberal governments after 1832. They were also known as Broad Churchmen (Kitson Clark, 1973; Brent, 1987).
80 J. R. Seeley quoted by Kitson Clark (1973: 235).
81 Coleridge's idea of a national clerisy, a corps of teachers within a rejuvenated Church responsible for the spiritual and ethical development of the nation, became the inspiration for a whole generation of clergy: 'The Clerisy of the nation, or national Church, in its primary acceptation and original intention, comprehended the learned of all denominations, the sages and professors of the law and jurisprudence, of medicine and physiology, of music, of military and civil architecture, of the physical sciences, with the mathematical as the common organ of the preceding; in short, all the so-called liberal arts and sciences, the possession and application of which constitute the civilization of a country, as well as the theological' (*The Constitution of Church and State*, London: W. Pickering, 1839), pp. 49 and 70.
82 Arnold, a Liberal Anglican and Christian Socialist, was one of the prominent educationalists of his times. When headmaster of Rugby School, he dedicated the school to the education of a national elite drawn from the commercial middle class (from which emerged Benjamin Jowett or Thomas Hughes). Several Arnoldians taught at Maurice's Working Men's Colleges.

of Anglicanism.[83] From the 1850s, women's parochial influence never stopped increasing: countless Sunday Schools (which entailed the training of women teachers), settlements (where female residents outnumbered males),[84] philanthropic, cultural, and business associations (run by or with women), in addition to the paid employment of spinsters in foreign missions, not only feminized the Church but provided a favourable intellectual climate for women's emancipation.[85] It opened a new 'avenue of real if narrowly defined power' for women of all classes (Davidoff, 2002: 147),[86] exemplified by the emergence of figures like the Salvationists Josephine Butler[87] and Ellis Hopkins, and housing reformers like Octavia Hill and Beatrice Potter (Webb). Hill was roped in the relief of distress by W. A. Fremantle, dean of Ripon (Kitson Clark, 1973: 276), and Potter by the Barnetts, founders of Toynbee Hall.[88] The Church's social gospel, relying on the large involvement of lay men and women, all permeated by the same sense of social mission and duty, eventually provoked a skirmish over their representation in the parochial church councils. The first expression of Church feminism started indeed with debate on women's right to vote for representatives (in fact some parishes allowed them both to sit on councils and to vote), leading in 1898 to a formal petition by churchwomen against the ban on female candidates for election

[83] Interestingly A. C. Tait, Rugby headmaster and Broad Church bishop, ordained the first deaconess, Elizabeth Ferard, in 1861 (Gill, 1994).

[84] The idea of university settlements originated with Edward Denison, a law student who lived amongst the poor in the East End. Settlements offered women new educational opportunities. The Women's University Settlement (1887) provided them with a specific training. See Vicinus (1985) or Scotland (2007) for details.

[85] It was thanks to her work in Katherine House that Emmeline Pethick-Lawrence gained her 'first experience of that emancipation of mental and practical powers which is to be found by working as a free person in a community of equals', *My Part in a Changing World* (London: Gollancz, 1938), p. 72.

[86] Mandler showed it also served as a vent for upper-class women who had ambitions for a public role, 'From Almack's to Willis's: Aristocratic Women and Politics, 1815–1867' (Vickery, ed., 2001).

[87] She took up arms against the Contagious Diseases Acts out of commitment to Evangelical Anglicanism.

[88] Canon Samuel Barnett's parish, and Toynbee Hall (1884) founded by Arnold Toynbee (a student of Green and assistant of Barnett), were both described by Herbert Asquith as 'a research laboratory for social reformers' (Leighton, 2004: 274). Barnett's views aired in the *Manchester Weekly Times* were later reprinted in *Practicable Socialism* (1915).

to councils. Dignitaries like Charles Gore, Edwyn Hoskyns, and William Cosmo Gordon Lang joined T. H. Green and Scott Holland in the protest against women's unjust exclusion from Church suffrage. In 1909, radical clerics, many of them working in settlements, convened to create the Church League for Women's Suffrage in support of the suffragettes. Its *Monthly Paper* relentlessly criticized the Church's failings [I, 8]. Amongst the ardent Anglican women agitating for the vote both in Church and State were Maude Royden, Louisa Corben, and Louise Creighton – whose public life was proof that there was no incompatibility between loyalty to one's family and the development of one's individuality.[89]

More emancipating seeds were sown by the birth of Christian Socialism in 1848, a counter-offensive against the disunity of Church and State, led by the ex-Unitarian F. D. Maurice [II, 2]. Christian Socialism was part of the controversy over education that divided Anglicans and Nonconformists, but primarily conceived as a moral movement of the working classes, largely in reaction against the radical political programme of Chartism.[90] Although the movement lost momentum from 1854 following internal discords, its intellectual influence remained profound throughout the century. Aimed at the spiritual reformation of society, it proposed a socially responsible Christianity, with Church and State working as close allies. In *The Kingdom of Christ* Maurice blamed the rise of Socialism and Chartism on the Church's failure to speak for the poor.[91] Inspired by Coleridge's organic view of society, he recommended 'active Charity', urging the clergy to undertake good works in their parishes. The propagation of a 'Practical Christianity', predicated on the belief that human brotherhood was the true guide of any social

89 In 1895 Creighton became president of the National Union of Women Workers which affiliated women working for philanthropic organizations.
90 Maurice's priorities were neither political nor economic but educative and ethical: 'Society is not to be made anew by arrangements of ours, but is to be regenerated by finding the law and ground of its order and harmony, the only secret of its existence, in God' (Norman, 1987: 30). His ultimate objective was to make political activity unnecessary.
91 Evidently inspired by Owen's movement, the Christian Socialists regarded it as the duty of the Church to condemn the selfish principles of individualism and competition. They were not opposed to the political economy as such, but promoted co-operative enterprises in the hope of fostering social harmony (see Maurice's *Social Morality*, 1869). Their associations set up for tailors and seamstresses eventually failed. Holyoake co-operated with the Christian Socialists.

organization, appealed to virtually any Christian philanthropist. Not only did it raise hopes in women for more Christian relations between the sexes but it also persuaded them that social work was synonymous with good citizenship,[92] as attested by the writings of settlement workers Ethel Portal in Bethnal Green, Alice Busk in Southwark,[93] and Elisabeth Blackwell ('Christian Socialism: Thoughts Suggested by the Easter Season, 1882'). Philanthropy and politics were hardly kept separate in parochial work. The Rev. William Tuckwell[94] exemplifies the radical clerics who criticized the Church for failing to respond to the social crisis; a fervent advocate of stringent social and political reform (including male and female suffrage), he led several campaigns to improve women's working conditions. The Methodist Rev. J. S. Lidgett's settlement in Bermondsey took pride in setting up a Working Men and Women's College. The reform of married women's property rights was facilitated by the reports gathered by the Rev. Septimus Hansard in Bethnal Green, which were produced in Parliament as evidence of abuse of male authority during the 1868 debates.

Even more importantly, Maurice's *Theological Essays* (1853) exacerbated the mid-Victorian 'warfare of conscience with theology' (Griffin, 2014: 122), i.e., the rejection of the teachings of Scripture if they came in conflict with one's conscience.[95] Millicent Fawcett remained significantly indebted all her life to Maurice, 'a modern Isaiah' for awakening 'new

---

92 The (strongly Greenite) Christian Social Union formed in 1889 by Gore, Holland, and Westcott encouraged women to work in local government. In 1894 it founded the Women's Industrial Committee, a pressure group for the improvement of their wages and working conditions.

93 Various testimonies of Christian Socialist women can be found in J. E. Hand (ed.), *Good Citizenship* (1899).

94 He was the father of the activist Gertrude Tuckwell, the first woman magistrate. He related his work as a county rector in *Reminiscences of a Radical Parson* (1915). Another (more eccentric) prominent social activist (also a disciple of Maurice, and supporter of secularist causes) was the Rev. Stewart D. Headlam: he promoted female equality in education, employment, and the law (*The Service of Humanity and Other Sermons*, 1882; *Christian Socialism*, Fabian Tract 42, 1892), and was elected to the London School Board with Annie Besant in 1882.

95 The crisis of faith was precipitated by works of revolutionary Christology such as the German D. F. Strauss's *Life of Jesus* (1835), translated by George Eliot, and Ernest Renan's *Life of Jesus* (1863) which inspired Seeley's *Ecce Homo* (Leighton, 2004: 136).

thoughts' in her.[96] Emily Davies, Annie Besant and Elisabeth Chapman acknowledged that their activism had sprung from obedience to their consciences, and the moral example set by Jesus Christ. W. T. Blair denounced both the Pauline sanction of slavery and women's subjection as incompatible with the idea of a just God (*Female Suffrage*, 1876). Even the socially conservative F. J. A. Hort found it impossible to endorse submission to male authority when abusive (*Village Sermons in Outline*, 1900). Christian Socialists were strong allies in the development of women's sphere of influence. The lawyer J. M. Ludlow (considered by Maurice as the true founder of the movement) pioneered the development of women's ministry (*Women's Work in the Church*, 1865) and suggested the opening of crèches for the children of working mothers;[97] the charismatic Methodist preacher Hugh Price Hughes set up sisterhoods.[98] The propagation of Christ's nature as partly feminine by Thomas Hughes [I, 8; III, 5; IV, 8] became central in the diffusion of new practices of manliness and femininity. The prescriptive marriage literature mapped out new forms of social and familial order. E. J. Hardy's *How to Be Happy Though Married* (1886) marked the beginning of a less tyrannical and more Christian type of subordination. A more restrained exercise of male authority was recommended by J. R. Miller's *Secrets of Happy Home Life* (1894). George Bainton's *The Wife as Lover and Friend* (1895) and the Rev. J. G. Greenhough's *Our Dear Home Life: Homely Talks on Courtship, Marriage and Family Life* (1896) also praised the values of comradeship, compromise, and love in relationships. The great number of couples who became renowned exemplars of successful companionate marriages was one of the hallmarks of the emancipation movement. The transformation of domestic masculinities no doubt accounted for the granting of

96 *What I Remember* (London, T. Fisher Unwin, 1924), pp. 43–4.
97 'Labour and the Poor', *Fraser's Magazine*, 41 (January 1850), 2.
98 Hughes and his wife invented the Sisterhood of the People, an undenominational, non-ecclesiastical order which, in 1894, started recruiting educated women desirous to work among the poor. The intent was overtly political: while offering women a sphere of social service in keeping with T. H. Green's spirit, it gave them a space where they gained social knowledge and influence, asserted their public roles and advanced their cause. Emmeline Pethick and another fifty sisters worked in Hughes's West London mission in 1887. The 'Sisters' were copied in several cities. From 1885 Hughes opposed the Contagious Diseases Acts and conducted a social reform crusade in the *Methodist Times*. He also promoted women's higher education and suffrage, and argued for equality between the sexes at work and by law.

the franchise to married women in local politics (1894 Local Government Act), and helped shift some of the ideological arguments in the opposition to parliamentary suffrage (Griffin, 2014: 314).

One of the greatest achievements of Christian Socialism was of course its remarkable contribution to the advance of education in England. In 1848, Maurice pioneered the foundation of Queen's College in London, the very first college for women in England [II, 2]. The Working Man's College in London (1854) was purpose-built for the intellectual and moral elevation of labouring men by university-trained men. It was Maurice's and John Westlake's concrete response to his ideal of social harmony and economic cooperation.[99] It inspired a similar college in Leicester in 1860, and the foundation of the London Working Women College in 1864 by the Unitarian Elisabeth Malleson. Women benefited greatly from the movement for university reform and expansion in which many of Maurice's disciples were involved. Started in 1850 by a group of Arnoldians sitting on the Royal Commission appointed to inquire into Oxford University, it found new advocates in a breed of charismatic dons – Benjamin Jowett, T. H. Green,[100] and Mark Pattison at Oxford, F. D. Maurice and Henry Sidgwick at Cambridge[101] – who all regarded the universities as the chief vehicles for societal reform.[102] In 1867 Miss

---

99 Westlake was remembered as an unflinching liberal who 'promoted every movement for the extension of the sphere of the activities of women and the removal of their disabilities', A. V. Dicey et al., *Memories of John Westlake* (London: Smith Elder, 1914), p. 62.
100 With wife Charlotte, Green was one of the founders in 1879 of Somerville Hall, partly funded by the London Ethical Society (1887), itself a nest of Greenites. He was also member of the 'Lectures for Women' Committee at Oxford in 1873. Middle-class reformers of girls' education, like Miss Buss, Sophie Bryant and the social activist Eleanor Rathbone, were ardent disciples of Green. On Green's many practical contributions to women's education see Anderson (1991: 679–82).
101 Professor Sidgwick was indefatigable in coaching women. He was instrumental in the promotion of Ann Clough, in the creation of Newnham College (1875) and of special examinations for women to facilitate their university access. The couple formed by Henry and his wife embodied a highly intellectualized marital friendship. Together they supported women's suffrage and campaigned for women's full university membership in the 1880s and 1890s.
102 The group of new dons began to take measures to bring students back to the authority of the colleges and restore the moral influence of the teacher. They demanded the end of obsolete regulations, the broadening of the curriculum, the removal of civil disabilities, or the lowering of fees in

Clough's North of England Council for Promoting the Higher education of Women launched a course of lectures for women in the cities of the North, with the help of James Bryce, James Stuart, George Butler, Sir Joshua Fitch, and Thomas Markby. Henry Sidgwick, aided by local professors, started the same scheme in Cambridge: the committee of the Association for the Higher Education of Women comprised the astronomer J. C. Adams, the mathematician Arthur Cayley, who became chairman of Newnham, the philosopher Henry Jackson and the classicist R. C. Jebb (both members with Sidgwick of the Cambridge Apostles, F. D. Maurice's arcane society for the intellectual elite). The teachings of the economist Alfred Marshall (*Lectures to Women*, 1873) raised the academic aspirations of many female students. Marshall was a member of the Grote Club, a gathering of reformist dons also headed by Maurice. The contributions to new structures of knowledge for girls, whether by Charles Kingsley [II, 4], Llewelyn Davies [II, 7], Canon John Percival,[103] or Jowett's student, Charles S. Roundell, one of the founders of the Girls' Public Day School Company (1872) which launched over thirty girls' schools, were a response to new social and economic needs.[104] Once the education of girls became a public concern, its provisions took a real turn for the better, substantiating Dyhouse's conclusion that 'in the reform of girls' secondary schools, as much as in the area of higher education ... the lead was often taken by men' (1981: 64). It was at a parish meeting called by Canon Thomas Dale and David Laing[105] that

---

order to attract the 'intellectual capital' of the nation. See for instance the Cambridge Apostle F. W. Farrar (*Essays on Liberal Education*, 1867) and J. R. Seeley's lectures [IV, 4].

103 When at Rugby, he appointed the first woman teacher, Marie Bethell Beauclerc. He helped create Clifton High School for Girls in Bristol, and offered scholarships for girls (to which T. H. Green contributed with his personal funds). He was succeeded in the task by Canon James Maurice Wilson. Both men belonged to the Church League for Women Suffrage.

104 In 1844 the cotton merchant George Holt, also a supporter of women's rights, gave one of his mansions to host the first school for girls in Liverpool. The Brewers' and Clothworkers' Companies gave substantial funds to Miss Buss's school in 1872. The businessman Henry Nash successfully lobbied for the creation of a girls' grammar school in Berkhamsted in 1884 (Fletcher, 1980).

105 Laing was secretary to the Governesses' Benevolent Institution, created in 1843, originally to rescue aged governesses with no means of support. The need for women to qualify properly for the teaching profession led to the creation of Queen's College, of which Laing was one of the founders.

the North London Collegiate School for boys was founded in 1850, and inspired Miss Buss, Laing's protégée, to open one for ladies. Cheltenham Ladies' College (1853) was created by three clergymen and one doctor, anxious to cater for the education of the daughters of the middle class; Worcester High School for girls was set up by the Rev. Canon William Butler (1883) with the same intent.[106] If the movement for the better education of women 'can only safely be studied as an aspect of the reform of secondary and higher education for men and boys during the same period' (Bryant, 1979: 76),[107] its development will never be properly understood without taking into account 'the overarching fact that it was primarily a religious movement ... a passionate attempt to give meaning to life, to rescue women from their "unloved, unapplied existences" ... and to assert the broad and practical doctrines of what is today called Christian Stewardship', embraced by both sexes (*Ibid.*: 72).

The new approach to Scripture

Religious debates are now fully established 'as intellectual-cultural discourse in relation to social history' and recognized as one of the major 'sources' of political and social ideas (Leighton, 2004). The reading of the Bible as a historical document and its corollary, the rejection of the principle of inerrancy, was the result of an ongoing criticism[108] which engaged clerics from all denominations and became more audacious as religion came in conflict with scientific discoveries (geology and zoology in particular). The phenomenon has been described as the 'historical turn in biblical scholarship' (Griffin, 2014: 112). The role of biblical criti-

---

106 The Liberal barrister Canon Hugh Robinson (note 154) was instrumental in the creation of eight girls' schools in Yorkshire.
107 Carol Dyhouse (1981) has warned against the assumption that the improvement of women's schooling arose out of a feminist concern; her study showed the conservatism of the first institutions regarding women's roles.
108 Joseph Priestley's 'historical method' was gradually supplanted by the combined influence of the German school of 'higher criticism', of American transcendentalism, and of Alexander Geddes's *Critical Remarks on the Hebrew Scriptures* (1800) which treated the Creation as a myth. The 'new Unitarianism' developed by divines like James Martineau, J. H. Thom, and J. J. Tayler was German-inspired. It cast doubts on the authorship and the dating of the Bible, and encouraged a reinterpretation of God's commandments in their cultural context.

cism was crucial in the development of Victorian political culture and social practices and hence in the transformation of gender relations. Critical commentaries on the Pauline Epistles led to a fundamental questioning of patriarchal hierarchy, and campaigners for women's rights did not fail to put that to good use in the legitimation of their cause, as did for instance the Rev. Hon. E. Lyttelton's 'Women's Suffrage and the Teaching of St Paul',[109] Elisabeth Rachel Chapman's 'St Paul & the Woman's Movement',[110] or Charles Gore's *St Paul's Epistle to the Ephesians* (1898) which recommended the protection of wives against cruel husbands by law. Paradoxically, without any original intent, Scripture became a new site of feminist debate which ultimately challenged the Christian prescriptive gender norms. The new interpretation of biblical teachings on the position of women and the analysis of Jesus's treatment of female characters provided a new basis to dispute definitions of masculinity and femininity. Drawing upon the histories of civilization which treated woman's position in society as a measure of human progress, Robert Aspland's *Beneficial Influence of Christianity on the Character and Condition of the Female Sex* (1812), H. W. Crosskey's (secular) approach in *A Defence of Religion* (1854),[111] and Baptist Francis A. Cox (*Female Scripture Biography*, 1817) argued that Christianity was a force that elevated woman's status (because it had put an end to Antique practices such as polygamy or infanticide). Like the Unitarian Baptist J. O. Squier's reinterpretation of Scripture (*The Character and Mission of Woman: A Lecture, Applicable to the New Marriage Law*, 1837), they encouraged a positive (even if still domestic) image of women. Secularists, on the contrary, denounced the Bible as the founding text of sexual oppression. Although not all as eccentric as Robert Taylor's *The Diegesis* (1829), a spate of critical works, testifying to a raging battle against orthodoxy, popularized the mythical and pagan roots of Scripture, and contended that the status of women had declined since the introduction of Christianity into the pagan world. Geoffrey Higgins's *Anacalypsis* (1836), Charles Hennell's *Inquiry Concerning the Origin of Christianity* (1838), Robert Cooper's *The Holy Scriptures Analyzed* (second edition 1840) and *The Infidel Textbook* (1846),

---

109 *Contemporary Review* (May 1896), 680–91.
110 The essay was published in *Marriage Questions in Modern Fiction, and Other Essays on Kindred Subjects* (1897) and testifies to the increasing development of a morality of justice, not of submission, within marriages.
111 Crosskey advocated a humanistic theism close to Holyoake's. He was president of the Birmingham Women's Suffrage Society for ten years.

Francis W. Newman's *Phases of Faith* (1850), Joseph Barker's *What Has the Bible Done for Woman?* (1863?), Bradlaugh's *The Bible: What It Is!* (1870), W. P. Ball's *The Bible Handbook* (1888), J. M. Robertson's *Christianity and Mythology* (1900),[112] Joseph McCabe's *The Religion of Woman: An Historical Study* (1905) proclaimed that only a secularized society, could emancipate women. Within the Established Church, *Essays and Reviews* (1860) written by seven Liberal Anglicans (such as Benjamin Jowett), also exhorted divines to treat the Bible 'like any other book' and reject woman's subordination as God's truth [I, 9; IV, 8]. The essays propagated the idea of progressive revelation and the theology of Incarnation;[113] they caused as much public controversy as Colenso's *The Pentateuch and the Book of Joshua* (1860). T. H. Green's 'Essay on Christian Dogma' (1858–1860) played its part against Christian dogmatism (but not its morality though).[114] F. W. Farrar's *Life of Christ* (1874), *Eternal Hope* (1878), and *The Bible: Its Meaning and Supremacy* (1897)[115] encouraged Christians to live socially useful lives.[116] Young High Church Oxonians did not resist the general contagion. The Lux Mundi group, identified with Charles Gore, Henry Scott Holland, and B. F. Westcott, endeavoured 'to succour a distressed faith ... to bring 'the Christian creed into its right relation to the modern growth of knowledge, scientific, historical, critical, and to the modern problems of politics and ethics'.[117] Published as a series of studies, *Lux Mundi* (1889) argued that it was time for the Church to move away from contemplation and adjust Christian beliefs to scientific discoveries, and to enter 'into the apprehension of the new social and intellectual movements of each age'[118] in order to reconquer its moral supremacy.

Such a prodigious development of exegetical works proved instrumental in moving the question of woman's status to centre stage.

112 He became editor of the *National Reformer* after Bradlaugh's death in 1891.
113 Benjamin Jowett's *Sermons on Faith and Doctrine*, delivered between 1871 and 1873, disseminated the image of Christ, an 'exemplar of God', as the perfect man.
114 R. L. Nettleship (ed.), *The Works of T. H. Green*, 3 vols (1886).
115 The books went through several editions and reached a wide audience. They greatly inspired the American feminist theologian Katherine Bushnell (*God's Words to Women*, 1918).
116 When Rector of St Margaret's, Farrar rallied large numbers of male and female parishioners to social causes. See R. Farrar, *The Life of F. W. Farrar* (London: James Nisbet, 1904), pp. 241–50.
117 Charles Gore (ed.), *Lux Mundi* (London: John Murray, 1904, first edition 1889), p. x.
118 *Ibid.*

Debates questioning religion occupied women's discussion platforms, and empowered many of them to produce their own narratives.[119] The flouting of the authority of Scripture destroyed one of the fundamental props of domestic ideology, inducing a gender dynamics which seriously undermined the hierarchical marital relationship. Without it neither could the emancipation movement have developed nor new ideas about femininity and masculinity emerged.

The Liberal reform agenda

The string of reforms affecting women's legal or political status between the Municipal Franchise Act (1869) and the repeal of the Contagious Diseases Acts (1886), including the series of Married Women Property Acts, was part of the marked increase of social and industrial legislation carried out by the Liberals in office, and known as 'the Social Turn'. A wide array of social reformers, differing in religious allegiances, were kept in the Liberal fold by the common faith that only a liberal society created and safeguarded the circumstances favourable to individual self-realization and co-operation.[120] The new party that emerged in 1859

---

119 See for instance the writings of women who declared their atheism: Emma Martin's *The Bible No Revelation* (1850?); Harriet Martineau's *Letters on the Laws of Man's Nature and the Development* (1851); Sophia Dobson Collet's *G. J. Holyoake and Modern Atheism* (1855); Sara Hennell's *Christianity and Infidelity* (1857); F. Power Cobbe, *The Theory of Intuitive Morals* (1859) or Annie Besant's *My Path to Atheism* (1877). The feminist reinterpretation of Scripture was a step towards self-determination: see Martine Monacelli-Faraut, 'Effacer la faute d'Eve: tentatives des militantes anglaises au dix-neuvième siècle pour (re) penser l'origine', *Résonances*, 11 (June 2010), 11–25.

120 'Religious and quasi-religious humanitarianism, emphasizing reciprocal social obligations and the moral regeneration of society, was one of the strongest impulses behind the social turn' (Leighton, 2004: 260). Charles Gore and Scott Holland identified the Liberal Party as the most practical vehicle for their 'socialist ends' (*Ibid.*: 261).

Being Conservative did not however necessarily imply hostility to change, as shown by the interest displayed by the Party in the working class (Disraeli's Tory democracy) and the voting of dramatic legislation such as the Custody of Infants Act (1839) or the Divorce Act (1857). Conservatives feature among the partisans of emancipation, as this collection shows, pointing to the need to avoid viewing liberalism and conservatism in a binary manner.

from the fusion of Whiggery and the Peelites led by Gladstone[121] was built upon the Whig tradition which had placed the welfare of the nation at the heart of the agenda.[122] An increasing sense of social responsibility towards the needy, a determination to do great things – including the emergence in Liberal political culture of 'a feminine ideal of peaceful improvement in the face of natural market forces'[123] – played a part in what historians have identified as the 'democratization of compassion' (Leighton, 2004: 229). This process was amplified by the entrenchment in the Party of Nonconformists,[124] whose notorious 'conscience' put considerable pressure to bear upon its members.[125] The party indebted to what T. H. Green called positive liberty (true freedom is where a man is free to do what he ought rather than what he pleases) saw itself as a 'moral' force at the centre of the state.[126] Liberal reforms were therefore often conscience-stricken, a response to a (morally intolerable) situation, inspired by the feeling that 'the state of the law has fallen far behind the current morality' (Griffin, 2014: 140).[127] As demonstrated by Griffin's examination of the parliamentary debates, the discovery that domestic abuse was no longer a working-class issue but a widespread social

---

121 His personality was crucial in the alignment of social reform with Liberalism between 1870 and 1900 (Leighton, 2004: 262–4).
122 The Foxite Lord John Russell regarded the Christian religion as the foundation of public spirit, good order, and virtuous government (*The Causes of the French Revolution*, 1832).
123 Embodied for instance by Henry Fawcett [III, 5]; see Boyd Hilton, 'Manliness, Masculinity and the Mid-Victorian Temperament', in Goldman, ed. (1989: 70).
124 Originally drawn to Liberalism by the hope that it would abolish their grievances, after mid-century they formed its 'largest, most active, and most high–principled section' (Richards, 1977: 387).
125 Based on the precept that 'what is morally wrong can never be politically right', the expression came into use in the 1890s (Bebbington, 1982: 40). The Christian Socialists faced the same moral challenge. In *Economic Morals* (1890), Scott Holland wrote: 'Economic science must succeed in being ethical, without ceasing to be scientific' (Leighton, 2004: 260). The Rev. Hugh Price Hughes, always prepared to assume the mantle of the Nonconformist conscience, pleaded for an intervening state in *Philanthropy of God* (1890).
126 Green's ethical idea of the common good was influential on British social thought from 1880 to 1914 (and particularly on H. P. Hughes). It acted as a bridge between religious denominations and political movements.
127 Lord Selborne quoted by Griffin. See also Kitson Clark (1973: 235, 279), and Richter (1964).

problem [III, 3; 4] affected the whole discourse on Victorian masculinity: it created a moral panic, compounded by the threat it posed to social hierarchy, which forced Liberal MPs to respond to the challenge.[128] The social legislation of the last quarter of the century represented a departure from earlier liberal objectives (such as the encouragement of individual self-reliance promoted by Samuel Smiles's *Self Help*), notably when it became clear that political economy had failed to deliver its promise and bring about economic, intellectual, and social progress to the whole nation. More and more Liberals came to revise their attitude regarding the role of the state and to regard 'interferences' as beneficial to social stability.[129] In practical terms it meant that the state's duty was to remove obstructions of opportunity to individual advancement so as to enable (free) citizens to make the best of themselves in the interest of the community.[130] The culture of social science which had permeated (New) Liberalism[131] led the Liberals in particular, and the Victorian public in general, to believe that it was possible to reform public morality through legislation, if one secured a rational, efficient, skilled administration of the State. One of the answers to the search for a perfect framework of laws and institutions was the creation of the National Association for the Promotion of Social Science (commonly known as the Social Science Association).[132] Conceived as a model for the organization and

128 Tensions between conscience and politics permeated the debates on mothers' custody rights, whether in Parliament or at the National Association for the Promotion of Social Science (Griffin, 2014: 140–59). See for instance Herbert Mozley, 'On the laws relating to the custody of children' (1882–1883), or T. Carlaw Martin's *The Custody and Guardianship of Children* (1884).
129 Green's idea of the state as a vehicle of moral improvement was inspirational to advanced Liberals (Leighton, 2004: 297).
130 It was defined by L. T. Hobhouse as 'a movement of liberation, a clearance of obstructions, an opening of channels for the flow of free spontaneous, vital activity' (*Liberalism*, 1909). Hobhouse made himself a reputation as an advocate of sex equality when a don at Oxford. See his political writings *Democracy and Reaction* (1904) or *Government by the People* (1910).
131 The science of society based on the discovery of the laws of social science can be traced back to many sources from Newton to Owen, Darwin, Ricardo, and Comte (Goldman, 2004: 294–7). It could be defined as the 'attempt to assert the right relation of social scientific data to practical ethics, and the art of government', Leighton (2004: 260). The Fabian Society (1884) contributed significantly to its development and application.
132 Interestingly its original name was the National Association for the Moral and Social Improvement of the People. Historians refer to it as 'the Victorian

application of social knowledge, it served between 1857 and 1886 as an 'outdoor parliament' (Goldman, 2004: 1),[133] mediating between politicians and public opinion,[134] and pressing the government into action.[135] This essential 'component of mid-Victorian culture and politics' (*Ibid.*: 4) was to become a major instrument of women's emancipation, following Lord Shaftesbury's decision to incorporate 'the whole female sex as our sympathizers and fellow labourers' (Bryant, 1979: 67).[136] Its five departments dealing with legal reform, penal policy, education, public health, and social economy provided middle-class women with the first significant and popular forum to advance their cause.[137]

    conscience in action' (Goldman, 2004: 38). This example of administrative interventionism, described by *The Times* (1 October 1860) as 'an incipient school for legislative interference in morals' (*Ibid.*: 6), confutes the myth of Victorian England as an age of laissez-faire. However there was 'no quantum change in the state's role; rather, state power was used to remodel institutions' (*Ibid.*: 250–73). See also Parry (2006). In other words, the Social Science Association was looking for laws that would make individuals capable of fending for themselves and taking their fate in their own hands, without fundamentally interfering in the market economy, or encroaching on individual liberty, and even less by taxing the ratepayers.

133 The Association contained a sprinkling of Tories but a majority of Whigs or radicals drawn from the 'friends of labour', Christian Socialist, Positivists, Liberals, Co-operatists – men like Fawcett, Mill, Kingsley, Ruskin, Maurice, Chadwick, Holyoake, etc. There were originally twenty-eight men (ten of them in government office) and fifteen women.

134 Making reforms 'palatable' to politicians, showing them how 'they meshed in with Victorian liberalism's interest in improving the morals of the poor' (Griffin, 2014: 110).

135 It was a major platform of deliberation. Hardly any socio-political question was excluded from its annual meetings: 'Not a single amendment in law, police, education, and the art of national health has ever been carried into effect which had not first been inculcated in season and out of season by the Social Science Association', *The Times*, 22 April 1886 (Goldman, 2004: 9). Its meetings, attended by hundreds of people, took place in all the major cities; their proceedings appeared in the press and were avidly read by thousands.

136 'Social science became part of the repertoire of the educated, independent-minded middle-class young woman of the 1860s and 1870s' (Goldman, 2004: 122).

137 Emily Davies wrote: 'The Association was of immense use to the women's movement in giving us a platform from which we could bring our views before the sort of people who were likely to be disposed to help in carrying them out' (Goldman, 2004: 47). Several pillars of the women's movement,

The Social Science Association was founded in July 1857 by Lord Brougham, with the barrister G. W. Hasting as general secretary, and Isa Craig as their assistant, with a view to co-ordinating the efforts of experts and politicians (lawyers, philanthropists, educationalists, etc., all leading figures from the political, administrative, and professional classes). It was responsible for the promotion of a great variety of reforms in favour of women which, gradually, enforced their legal rights and their access to secondary and higher education, to employment, and to training. Just before the opening of the 1869 congress in Bristol, Dr Charles Bell Taylor, outraged by the extension of the Contagious Diseases Acts to the civilian population, launched a national campaign for their repeal. After a meeting convened in protest of what he regarded as 'a most cruel, unjust and despotic measure' (Goldman, 2004: 129),[138] he formed a National Association, followed at the end of the year by the establishment of a Ladies Association, headed by Josephine Butler.[139] The male leadership of the campaign against the Contagious Diseases Acts was mostly Nonconformist and Freethinking: Liberal MPs Henry J. Wilson,[140] A. J. Mundella, and Jacob Bright,[141] the lawyer Sheldon Amos,[142] Ben Elmy,[143] Francis W.

Emily Faithfull, Bessie Parkes, Adelaide Procter, Jessie Boucherette, and Elisabeth Pease Nichol, held conferences there (126 women contributed a total of 269 papers, *Ibid.*: 217). They were admitted equally whether as members or as administrators for the first time (*Ibid.*: 119).

138 At the 1870 meeting three papers were read against the Contagious Diseases Acts: 'The Present State of the Contagious Diseases Acts'; 'The Policy of the Contagious Disease Acts 1866 and 1869', 'The Difference of Sex as a Topic of Jurisprudence and Legislation'.

139 She was encouraged to do so by her husband, the Rev. George Butler, who was exhorting women to fight their own battles (Bryant, 1979: 93).

140 Wilson led the repeal campaigns in the North of England. Abolitionists were less concerned however about women's rights than about the spread of immorality and the protection of women from male corruption: Wilson was treasurer of the National Vigilance Society which in 1889 prosecuted Emile Zola's publisher (Royle, 1980: 276).

141 Bright was also the Parliament leader of the suffrage campaign and a supporter of the Married Women's Property reform (1868–1874). In 1869 he obtained the municipal franchise for women.

142 He is the author of *A Comparative Survey of the Laws in Force for the Prohibition, Regulation and Licensing of Vice in England and Other Countries* (1877).

143 He edited the *Shield*, the journal of the repeal campaign against the Contagious Diseases Acts.

Newman,[144] William Shaen,[145] Robert Applegarth;[146] J. S. Mill came in person to testify to the meeting,[147] James Stansfeld ruined his career as Cabinet minister by accepting the official leadership of the movement in the Commons in 1875.[148] The Society for Promoting the Employment of Women (1859) was created after the recommendations of the Social Science Association's investigating committee on industrial employment. It assisted Emily Faithfull to set up the Victoria Press, where all employees were female (1862). The Women's Protective and Provident League, created by Emma Paterson to encourage female trade unionism (1874), benefited greatly from the helpful advice of the Co-operatists Thomas Brassey, Hodgson Pratt,[149] Henry Solly, Auberon Herbert, and J. H. Levy, a member of the Personal Rights Association. Following the 1874 Bristol meeting, five craft societies were born, and Emma was one of the first women to be admitted to the Trade Union Congress (1875). One of the most spectacular achievements of the Social Science Association has to be the 1870 Married Women Property Act. It was the result of a vigorous campaign started at the 1867 congress by George Hastings's paper against the common law regulating marriage, bringing to fruition the work of Barbara Leigh Smith, Matthew Davenport Hill (a friend of her father's and a suffragist since 1832), and Brougham's Law Amendment Society

144 He was a supporter of married women's property rights and of women's access to higher education.
145 Shaen was the founder and chairman of the National Association against the Contagious Diseases Acts from 1870 to 1886. He campaigned for suffrage and for the admission of women at university, and was involved in the foundation of Bedford, Girton, and Newnham Colleges, as well as of medical colleges.
146 Robert Applegarth, a working-class member of the royal commission investigating the Contagious Diseases Acts, became a convinced repealer after visiting military hospitals and several haunts of vice; he suggested that the Commission heard women's views on the subject. In 1869 Francis Newman tried to get women admitted to the Social Science Association meeting.
147 For details see Goldman (2004: 127–36).
148 Stansfeld was married to W. H. Ashurst's daughter. A Chartist sympathizer, suffragist, and radical MP for thirty-six years, he was celebrated by J. L. Hammond and, Barbara Hammond in *James Stansfeld: A Victorian Champion of Sex Equality* (1932). Duncan MacLaren was another MP in favour of the repeal.
149 Hodgson Pratt, a friend of Holyoake and Solly, chaired an organizational conference to implement her proposals.

in 1854 [III, 3]. The campaign was well prepared,[150] and overwhelmingly supported in Parliament by Liberals, amongst whom Thomas Hughes and Thomas Acland (Griffin, 2014). Most remarkable too was the role of the Social Science Association's Committee for Education. The Committee included every name in the field and was influential in the appointment of the Taunton Commission (1864) which led to the reforming of endowed schools (to which Lord Brougham had been attached since 1816). All the Taunton commissioners were personally engaged with the reform of middle-class education and proved attentive to the points of view of women educationists.[151] They had themselves given papers on the question in the 1860s. Henry Roby, in particular, the secretary of the Commission, turned out to be a most precious ally for Emily Davies.[152] The three men appointed to administer the Endowed School Acts (1869), 'the Magna Charta of girl's education',[153] were all committed reformers.[154] In 1865, banking on the success of an experiment started in 1863, a special committee helped secure girls' formal admission to Cambridge examinations (in Oxford the locals for girls were introduced later in 1873–1874). Last but not least, Sir Joshua Fitch, a friend of T. H. Green, J. L. Davies [II, 7], and James Bryce, deserves a special mention in this chapter, not only for his expert work as member of the SSA but also for his involvement with every phase of the struggle

150 The work of its preparatory Committee, which included John Westlake, Thomas Hare, Jacob Bright, G. J. Shaw-Lefevre and Russell Gurney, was lauded by Elisabeth Wolstenholme (Goldman, 2004: 126).
151 Matthew Arnold played no small part. His series of essays, *Culture and Anarchy* (1867–1868), pleading for a state-run system, made a lasting impression in the debates. Most grammar schools were Anglican foundations.
152 Roby was a Cambridge don and Liberal MP. He sent her confidential papers to help her campaign strategy, drafted Girton College's constitution, designed its scheme of studies, set its entrance paper, and stocked its library (Fletcher, 1980: 68). James Bryce, one of the university Liberals, member of Taunton Commission in 1865, and chair of it in 1895, marshalled support for Girton College. A tireless worker for the cause, he remained nevertheless opposed to suffrage.
153 Alice Zimmern, *The Renaissance of Girls' Education in England* (1898), p. 83.
154 Arthur Hobhouse [III, 4], Lord (G. W.) Lyttelton, and Canon Hugh Robinson. Lord Lyttelton and his colleagues were responsible for Schemes establishing forty-seven girls' grammar schools (Fletcher, 1980). Henry Winterbotham, MP for Stroud, is one of the forgotten promoters of girls' education; he defended the equal sharing of endowments between boys and girls (Fletcher, 1980: 26–7).

for women's education – whether in the University Extension Scheme, in the Cambridge Locals campaigns, in the foundation of Girton and of the Girls' Public Day School Company, or in the opening of the University of London to women students on equal terms with men, to quote only a few of his contributions. Remarked by Matthew Arnold, he was made a school inspector, and dedicated his life to improving pedagogy and raising schools' teaching standards. He became one of the most respected educationists of his times (his revelation of the abuses and inadequacy of the educational endowments in his seminal report for the Taunton Commission led to the reform of the system in 1869). Interestingly, *Lectures on Teaching* (1882) and *Educational Aims and Methods* (1900), a collection of his chief addresses, testify to the persistence of conservative viewpoints on women's roles – even in a recognized champion of women's education.[155]

Men's campaigns for birth control

The major means by which fertility was controlled were all known and written about in the eighteenth century, but private sexual practices became the subject of public debate only in the nineteenth century,[156] as a result of two preoccupying national issues, the population question and 'the crusade against poverty' (significantly the subtitle of the *Malthusian* after 1881). Before becoming an instrument for greater sexual freedom, 'the preventive check'[157] was first regarded as an instrument of social control against the reckless poor – providing yet another example of the hybrid character, both progressive and conservative, of the ideologies that ended up fostering women's rights. There was never any pure ideology in favour of birth control: it was buttressed with a social

---

155 Although Fitch secured a large share of endowments for girls' schools, supported women's suffrage and work, and had declared intellect to be 'of no sex', he exalted home as the centre of life.
156 A plethora of books were published on the subject by Chartists, Socialists and Liberals asking for a redistribution of land to fight against poverty, and arguing that raising the standard of living would check the rise of population (McLaren, 1978).
157 The term 'birth control' was actually coined in the twentieth century by Margaret Sanger. In 1921 Marie Stopes coined the phrase 'Constructive Birth Control' in an attempt to make contraception more acceptable in the public mind.

project, entangled with Malthusian economics, Freethought philosophy, or eugenics considerations.[158] However, for the first time, the radical critique of existing sex relations, i.e., the sexual subjection of women, the condemnation of the double standard, the reducing of women to childbearers, the plight of unwanted pregnancies, or mental and physical illnesses due to sexual frustration, prompted an unprecedented interest in the health of women. In the long run, this concern acted in favour of increasing women's control over their bodies.

Pauperism had been primarily diagnosed by Malthus and his disciples (*Essay on Population*, 1798)[159] as 'the reckless over-breeding of the poor', which charity and public relief aggravated, but which was fortunately kept in check by Madame Nature. His conclusions were very influential in the recommendations of the Old Poor Laws reformers. Although in the 1803 edition of his *Essay* he propounded restraint from marriage (not within marriage) as a remedy for overpopulation [IV, 6], and in the 1817 reprint actually reprobated artificial modes of checking population, paradoxically Malthus was to provide stimulus to the birth control movement. The first campaigner for the 'preventive check' to overpopulation was Francis Place,[160] a Utilitarian tailor (but father of fifteen!), whose ideas combined those of Jeremy Bentham, John Stuart Mill, Edward Wakefield, and William Godwin. In reaction to Malthus's favouring of moral restraint (i.e., that labourers should abstain from marriage until able to provide for a family), which Place regarded as debasing their class [IV, 2], he claimed on the contrary that sexual intercourse should start at an early age,[161] and denounced 'the class conspiracy' of the aristocrats (who made use of contraception) against the workers. Place wished

---

158 Or even dictated by military-economic considerations. In 1916, C. K. Ogden's *Uncontrolled Breeding, or Fecundity Versus Civilisation*, published under the pseudonym Adelyne More, argued that overpopulation was the main cause of war.
159 The Rev. Thomas Robert Malthus, an Anglican aristocrat, had in fact largely plagiarized the ideas of Sir James Steuart, Robert Wallace, and Joseph Townsend that population multiplies faster than subsistence, and that misery and natural catastrophes produce the necessary population adjustments.
160 His library in Charing Cross was the unofficial headquarters of English radicalism, from working-class leaders to radical MPs.
161 His argument that late sexual relations entailed mental disorders and the production of weak children was based on his own hospital enquiries (Fryer, 1965: 73).

to give them the means of avoiding Malthus's option.[162] His practical instructions on the artificial control of fertility in the *Diabolical Handbills* (1823) were an attempt to fight against the social inequality bred by overpopulation, and to bring about social and political change. They remained unsigned. The first to associate his name to the subject was Richard Carlile in 1826, allegedly after being converted by Place.[163] But his own case shows that birth control came about also as a side effect of the infidels' crusade against priestcraft:[164] birth control provided another opportunity to attack the Church and encourage freethinking, to rid people of the restrictive dictates of revealed religion and of the moral hegemony of the Church.

Birth control caused much concern both amongst the medical profession (anxious to preserve their reputation),[165] and in the ranks of the political economists. J. R. McCullough warned that, without self-denial and competition from the pressure of numbers, civilization could not progress, and that reduced births would force up wages. In the 1860s, birth control propaganda was dominated by social conservatives, anxious to defuse any form of socialist reform and to preserve the tenets of laissez-faire.[166] It did not however make the topic more respectable [IV, 4 and 6]. Henry Arthur Allbutt, a dermatologist and Freethinker, was struck off the medical register for publishing *The Wife's Handbook* (1886), which included a passage on contraception.[167] T. R. Allinson met

162 Two self-taught working men, William Campion and Richard Hassell, discussed it in their *Newgate Monthly Magazine* (1825–1826).
163 Carlile was initially afraid that contraception would favour debauchery, but a flood of letters from all over the country asking for information on the subject convinced him otherwise (Fryer, 1965: 75).
164 The publishers James Watson, Henry Hetherington, John Cleave, Edward Truelove, and Austin Holyoake distributed birth control tracts.
165 Only a handful of physicians endorsed birth control: Kate Mitchell, William Hitchman, and Walter Dunstan. Dr Elisabeth Blackwell proposed abstinence instead. Dr Mary Scharlieb referred to birth control as race suicide (McLaren, 1978: 111). Foreign medics, such as Auguste Forel, were more supportive (Monacelli, 2005).
166 'Œdipus' [Thomas J. Haslam], *The Marriage Problem* (1868); 'M. G. H.', *Poverty: Its Causes and Cure* (1870); Austin Holyoake, *Large or Small Families? On Which Side Lies the Balance of Comfort?* (1870); John Henry Palmer, *Individual, Family and National Poverty* (1875). Richard Harte (*On the Laws and Customs Relating to Marriage*, 1870), Cookson [IV, 6], and the phrenologist J. B. Keswick (*Woman: Her Physical Culture*, 1895) were far more 'feminist' in their intentions.
167 Like Allinson, he continued to practise unregistered. His book was one of the

the same fate for *A Book for Married Women* (1894). But nevertheless, by the turn of the century, women of all classes had a doctrine at their disposal holding that to limit the size of their families was both a right and a duty.[168]

Not until the prosecution of Charles Bradlaugh was birth control turned into a *cause célèbre* pushed in the women's movement. Bradlaugh's short-lived Malthusian League in 1861 had tried to popularize contraception but his Malthusian views were mainly an offshoot of the secularist movement's rationalist propaganda.[169] The trial, originally intended as publicity for Bradlaugh's campaigns, demonstrated an unexpected public interest in contraceptive methods.[170] The immediate re-establishment of the Malthusian League by C. R. Drysdale institutionalized the defence of birth control. The League (1877–1927) gained 220 new members in the week following the trial. However, its pamphlets and leaflets, of which

---

most popular to be published in Britain: ninety thousand copies were sold by 1907, and five hundred thousand by 1926. In *Artificial Checks to Population: Is the Popular Teaching of Them Infamous?* (1888), he remarked that only cheap birth control pamphlets aimed at the lower classes were being prosecuted. On the prosecution cases following the sale of those books, see Royle (1980: 276, 281).

168 The channels of information on birth control ranged from local shops to the advertising columns of mass circulation dailies, plus via a number of sex manuals (McLaren, 1978: 225–6). Ada Slack in the Women's Cooperative Guild fought for the right of women to control their bodies. In 1896, the pamphlet, *The Malthusian Handbook* (1893), advertised by Julia Dawson in the *Clarion*, sold out in a few weeks. Although this is not within our remit here, women's response to contraception was complicated by many factors, including a concern for respectability: E. Wolstenholme Elmy signed up to the Besant–Bradlaugh's defence committee, but Henry Fawcett refused to let his wife be a witness at the trial. It never followed a clear pro- or anti-birth control divide (Bland, 1995). Some women would even argue that birth control would benefit men by favouring sexual promiscuity.

169 See his pamphlets *Jesus, Shelley and Malthus* (1861), *Poverty and Its Effects on the Political Condition of the People* (1863), *Labour's Prayer* and *Why Do Men Starve?* (1865).

170 In America, Charles Knowlton's *Fruits of Philosophy* (1832) attacked the medical profession for its failure to deal with the question of procreation. The book had been selling seven hundred copies a year in Britain without government interference until 1876, when Charles Watts published a new edition containing lewd illustrations, and was prosecuted for obscenity. In 1877 Bradlaugh and Besant republished the book (updated with medical footnotes by G. Drysdale): five hundred copies sold in twenty minutes.

three million copies were distributed, did not actually provide practical information on contraception (until 1913), and the League limited itself to the enforcement of Malthusian economics.[171] The real propaganda work on conception prevention was carried out by Secularist lecturers within the League (W. H. Reynolds, its secretary, for instance), or working with it, like Joseph Symes, originally a Wesleyan minister, who framed birth control with 'the rights of women' in the *National Reformer*,[172] the editor George Standring, or Annie Besant, whose pamphlet *The Law of Population* (1877), sold 175,000 copies by 1891 (although after her conversion to Theosophy she rejected birth control) [I, 5].

The contagion of Eugenics provided yet another stimulus to birth control discussions [III, 6]. From the publication of Francis Galton, *Inquiries into Human Faculty and Its Development* in 1883, the new science permeated C. F. G. Masterman's *The Condition of England* (1909) or J. A. Hobson's *The Social Problem* (1901). Attacks against the socialists' refusal to promote contraception came from D. G. Ritchie [II, 8] and George Shoobridge Carr (*Social Evolution and the Evolution of Socialism*, 1895). If the Malthusian League was concerned with quantity, the eugenics movement was preoccupied with quality, but the League followed suit by calling for restrictions of the breeding of the unfit (the period is marked by a deluge of books and articles calling for policies to keep their number in check). Eugenicists advanced fresh arguments to explain why women and workers could not be left to determine their family size themselves, and the Fabians turned to a form of state-directed fertility control ('endowed motherhood'),[173] going as far as suggesting the 'nationalization' of the

---

171 Its regular journal, *The Malthusian* (1879–1921), persistently targeted the working classes: 'We want the poor to be taught to limit their families by the same contraceptive methods which most married couples in the richer classes are employing', 27:10 (15 October 1913), p. 73. Its middle-class contributors criticized the socialists for turning their backs on the iron laws of economics.

172 *National Reformer* (29 July 1877), p. 513. He was far more radical than most in his attack on the double standard, and pleaded for women's right to sexual enjoyment free from the fear of pregnancy, *National Reformer* (23 September 1877), p. 644.

173 Alarming Fabian tracts, 'The Decline in the Birth Rate' by Sidney Webb (131, 1907), or 'The Endowment of Motherhood' by H. D. Harben (149, 1910), voiced the middle classes' fear of physical degeneracy and race suicide. In the *New Age*, Beatrice Hastings advocated 'The Nationalisation of Mothers' (27 June 1907, p. 132).

breeding industry in order to discourage reproduction from the inferior stock.[174] Whether a right or a duty, birth control was therefore primarily an ideology of social management. The significant decline in birth rate between 1876 and 1936,[175] particularly in the upper and middle classes, was due less to propaganda than to adjustments to new socio-economic conditions (Fryer, 1965: 176–9): legislation had made working of children under ten illegal (1867) and education compulsory (1870), depriving the working class of children's wages; skilled workers were keen to preserve their standards of comfort, and the middle classes wanted all their children to have an education. In other words, birth control was adopted not so much because it was desirable *per se* but because it had become necessary.

Men's campaigns for women's suffrage

For several reasons the franchise question stands apart: singularly, except for occasional papers, it was never debated by the Social Science Association, which took no official position on the subject. In order to maximize parliamentary support, the women's vote was never presented as a party issue,[176] and defied traditional alliances.[177] As Pugh pointed out

174 The Drysdales (including their son C. Vickery Drysdale) were convinced eugenicists and promoted birth control (see Alice Vickery's 'On the Position of Women, as Affected by Large Families' in the *Malthusian*, 1880). They helped establish a college for the medical training of women, and supported a wide range of women's rights.
175 In the 1860s there were 6.16 births per marriage, in 1915, 2.43. Lewis-Faning's Royal Commission on Population reported that forty per cent of married women between 1910 and 1919 were using contraceptive methods.
176 Or perhaps as '*anti*-party' Pugh argued (2000: 22).
177 As revealed by the political allegiances of the men who introduced suffrage bills: Jacob Bright (Liberal, 1870); Leonard Courtney (Liberal, 1879); Hugh Mason (Liberal, 1881); William Woodall (Liberal, 1884); Baron Dimsdale (Conservative, 1888); W. S. B. McLaren (Liberal, 1888); Sir Albert Rollit (Conservative, 1982); Charles McLaren (Liberal, 1893); F. Faithfull Begg (Conservative, 1896); Bamford Slack (Liberal, 1905); Sir Charles Dilke (Liberal, 1906); W. H. Dickinson (Liberal, 1907 and 1913); Henry York Stanger (Liberal, 1908); Geoffrey Howard (Liberal, 1909); D. J. Shackleton (Labour, 1910); Sir George Kemp (Liberal Unionist, 1911), and James Tynte Agg-Gardner (Conservative, 1912). Two bills were introduced in the Upper Chamber by Lord Denman (1887) and Lord Templetown (1897).

(2000), Conservatism turned out to be as an unexpected ally, and Liberalism an unexpected enemy, (the subject causing a lot of friction within the Liberal Party itself). Although a long-standing historical claim,[178] female suffrage was not a national topic until Russell's Liberal government introduced a new parliamentary reform bill in 1866. It was then officially embraced by the ladies of Langham Place. From then on franchise bills were presented almost every year, but the question did not significantly reappear in the parliamentary debates until the 1884 Reform Act. In the end, and much to the Pankhursts' dismay, the vote was less the victory of the vindication of a woman's right than part and parcel of the recognition of the principle of individual representation.[179] With the brief interval of the two Conciliation Bills designed to enfranchise women specifically (but rapidly abandoned, which infuriated the suffragettes), the women's vote was never seriously entertained by Asquith's government. It became a practical necessity when women's inclusion on the electoral registers appeared to the Liberals as one of the keys to wider economic and political changes.[180] Millicent Fawcett had suspected suffrage would come not 'as an isolated phenomenon' but 'as a necessary corollary of the other changes which have been gradually and steadily modifying, this century, the social history of our country'.[181]

The pro-suffrage campaigns (including campaigns against it) are however an interesting example and perhaps one of the best illustrations of 'co-partnership'[182] between the sexes. They were started by, and based on, celebrated husband/wife, father/brother/daughter co-operation, a telling evidence of close and dynamic interaction between the male and

---

178 Thomas Starling Norgate endorsed women's suffrage in the *Cabinet* (1795). Henry Hunt presented Mary Smith's suffrage petition to Parliament in 1832.
179 Rover remarks that 'the development of political thought away from the representation of interests and towards individual rights was necessary before women could hope to have the vote' (1967: 13).
180 Pugh (2000) remarked that when education, health, and poor relief (issues which were considered within female expertise) became central to national politics, they gave women a stronger claim to the vote. After the 1885 Reform Act, the updating of the messy electoral registers was also a pressing need, which explains the nine bills in 1888 attempting to change the registration system.
181 'Women's Suffrage: A Reply', *The Nineteenth Century*, 107 (1886), 746.
182 Sir Alfred Mond, in the Men's League for Women's Suffrage's *Monthly Paper*, 38 (November 1912).

the female sex, irrespective of denominations,[183] parties,[184] and classes.[185] This is substantiated by the unprecedented number of leagues set up throughout the country in its support (and whose papers would deserve greater exploration).[186] With the exception of Mrs Pankhurst's Women's Social and Political Union, which counted only one (financially invaluable) male member, Frederick Pethick-Lawrence,[187] and of Charlotte Despard and Teresa Billington-Greig's Women's Freedom League, the suffragist movement remained mixed. Until 1912, co-operation between male and female suffrage societies was recorded as harmonious and effective.[188] Christabel Pankhurst initially welcomed men's collaboration. Duval's work on women's behalf [III, 8][189] was first highly appreciated by the journal *Votes For Women*: 'Their action had emphasized the fact that the campaign to secure votes for women was not a sex war; it was a great fight that was being undertaken by men as well as women ... Their action should be written in the annals of the fight in letters of gold.'[190] The Church

183 The Church League for Women's Suffrage (1909) [I, 9]; the Free Church League for Women's Suffrage (1910) with the Rev. Charles Fleming Williams and his wife; the Catholic Women's Suffrage Society (1911) with Joseph Clayton and Francis Meynell as members; the Jewish League for Woman Suffrage (1912) with Laura and Leonard Frankin.
184 A Liberal Men's Association for Women's Suffrage was formed in protest against Asquith's policy in 1913.
185 The Rebels' Social and Political Union and the East London Men's Society were largely working-class associations.
186 The lawyer Herbert Jacobs's Men's League for Women's Suffrage (1907) attracted high-ranking professionals, clergymen, and the literati (Edward Carpenter, George Bernard Shaw, Thomas Hardy, John Galsworthy). The Men's Committee for Justice to Women (1909) was led by Captain Gonne, the Men's Political Union (1910) by Victor Duval. Victor Prout's Men's Federation for Woman Suffrage (c. 1912) was close to Sylvia Pankhurst; the Men's Society for Women's Rights (1912) was founded by the editor A. W. G. Jamrach. On regional suffragism see Crawford (2006).
187 He was treasurer of the Women's Social and Political Union, and financed their journal *Votes for Women*.
188 Sylvia Pankhurst, *The Suffragette Movement* (London: Longmans, Green & Co, 1931), pp. 268, 379–80, 471.
189 Monacelli, 'Victor Duval (1885–1945) et la *Men's Political Union*' (in Monacelli, ed., 2010).
190 *Votes for Women* (4 November 1911), p. 66 and 29 December 1911, pp. 210–11. E. Robins, Annie Kenney, Mary Richardson, S. Pankhurst, and E. Pethick Lawrence all recognized men's contributions, even if sometimes equivocally.

leagues were co-funded by men and women, and so were the People's Suffrage Federation (1909),[191] the London Graduates' Union for Women's Suffrage (1909), the National Political League for Men and Women (1911), the Votes for Women Fellowship (1912), the Northern Men's Federation for Women Suffrage (1913–1919) and, of course, the United Suffragists (1914) by Henry Nevinson and H. J. Gillespie.[192] In June 1907, the *Women's Franchise* founded by the journalist J. E. Francis was intended to be 'the joint organ of all the suffrage societies', male or female. Significantly the Manchester National Society for Women's Suffrage (1865) with Richard M. Pankhurst,[193] Jacob Bright, Max Kyllmann, and the Rev. S. A. Steinthal on the executive committee, Ben Elmy's Male Electors' League for Women Suffrage (1897) or the Men's League for Women's Suffrage (1907) all predate the (male or female) Antis' leagues (1910).[194] A number of men jeopardized their careers or lost their assets in support of the vote, like Dr Victor Horsley, Leonard Courtney,[195] Frederick Pethick-Lawrence, the businessman Godwin Clayton, the police magistrate Cecil Chapman, and the publisher J. E. Francis. Keir Hardie, George Lansbury, and Philip Snowden supported the vote against their party policy.[196] The role of the Conservatives in the campaigns has also undergone serious revision (Auchterlonie, 2007). The support of Tories like Richard Sherwood on the Isle of Man (where women obtained the vote in 1881), Lord Salisbury, Lord Selborne, Robert Cecil, Lord Lytton, the Fourth Viscount

191 The People's Suffrage Federation (1909) was founded by Labour men and women; Arthur Henderson, Margaret Bondfield, and Mary Macarthur were amongst its members.
192 Men and women sat in equal numbers on its committee.
193 The lawyer Richard (Dr) Pankhurst undeniably features amongst the 'champions' of women's emancipation. He was a mentor to his wife, and Lydia Becker's legal adviser. He drafted the amendment which included women in the Municipal Corporation Bill in 1869, the first suffrage bill (1870), and both the Married Women's Property Acts of 1870 and 1882. R. Pankhurst introduced the concept of 'feme sole' in the draft but it was abandoned.
194 The majority of Conservative MPs refused to follow Cromer and Curzon.
195 Leonard Henry Courtney, an uncompromising Liberal, was married to Beatrice Webb's sister. In 1884 he supported Woodall's bill against party policy, and remained a suffragist to his death.
196 Snowden was secretary of the 1910 Conciliation Committee and published a suffrage pamphlet, *The Dominant Issue* (1913). On Hardie's suffrage activism in the party and the Women's Social and Political Union, see Morgan (1975). Lansbury became a suffrage militant in 1912 and resigned his seat rather than toe Labour policy.

Templetown, and Captain Justinian Edwards-Heathcote disproves the claim that suffrage was an exclusive offshoot of liberalism. One of the (unexpected) developments of the Conservative Primrose League (1884) was that it became 'an advertisement for the political talents of women', thus successfully trained in electioneering tactics and party politics (Pugh, 2000: 111).[197]

The large body of literature available on the suffrage case has not only opened new perspectives on the subject but also forced a reassessment of the opposition to the women's vote: 'Between 1867 and 1885 it had been possible to object to women's suffrage because it seemed genuinely incompatible with the dominant interpretations of the nature of the political system, but by the turn of the century the constitutional doctrines of both major political parties seemed to demand the enfranchisement of at least some women' (Griffin, 2014: 308). Griffin recently pointed out the fluctuations in prominence and credibility of the arguments for or against suffrage (2014: chap. 9). He convincingly argued that, until the Liberals moved to the principle of 'one man, one vote',[198] the 'languages of representation' used by suffragist MPs in the debates (class, interests, property, household suffrage) all proved a dead-end. As suggested above, the question of suffrage could not gain political kudos, let alone triumph, until the arguments related to domestic ideology[199] and Scripture (the inherited patterns of sexual behaviour that underpinned the opposition to the vote) had crumbled. T. H. Green's influential theory of citizenship and social service, at the core of the nineteenth-century Social Gospel, adds a very plausible explanation to the opposition to female parliamentary franchise: men and women who were satisfied with women's increasing political involvement in community work[200] targeted more urgent fields of emancipation. The inadequacy of

197 From the 1880s, women's suffrage was for the Conservatives a means of strengthening their battle against socialism. Although the League did not actually campaign for suffrage, George Renwick, the president of the Newcastle council, and Faithfull Begg declared themselves suffragists.
198 This then accounts for the majority of votes in Parliament in favour of suffrage by the 1890s.
199 The vote of wives interfered with 'coverture', and marital authority, a central tenet of domestic ideology. If restricted to spinsters, it meant giving 'votes to the class of women who had no wrongs in order to redress the wrongs of that class to which it gave no votes' (Griffin, 2014: 226), a factor which compounded the issue.
200 Green opposed suffrage, convinced that 'the growth of women's power in

female schooling in the 1860s unfortunately validated the argument that the right to vote could be exercised only by an educated person. Finally one of the prerequisites for women's suffrage seems to have been the introduction of the secret ballot (it was then impossible for men to claim women knew how their husbands voted). Significantly it promoted the representation of individuals rather than classes, and converted several male Antis to suffragism (Griffin, 2014: 248–9).

There is little doubt that the nineteenth-century fight for women's rights took place against a complex backdrop of compelling social, religious, political, and economic factors that encouraged its development, and accelerated the erosion of gender stereotypes. Belittling women's achievements was never the intention of this book. The history of women's emancipation is becoming more securely grounded in its intellectual context; it is only fair that its male protagonists should have their share of the limelight.

---

such a state as England should be through local government' (Anderson, 1991: 683–5). Mrs Humphry Ward, the leader of the Women Antis, was a Greenite. By 1900 1,589 women were serving in elected local government as against seventy-nine in 1880 (Anderson, 1991: 688).

I
Comrades in struggle

> If woman is not free, man must ever be a slave.
> Goodwyn Barmby

1 'Arouse! Awake! Rescue your sex'

William Thompson (1775–1833) has been celebrated in history as 'Britain's pioneer socialist, feminist, and co-operator' (Pankhurst, 1954). Although born into the wealthy Anglo-Irish Ascendancy, he was an enlightened landlord and supported Catholic emancipation. Thompson was one of the early critics of capitalism and of Malthus's theories. His *Inquiry into the Principles of the Distribution of Wealth Most Conducive to Human Happiness; Applied to the Newly Proposed System of Voluntary Equality of Wealth* (1824) makes him second to Owen as the leading theorist of Co-operativism.[1] The *Appeal* – in Thompson's own words, an amalgamation of his own ideas and those of Anna Wheeler, with whom he maintained a deep and long-term friendship – is one of the most revered texts of socialist feminism, and regarded as its first manifesto. A full diatribe against men's universal tyranny over women, a condemnation of the double standard, a plea for women's civic rights, the *Appeal* is also a vehement denunciation of the marriage code, 'the disgrace of civilisation' (p. xiv), and a scathing attack against women's 'unindividualization'. It came as a powerful sequel to Thompson's former advocacy of sex equality and birth control (presented as 'individual prudence' or 'gentle' exercise) in his *Practical Directions for the Speedy and Economical Establishment of Communities on the Principles of Mutual Co-operation, United Possessions and Equality of Exertions and the Means of Enjoyments*, 1830. Thompson's writings on

---

[1] Lovett and Thompson co-founded the British Association for the Spread of Co-operative Knowledge.

sex equality resonate with Jeremy Bentham's Utilitarian principles: 'The interests therefore of all human beings, their real comprehensive interests, calculating all the consequences of their actions and pursuing that which will promote preponderant good, thus reconciling individual with general welfare, ought to be pursued for all, and for all classes; the interests of women for their own sakes, the interests of men for theirs' (p. 166). But they are also related to his opposition to private property. Thompson regarded women's full emancipation as impossible until the adoption of a new political economy and social arrangements – 'the system of Association, or of Labor by Mutual Co-operation ... the only one which will complete and forever insure the perfect equality and entire reciprocity of happiness between men and women' (p. 199). In *Labor Rewarded. The Claims of Labor and Capital Conciliated: or, How to Secure to Labor the Whole Products of Its Exertions* (1827) he attempted to sketch an ideal government with co-operative communities, maximized freedom, and altered marriage laws. But Thompson knew that the achievement of gender equality required more than replacing the 'science of producing wealth by individual competition' by 'the social science, or the science of promoting human happiness' (p. xiv). He was acutely aware that men would have to rethink and refashion their own sense of manhood: 'To wish for the enjoyment of the higher pleasures of sympathy and communication of knowledge between the sexes, heightened by that mutual grace and glow, that decorum and mutual respect, to which the feeling of perfect, unrestrained equality in the intercourse gives birth, a man must have heard of such pleasures, must be able to conceive them, and must have an organization from nature or education, or both, capable of receiving delight from them when presented to him' (p. xiii). This is perhaps one of the most challenging and innovative qualities of the *Appeal*.

William Thompson, *Appeal of One Half the Human Race, Women, Against the Pretensions of the Other Half, Men, to Retain Them in Political, and Thence in Civil and Domestic, Slavery* (London: Longman, Hurst, Rees, Orme, Brown, and Green, 1825), pp. 208–11

The removal of all *partial* existing restraints of law of custom, and the unfolding of the career of equal exertion to women and men, instead of being any obstacle to your ['Women of England'] further advancement under the system of Mutual Co-operation, would be the most certain step towards the progress of it, would prepare you to perceive its benefits, and render you anxious on the first opportunity to embrace them. No wretches ever passed from a state of slavery to a system of freedom without more or less of mental excitement, without more or less of alarm, to the timid amongst their masters. These are partial and necessary evils, swelling almost into blessings from the immensity of preponderant good by which they are followed. Regard them not. Truth, benevolence, the interest of the whole human race, are on your side. Persevere, and you must be free. If to your intelligence and efforts, this mighty change in human affairs shall be indebted, you will lay men under an obligation of gratitude to you, in comparison with which, the past use of your mere animal charms would be like the fretful dream of the morning.

Nor will your fellow-creatures, men, long resist the change. They are too deeply concerned to continue long to oppose what palpably tends to their happiness: they are too deeply concerned not to be compelled to re-consider the barbarous systems of laws and morals under which they have been brought up. In justice, in pity to them, submit no longer; no longer *willingly* submit to their caprices. Though your bodies may be a little longer kept in servitude, degrade not yourselves by the repetition of superfluous vows of obedience: cease to kiss the rod: let your *minds* be henceforth free. The morn of loosening your physical chains will not be far distant.

Wretched as is, as has always been, your political, civil, domestic, and individual position – what reason have you to believe it likely to be improved without the energetic co-operation of your own exertions, without your own unshrinking determination?

Mark the effect on human character of that system of education pursued at all our public seminaries, exclusively devoted as they are to the males of our race. Can the tiger passions, so sedulously cultivated in our youths at their public schools, to be hereafter exercised on their fellow-men, give any promise of more kindly treatment to your sex, who are so entirely in their power, in whose favour no restrain of law exists, no punishment for injury, except indeed the deadly blow be given – though even then a loop-hole of retreat can be found for the murderer? Arouse! Awake! Rescue your sex, your species, from the frightful circumstances that surround and degrade you: – demand your rights; or man, ungenerous man, intoxicated with his power, may become still more presumptuous, and no longer measure or calculate the effect of his actions towards you, relying on your apathetic submission, while improvement in every other department of human exertion is on the advance.

Behold our youths brought up in the indulgence of all the cruel and ferocious passions, as inimical to the development of the higher intellectual faculties as they are revolting to reason and humanity – sad proof of the short-sighted ignorance of their teachers! Behold them hence taught, nay compelled to believe, that all who want force to oppose to theirs, are by nature made over to them as objects of oppression, of sport, and contempt.

Demand them with confidence and dignity your portion of the common rights of all:—assume the high post that nature has assigned you; become the respectable and respected mothers and instructors of men; arrest this education of brutality; and cease to be the mere degraded instruments of men's sensual pleasure.

Do not those male portions of the human race who are oppressed by their fellow-men, occasionally see and feel their wrongs? Do they not occasionally break in upon the debasing slumbers of their foolish and wretched oppressors, by communing about their wrongs, by remonstrating and petitioning for their removal?

When will you, the most oppressed and degraded of the human race – for no vice, for no crime degraded and oppressed – see your wrongs, commune about them, break in upon the leaden slumbers of your masters, and remonstrate and petition for their removal? When will you remonstrate and demand that the same enlarged education, which ought to be afforded to all men, should also be afforded to you? That all exclusive laws restraining your exertions should be repealed? That your persons, in whatever situation in life should be equally protected from *assault*, imprisonment, or restrain of any kind, with those of men? That, whether married or not, your actions, like those of men, should be regulated by your own notions of propriety and duty, restrained only by equal and just laws? That the same punishments, whether legal or moral, and no more than the same punishments, should be awarded to you, for the same vices or crimes, that are to men awarded? And that the same political and civil rights that men enjoy should be secured to you, because from the comparative want of strength you are more in need than men, of such legal protection?

The slow advance that man makes in obtaining his own liberties is a proof of what is called the retributive justice of nature, of the unerring tendency of injustice to produce accumulated evils. He wishes to obtain liberty for himself; yet selfishly conspires to exclude from its blessings one half his race. What is man, that he can pretend to change these tendencies and produce two contrary effects – your degradation and his own happiness – by means not only inadequate, but also opposed to the nature of things and to each other?

Shall he obtain liberty and happiness for himself, whilst resolved to deny it to the other half of his species? Can he ever become consistently just to his fellow-creature man, whilst he remains uniformly unjust to his fellow-creature woman? No, no; the principle of justice must be equal in its operation, extending to the whole human family, before men can reasonably hope any result from their labors, but that self delusion which mocks them with *an ideal advance*, whilst yet chained down by their oppression of you to misery, vice, and eternally recurring disappointments.

O woman, from your auspicious hands may the new destiny of your species proceed! The collective voices of your sex raised against oppression will ultimately make men themselves your advocates and debtors.

2 'Throw off the degrading yoke'

Reginald John Richardson (1803–1861), originally a Salford master joiner, claimed to have taken part in every working-class movement of his times. Present as a boy at the Peterloo massacre, a Luddite at twenty-three, he was one of the leading agitators for the Reform Act in 1832, and the founder of the Anti-Poor Law Association in South Lancashire in 1837. A year later, he took part in the organization of the first Chartist convention on Kersal Moor. By then the radical rioter had become a good literate debater, and Richardson served as editor of the *Dundee Chronicle* (1841–42). In theory Chartists who demanded the vote as a universal right included female enfranchisement (in the early years over 150 female Unions were formed throughout Britain).[2] Suffrage however was removed from their social programme, the People's Charter, as a strategy to rally more potential supporters, but Richardson held fast to his beliefs in equality and justice, and addressed the question head on by affirming women's natural, civil and political rights. Confronting the Bible on the question of woman's subordination, he regarded the word 'helpmeet' as the basis for the equality of the sexes (a conception of the sexes as different and complementary [I, 7]), and argued that a husband's

---

2 Few female Chartist sections had a separate agenda from their husbands' and they remained primarily concerned about bettering homes for their families.

power over his wife could derive only from her consent (which incidentally accounts for Richardson's support of single women franchise). Of a bellicose nature, and supportive of 'physical force', Richardson was arrested on charge of sedition and served a nine-month prison sentence, during which he wrote 'The Rights of Women', a pro-suffrage pamphlet published in 1840 in Edinburgh, London, and Manchester. Feargus O'Connor reviewed the publication very eulogistically (women's political rights, he wrote, were set forth 'with a lucidity and clearness which nothing but the most determined obstinacy and blinded selfishness will be able to resist'),[3] even if by 1849 he became hostile to female franchise. Several feminist votaries in his National Association, like the republican W. H. Linton, the abolitionist James Haughton, or the Whig politician William Biggs, took advantage of the Chartist agitation to stimulate public debates on domesticity and democracy. Goodwyn Barmby demanded 'unsexual Chartism' in the first issue of *Promethean* (1842). The *Star in the East*, James and Caroline Hill's paper, lambasted the Chartists for paying lip service to the liberal principles they professed publicly. Richardson's high-spirited pamphlet urging women to 'band *themselves* together to oppose the progress of despotism' is almost unique amongst Chartists, and ranks amongst the best examinations of women's socio-political subjection. Although it typified the (widely shared) Chartists' acquiescence in gender roles (the ideal of marriage, the praise of domestic life and duties), it never screened Richardson's confidence in female reasoning power, nor did it belittle his plea for women's political emancipation, even if it was motivated by a concern for working-class respectability. Chartism may have been short-lived (it dissolved in 1848), but it raised the consciousness and confidence of many working-class women on whom its activities relied.

R. J. Richardson, *The Rights of Woman: Exhibiting Her Natural, Civil, And Political Claims to a Share in the Legislative and Executive Power of the State* (Edinburgh: J. Duncan, 1840), pp. 8–11

Having shown, in a clear and forcible light, the abstract right of woman to equality with the man, in all cases except where restrained by her own free will, I now proceed to show you my opinions upon what I may be allowed to term, the physical inequality of woman; and in order that I may strengthen my vindication of the rights of woman, I shall prove she is not deteriorated or reduced in consequence of her physical weakness.

3 *Northern Star* (30 January 1841), p. 3.

Physiologists tell us that woman is physically weaker than man, and our common observations justify that opinion. Her natural organization befits her for other services to the human race equivalent to those performed by man, whilst the latter is gifted with a strong osseous structure, capable of bearing greater hardships, firm muscular fibre, strong tendons capable of great elasticity, powerful nerves enabling him to bear great trials, abundant secretions necessary to supply the wasting of his vigorous frame, copious streams of the vital fluid, with strong digestive powers to supply the means of life, and lastly, his superior strength of body and mind all combined, befit him for the hardy toils and dangers which he is doomed to endure, in consequence of the primitive curse; but the woman, has also her physical excellences peculiar to her sex, equally as important to the human race. It is true, she is less fitted by nature to endure toil and danger than man; but contrast his bold and rugged form with her soft and graceful person, his high commanding voice with her mild and soothing tones, his inflexible will with her yielding disposition, his boisterous passions with her insinuating and fascinating powers of love; combine them all, and what an agreeable compound do they form! their essence is the spring of life, the fountain of social order, the reservoir from whence all the happiness of mankind flows, the stream that irrigates with all the kind offices of nature the community through which it takes its course. In one line of the poet: –

'Woman, lovely woman, nature formed you to temper man!'

Why should man trample upon her, because she is physically unable to meet him upon equal terms? Why does he look down upon her, when she is the ordained of God to minister to his happiness? Why does he consider her inferior to himself, when without her he would be miserable; in fact, his race could not be perpetuated in accordance with the divine injunction, that bade him 'go forth, multiply and replenish the earth?' Why does he, professing Christianity, draw an invidious line of demarcation betwixt himself and woman, creating a distinction which the Great Creator of the universe, in the fulness of his wisdom, sought not to make other than male and female? Why does he seek to make her his slave, whom God designed should be his helpmate? Why, in the name of innocence, love, and truth, whose virtues are inherent in woman, should she be deemed incapable of participating in the election of her lawgivers and rulers? Surely God, in his infinite goodness and wisdom, hath not so decreed! Then why should man, – restless, ambitious, and lordly man, – presume to set upon helpless and innocent woman the mark of slavery, and deprive her of all the rights, privileges, franchises, and functions, which he usurps and monopolizes, to the grievous injury of her whom it is his natural duty to protect? Away with all equivocation! perish all evasions! Tell me not that woman is the natural slave of man! Insult not human reason by declaring her unequal to her fellow-man! degrade not human nature by proclaiming to the world that woman, because she is physically unequal, that she is uncapable of judging between right and wrong, virtue and vice, or of the causes that promote happiness or misery, peace or war, pleasure or pain, wisdom or folly! Equivocation and evasion are sure denotements of knavery. To call woman a slave, is the language of a coward and a tyrant; to say that she is not naturally gifted with the powers of ratiocination, is the egregious folly of a blasphemer and a libel upon humanity itself.

Admit at once that woman *is not the slave of man*, and we elevate her from her degraded position and recognise her as a fellow creature; say that *she is equal to man*, in every respect, and we fulfil the sacred ordinance of God. Proclaim that she *is endowed with reasoning faculties*, and we take her into our councils. These three admissions constitute the principles of human government: Liberty, Equality, and Knowledge. They are the Rights of Man, the Rights of Woman, and of the Human Family: those who would subvert them are enemies to the human race, unworthy the name of man, and of the affections of endearing woman.

It is much to be regretted that women, in all ages, have yielded to the tyranny of men, and were it not that my doctrines were founded upon the eternal basis of truth and deduced from principles of natural law, I should feel inclined to admit that custom, slavish and barbarous as it is, has sanctioned their subjugation; but surely there is a time for redemption, a time when reason will prevail over tyranny, and manumize the fairest portion of the human race! – a time, when men will redeem their own character from the foul blot that shadows their noble nature by at once admitting women to share in the legislative power of their common country – a time when, at least, our own countrymen, urged forward by their mothers, sweethearts, wives, and daughters, will throw off the degrading yoke, that not only deprives a great majority of themselves of the elective franchise, but almost totally disqualifies the whole of the women, thereby holding them in political thraldom.

3 The root causes of women's subjection

As one of the most prominent and influential liberal intellectuals of the Victorian age, James Stuart Mill (1806–1873) does not need much introducing. Mill was an exceptionally bright scholar, the author of leading philosophical and political essays such as *Principles of Political Economy, with Some of Their Applications to Social Philosophy* (1848); *On Liberty* (1859); *Considerations on Representative Government* (1861), *Utilitarianism* (1863). He became a women's champion on presenting Barbara Bodichon's suffrage petition to Parliament in 1867, and proposing an amendment to the Second Reform Bill to include female enfranchisement (on the same terms as men). His advocacy of women's rights originated in a belief in the sovereignty of the individual and a profound dislike of tyranny, whether social or domestic (although while working for the British East India Company from 1823 to 1858, Mill recommended 'benevolent despotism' over the colonized). Mill showed a commitment to sex equality in his early contributions to the *Westminster Review* in 1824, and was jailed for distributing Francis Place's pamphlets on birth control (in the *Black Dwarf* he publicly vindicated the 'check' of population as highly moral and virtuous, a point also addressed in *Principles of Political Economy*).[4] But as he admitted in his *Autobiography* (1873), his long-term relationship with the feminist Harriet Taylor turned what was 'little more than an abstract principle', indebted to the ideas of the Saint Simonians, Owen, and Fourier,[5] into a full endorsement of women's political and economic rights. *The Subjection of Women* (1869), the outcome of a common 'fund of thought' with Harriet, is recognized with Thompson's *Appeal* as the one of the founding texts of nineteenth-century feminism.[6] Mill analysed the

---

4 Mill denounced as barbarism 'the *right* to a person of another'. The debate appeared in the *Black Dwarf* (November 1823 – January 1824) between Wooler, the editor, Francis Place and Mill, writing as 'A.M.'. His father, James Mill, had made references to birth control in *Elements of Political Economy*, 1821, and the *Supplement of the Encyclopaedia Britannica*, 'Colony', 1824. So did the *Edinburgh Review*, 38:75 (February 1823).
5 In the 1830s the French Saint Simonians propagandized their own socialism in England thanks to Anna Wheeler's translations in *The Crisis*. Charles Fourier's books were promoted by Hugh Doherty in his short-lived *Morning Star* in 1840.
6 T. H. Green's *Prolegomena to Ethics* (1883) and *Lectures on the Principles of Moral Obligation* (1895) deserve the same recognition for their unequivocal rejection of patriarchy, and forceful promotion of women's positive equality and liberty regarding adultery, marriage and family relations (Anderson, 1991).

various social mechanisms that kept women in bondage; he proclaimed their intellectual capacities as equal to men's, and encouraged them to prove their mettle in all professions (although he excluded married women). Mill did not fail to raise the nature-versus-nurture debate, central to the Woman Question: 'What is called the nature of women is an eminently artificial thing – the result of forced repression in some directions' (p. 38). Mill considered that unequal sex relations were an impediment to human improvement. Emancipation was neither for him nor for that matter for any other contemporary social reformer – an end in itself. However Mill's plea for the birth of a new society based on the principles of justice and freedom, 'the first and strongest want in human nature' (p. 178), went well beyond Bentham's *felicific calculus*: 'The most direct benefit of all', he wrote, was 'the unspeakable gain in private happiness to the liberated half of the species' (p. 178). The book provoked a lot of controversy and rather hostile press reactions, including from Mill's friends: the anti-suffragist novelist Margaret Oliphant found the description of woman's oppression in wedlock grossly exaggerated; her review of the book in the *Edinburgh Review*, 130 (1869) was particularly virulent.

John Stuart Mill, *The Subjection of Women* (London: Longmans, Green, Reader, and Dyer, 1869), pp. 26–31

All causes, social and natural, combine to make it unlikely that women should be collectively rebellious to the power of men. They are so far in a position different from all other subject classes, that their masters require something more from them than actual service. Men do not want solely the obedience of women, they want their sentiments. All men, except the most brutish, desire to have, in the woman most nearly connected with them, not a forced slave but a willing one, not a slave merely, but a favourite. They have therefore put everything in practice to enslave their minds. The masters of all other slaves rely, for maintaining obedience, on fear; either fear of themselves, or religious fears. The masters of women wanted more than simple obedience, and they turned the whole force of education to effect their purpose. All women are brought up from the very earliest years in the belief that their ideal of character is the very opposite to that of men; not self-will, and government by self-control, but submission, and yielding to the control of other. All the moralities tell them that it is the duty of women, and all the current sentimentalities that it is their nature, to live for others;

to make complete abnegation of themselves, and to have no life but in their affections. And by their affections are meant the only ones they are allowed to have – those to the men with whom they are connected, or to the children who constitute an additional and indefeasible tie between them and a man. When we put together three things – first, the natural attraction between opposite sexes; secondly, the wife's entire dependence on the husband, every privilege or pleasure she has being either his gift, or depending entirely on his will; and lastly, that the principal object of human pursuit, consideration, and all objects of social ambition, can in general be sought or obtained by her only through him, it would be a miracle if the object of being attractive to men had not become the polar star of feminine education and formation of character. And, this great means of influence over the minds of women having been acquired, an instinct of selfishness made men avail themselves of it to the utmost as a means of holding women in subjection, by representing to them meekness, submissiveness, and resignation of all individual will into the hands of a man, as an essential part of sexual attractiveness. Can it be doubted that any of the other yokes which mankind have succeeded in breaking, would have subsisted till now if the same means had existed, and had been so sedulously used, to bow down their minds to it? If it had been made the object of the life of every young plebeian to find personal favour in the eyes of some patrician, of every young serf with some seigneur; if domestication with him, and a share of his personal affections, had been held out as the prize which they all should look out for, the most gifted and aspiring being able to reckon on the most desirable prizes; and if, when this prize had been obtained, they had been shut out by a wall of brass from all interests not centering in him, all feelings and desires but those which he shared or inculcated; would not serfs and seigneurs, plebeians and patricians, have been as broadly distinguished at this day as men and women are? and would not all but a thinker here and there, have believed the distinction to be a fundamental and unalterable fact in human nature?

The preceding considerations are amply sufficient to show that custom, however universal it may be, affords in this case no presumption, and ought not to create any prejudice, in favour of the arrangements which place women in social and political subjection to men. But I may go farther, and maintain that the course of history, and the tendencies of progressive human society, afford not only no presumption in favour of this system of inequality of rights, but a strong one against it; and that, so far as the whole course of human improvement up to this time, the whole stream of modern tendencies, warrants any inference on the subject, it is, that this relic of the past is discordant with the future, and must necessarily disappear. For, what is the peculiar character of the modern world – the difference which chiefly distinguishes modern institutions, modern social ideas, modern life itself, from those of times long past? It is, that human beings are no longer born to their place in life, and chained down by an inexorable bond to the place they are born to, but are free to employ their faculties, and such favourable chances as offer, to achieve the lot which may appear to them most desirable. Human society of old was constituted on a very different principle. All were born to a fixed social position, and were mostly kept in it by law, or interdicted from any means by which they could emerge from it. As some men are born white and others black, so some were born slaves and others freemen and citizens; some were born patricians, others plebeians; some were born feudal nobles, others commoners and *roturiers*. A slave or serf could never make himself free, nor, except by the will of his master, become so. In most European countries it was not till towards the close of the middle ages, and as a consequence of the growth of regal power, that commoners could be ennobled. Even among nobles, the eldest son was born the exclusive heir to the paternal possessions, and a long time elapsed before it was fully established that the father could disinherit him. Among the industrious classes, only those who were born members of a guild, or were admitted into it by its members, could lawfully practice their calling within its local limits; and nobody could practice any calling deemed important, in any but the legal manner – by processes authoritatively prescribed. Manufacturers have stood in the pillory for presuming to carry on their business by new and improved methods. In modern Europe, and most in those parts of it which have participated most largely in all other modern improvements, diametrically opposite doctrines now prevail.

4 Against the sexual double standard

From the 1830s, sexual licence had been a widely debated subject in Unitarian quarters. Vehement campaigns were engaged by William Shaen, William Biggs, and James Stanfeld (members of the Associate Institution for Improving and Enforcing the Laws for the Protection of

Women, 1844)[7] against those they called 'a worse set of masters than any negro slaveowners'.[8] Until the 1860s all rescue workers had been men, but women were gradually invited to join forces with them (Bessie Rayner Parkes was one of the first to work in the Westminster slums). Several unsuccessful efforts had been made to curtail prostitution by law: the London Society for the Protection of Young Females submitted a bill in 1842 to the Home Secretary; the Bishop of Exeter introduced a bill in the Lords on 17 May 1844, followed by Lord Brougham's Protection of Women Bill (25 July 1849). When W. T. Stead (1849–1912) took the editorship of the *Pall Mall Gazette* in 1883, he was a seasoned journalist, determined to use the newspaper for his own crusades. Stead was a deeply religious man, particularly concerned about criminal vice and the plight of the fallen woman. As editor of the Darlington *Northern Echo* (1871–1880), then the most influential voice of radicalism and the Nonconformist conscience in northern England, he had attracted public attention to injustices with incisive leaders and articles. Stead supported Josephine Butler's campaign for the repeal of the Contagious Diseases Act with a sense of mission. When Parliament abandoned the Criminal Law Amendment Bill for the third time, he felt 'an imperious sense of public duty' to try and force the bill through by printing a series of statements on child prostitution in London.[9] Between 6 and 10 July 1885, his articles entitled 'The Report of our Secret Commission' caused a public sensation, raising the paper's readership to unprecedented heights. However, in order to prove his case against those who 'trafficked in womanhood', he arranged the purchase of a thirteen-year-old girl (whom Butler had persuaded Rebecca Jarrett, a prostitute, to procure). He was later found guilty of abduction and was thrown into jail for three months (an experience he claimed was the happiest of his life). Ironically the series of articles was republished (slightly abridged, on 29 July 1885, under the title 'The Maiden Tribute of Modern Babylon'),

---

7 Radical Unitarians as well as Conservative churchmen and politicians collaborated to the association. Its journal, the *Female Friend*, was committed to the defence of women's rights. *Magdalenism* (1840) by the surgeon William Tait was the first detailed study of the causes, extent and consequences of prostitution in Edinburgh.
8 *People's Journal*, 2:31 (1 August 1846), p. 9.
9 Encouraged by Benjamin Scott, Chamberlain of the city of London, an anti-vice campaigner, a member of the Gospel Purity Association (1885), and a Contagious Diseases Acts repealer (*A State of Iniquity: Its Rise, Extension and Overthrow*, 1890).

after a committee of investigation composed of MPs Samuel Morley and R. T. Reid, the Archbishop of Canterbury, the Cardinal Archbishop of Westminster, and the Bishop of London declared Stead's statements 'substantially true'. No good tree bears bad fruit. The law which raised the age of consent from thirteen to sixteen was passed the following August. Single-handedly he had achieved what he called 'government by journalism'.[10] His aspiration to turn the press into 'the eye and the ear and the tongue of the people' had come true. But this success was also an indicator that public opinion perceived the prostitute as an innocent victim.[11] Stead's judges significantly thanked him for services rendered to the nation, i.e., for 'securing the passage of a much needed law for the protection of young girls'.[12] Stead also supported suffrage and promoted women's access to journalism in the *Review of Reviews*[13] which he founded in 1890, before tragically perishing in the sinking of the *Titanic*.

W. T. Stead, 'The Maiden Tribute of Modern Babylon' (*The Report of the Pall Mall Gazette's Secret Commission*), Pall Mall Gazette (29 July 1885), p. 2

This very night in London, and every night, year in and year out, not seven maidens only, but many times seven, selected almost as much by chance as those who in the Athenian market-place drew lots as to which should be flung into the Cretan labyrinth, will be offered up as the Maiden Tribute of Modern Babylon. Maidens they were when this morning dawned, but to-night their ruin will be accomplished, and to-morrow they will find themselves within the portals of the maze of London brotheldom. Within that labyrinth wander, like lost souls, the vast host of London prostitutes, whose numbers no man can compute, but who are probably not much below 50,000 strong. Many, no doubt, who venture but a little way within the maze make their escape. But multitudes are swept irresistibly on and on to be destroyed in due season,

10 'Government by Journalism', *Contemporary Review*, 49 (May 1886).
11 Stead founded the National Vigilance Association the same year, supported by Sophia Dobson Collet, Sara Hennell, and Annie Besant whom he had defended during her trial. In contrast with Stead, T. H. Green's prescription against prostitution was women's economic independence ('The Development of the Moral Ideal', *Prolegomena*).
12 Recorded in *My Father, Personal and Spiritual Reminiscences* by Estelle Wilson Stead (London: Heinemann, 1913), p. 133.
13 'Young Women in Journalism', *Review of Reviews*, 6 (October 1892).

to give place to others, who also will share their doom. The maw of the London Minotaur is insatiable, and none that go into the secret recesses of his lair return again. After some years' dolorous wandering in this palace of despair – for 'hope of rest to solace there is none, nor e'en of milder pang,' save the poisonous anodyne of drink – most of those ensnared to-night will perish, some of them in horrible torture. Yet, so far from this great city being convulsed with woe, London cares for none of these things, and the cultured man of the world, the heir of all the ages, the ultimate product of a long series of civilizations and religions, will shrug his shoulders in scorn at the folly of any one who ventures in public print to raise even the mildest protest against a horror a thousand times more horrible than that which, in the youth of the world, haunted like a nightmare the imagination of mankind. Nevertheless, I have not yet lost faith in the heart and conscience of the English folk, the sturdy innate chivalry and right thinking of our common people; and although I am no vain dreamer of Utopias peopled solely by Sir Galahads and vestal virgins, I am not without hope that there may be some check placed upon this vast tribute of maidens, unwitting or unwilling, which is nightly levied in London. Much of all this vice may be inevitable, and with that I have nothing to do. But I do ask that those doomed to the house of evil fame shall not be trapped into it unwillingly, and that none shall be beguiled into the chamber of death before they are of an age to read the inscription above the portal – 'All hope abandon ye who enter here.' If the daughters of the people must be served up as dainty morsels to minister to the passions of the rich,[14] let them at least attain an age when they can understand the nature of the sacrifice which they are asked to make. And if we must cast maidens – not seven, but seven times seven – nightly into the jaws of vice, let us at least see to it that they assent to their own immolation, and are not unwilling sacrifices procured by force and fraud. That is surely not too much to ask from the dissolute rich. Even considerations of self-interest might lead our rulers to assent to so modest a demand. For the hour of Democracy has struck, and there is no wrong which a man resents like this. If it has not been resented hitherto, it is not because it was not felt. The Roman Republic was founded by the rape of Lucrece, but Lucrece was a member of one of the governing families. A similar offence placed Spain under the

14 The specific targeting of the sexuality of the upper classes ended up sapping the moral authority of the governing elites. See also the Rev. Edward Lyttelton's *Training the Young in the Laws of Sex* (1900).

domination of the Moors, but there again the victim of Royal licence was the daughter of a count. But the fathers and brothers whose daughters and sisters are purchased like slaves, not for labour, but for lust, are now at last enrolled among the governing classes – a circumstance full of hope for the nation, but by no means without menace for a class. Many of the French Revolutionists were dissolute enough, but nothing gave such an edge to the guillotine as the memory of the *Parc aux Cerfs*; and even in our time the horrors that attended the suppression of the Commune were largely due to the despair of the *femme vengeresse*. Hence, unless the levying of the maiden tribute in London is shorn of its worst abuses – at present, as I shall show, flourishing unchecked – resentment, which might be appeased by reform, may hereafter be the virus of a social revolution. It is the one explosive which is strong enough to wreck the Throne.

Liberty for vice, repression for crime

To avoid all misapprehension as to the object with which I propose to set forth the ghastly and criminal features of this infernal traffic, I wish to say emphatically at the outset that, however strongly I may feel as to the imperative importance of morality and chastity, I do not ask for any police interference with the liberty of vice. I ask only for the repression of crime. Sexual immorality, however evil it may be in itself or in its consequences, must be dealt with not by the policeman but by the teacher, so long as the persons contracting are of full age, are perfectly free agents, and in their sin are guilty of no outrage on public morals. So far from demanding any increased power for the police, I would rather incline to say to the police, 'Hands off,' when they interfere arbitrarily with the ordinary operations of the market of vice. But the more freely we permit to adults absolute liberty of vice to adults, the more stringent must be our precautions against the innumerable crimes which spring from vice, as vice itself springs from the impure imaginings of the heart of man. These crimes flourish on every side, unnoticed and unchecked. To extirpate vice by Act of Parliament is impossible; but because we must leave vice equally free that is no reason why we should acquiesce helplessly in the perpetration of crime. And that crime of the most ruthless and abominable description is constantly and systematically practised in London without let or hindrance, I am in a position to prove. Those who are constantly engaged in its practice naturally deny its existence. But I speak of that which I do know, not from hearsay or rumour, but of my own personal knowledge.

5 'A thousand-times-told tale'

Because of an unfortunate penchant for money and women which allegedly drove his partner Eleanor –Karl Marx's younger daughter – to commit suicide, Edward Bibbens Aveling (1851–1898) has gone down in history as a very controversial figure of socialism, and obviously even more so of 'feminism'. However, Aveling and Eleanor are indissociable icons of Victorian militancy. Irresistibly drawn to each other and united by common tastes, they deliberately flaunted social conventions by living together, although Edward was still married.[15] Aveling met Eleanor in 1872, when teaching physics and botany at Miss Buss's North London Collegiate School for Ladies, before becoming a distinguished science academic at University College, London, and a celebrated popularizer both of Darwin's ideas (*National Reformer*, 1879–1880) and of Marx's views. Aveling rapidly moved from a Nonconformist background to freethinking and atheism: with Charles Bradlaugh and Annie Besant he was one of the three pivots of the National Secular Society in 1879, and true to his principles refused to pledge religious alliance for the sake of a career at King's College. Eleanor and Aveling became kindred spirits when both members of Hyndman's Social Democratic Federation (SDF), the first Marxist party in Britain, which they left in 1884 for the more internationally oriented Socialist League. They proved indefatigable and effective workers for the cause of socialism, including in America, relentlessly haranguing crowds together, and regularly coupling their names in publications.[16] The SDF's concern for the resolution of the class or social question always took primacy over the woman question (with the exception of Keir Hardie; Hyndman was notoriously opposed to women's rights, and Belfort Bax was an active member of the Men's Anti-Suffrage League).[17] The pamphlet below, reproduced in the *Westminster Review*,

---

15 Illicit unions in freethinking socialist milieux ranged from *ménages à trois* to free unions (Alice Vickery and Charles Drysdale, G. Aldred and Rose Witcop, Elisabeth Wolstenholme and Ben Elmy, George Eliot and George Henry Lewes, Emma Martin and Joshua Hopkins were notorious exemplars). The Legitimation League (1893) and its journal, the *Adult* (1897–1898), campaigned for free unions and the legal protection of children born outside of wedlock (Frost, 2008).
16 Katherine and John B. Glasier, also members of the Socialist League, devoted their lives to the socialist cause. Although they prided themselves on an egalitarian marriage, they opposed women's votes (Thompson, 1971).
17 Robert Blatchford, at first an advocate of woman's cause, opposed suffrage vehemently in the *Clarion* in the 1890s because, typically too, he thought it would weaken the case for men's rights.

testifies to the differing ideological strands which existed within the party regarding women's rights (further exemplified by Herbert Burrows's *The Future of Woman*, 1909, which opposed differentiated gender roles).[18] But it is also interestingly far more explicit on women's subordination as a sex, and far more critical of 'the organized tyranny of men' than Eleanor's original review of August Bebel's *Woman – Past Present and Future* which had toed the party line.[19] Their joint version of the pamphlet undeniably points to Aveling's contribution in the denunciation of the expropriation of women 'as to their rights as human beings'. Drawing upon their own partnership based on co-operation and mutual admiration ('the treatment of such a question as this is best when it is that of man and a woman thinking and working together'), and following W. T. Stead's revelations on the white slave trade, they made their pamphlet intentionally provocative, particularly regarding marriage, prostitution, and chastity. Both however were convinced that 'equality without distinction of sex' was impossible until the capitalist system of production was brought to an end. Aveling was, besides, one of the few socialists committed to birth control, which he defended in articles in *Justice*, in *Commonweal*, and in the pamphlet *Darwinism and Small Families* (1882).[20] In 1883, he unsuccessfully staged a press campaign in protest against Annie Besant and Alice Bradlaugh's exclusion from the University of London.

Edward Aveling and Eleanor Marx Aveling, 'The Woman Question. *From a Socialist Point of View*', *Westminster Review*, new series, 69 (January and April 1886), 210–13

We will suppose all women, not only those having property, enabled to vote; the Contagious Diseases Act repealed; every calling thrown open to both sexes. The actual position of women in respect to men would

18 This points to the persistence of the Owenite tradition within the sexually conservative mainstream of the socialist associations.
19 Supplement of the *Commonweal*, 1:6 (July 1885), 63.
20 Other exceptions were Daniel Chatterton (*Babies and Bunny Rabbits: A Popular Educator*, 1884?), the Rev. Stewart Headlam (in the 1880s he made several pleas in favour of birth control in the *Malthusian*), J. M. Robertson (*Socialism and Malthusianism*, 1885), and Fabian George Standring in his journal *Birth Control* (1919). In socialist ranks opposition to the discussion of fertility control and the population question was endemic. They were considered as false issues impeding the progress of labour. Marx referred to Malthus as 'a shameless sycophant of the ruling class'. English Marxists opposed the Malthusian League.

not be very vitally touched. (We are not concerned at present with the results of the increased competition and more embittered struggle for existence.) For not one of these things, save indirectly the Contagious Diseases Act, touches them in their sex relations. Nor should we deny that, with the gain of each or all of these points, the tremendous change that is to come would be more easy of attainment. But it is essential to keep in mind that ultimate change, only to come about when the yet more tremendous social change whose corollary it will be has taken place. Without that larger social change women will never be free.

The truth, not fully recognised even by those anxious to do good to woman, is that she, like the labour-classes, is in an oppressed condition; that her position, like theirs, is one of unjust and merciless degradation. Women are the creatures of an organised tyranny of men, as the workers are the creatures of an organised tyranny of idlers. Even where thus much is grasped, we must never be weary of insisting on the non-understanding that for women, as for the labouring classes, no solution of the difficulties and problems that present themselves is really possible in the present condition of society. All that is done, heralded with no matter what flourish of trumpets, is palliative, not remedial. Both the oppressed classes, women and the immediate producers, must understand that their emancipation will come from themselves. Women will find allies in the better sort of men, as the labourers are finding allies among the philosophers, artists, and poets. But the one has nothing to hope from man as a whole, and the other has nothing to hope from the middle-class as a whole.

The truth of this comes out in the fact that, before we pass to the consideration of the condition of women, we have to speak this word of warning. To many, that which we have to say of the Now will seem exaggerated; much that we have to say of the Hereafter, visionary, and perhaps all that is said, dangerous. To cultured people, public opinion is still that of man alone, and the customary is the moral. The majority still lays stress upon the occasional sex-helplessness of woman as a bar to her even consideration with man. It still descants upon the 'natural calling' of the female. As to the former, people forget that sex-helplessness at certain times is largely exaggerated by the unhealthy conditions of our modern life, if, indeed, it is not wholly due to these. Given rational conditions, it would largely, if not completely, disappear. They forget also that all this about which the talk is so glib when woman's freedom is under discussion is conveniently ignored when the question is one of woman's enslavement. They forget that by capitalist employers this very sex-helplessness of woman is only taken into account with the view of lowering the general rate of wages. Again, there is no more a 'natural calling' of woman than there is a natural law of capitalistic production, or a 'natural' limit to the amount of the labourer's product that goes to him for means of subsistence. That, in the first case, woman's 'calling' is supposed to be only the tending of children, the maintenance of household conditions, and a general obedience to her lord; that, in the second, the production of surplus-value is a necessary preliminary to the production of capital; that, in the third, the amount the labourer receives for his means of subsistence is so much as will keep him only just above starvation point: these are not natural laws in the same sense as are the laws of motion. They are only certain temporary conventions of society, like the convention that French is the language of diplomacy.

To treat the position of women at the present time in detail is to repeat a thousand-times-told tale. Yet, for our purpose, we must re-emphasise some familiar points, and perhaps mention one or two less familiar. And first, a general idea that has to do with all women. The life of woman does not coincide with that of man. Their lives do not intersect; in many cases do not even touch. Hence the life of the race is stunted. According to Kant, 'a man and woman constitute, when united, the whole and entire being; one sex completes the other.' But when each sex is incomplete, and the one incomplete to the most lamentable extent, and when, as a rule, neither of them comes into real, thorough, habitual, free contact, mind to mind, with the other, the being is neither whole nor entire.

Second, a special idea that has to do with only a certain number, but that a large one, of women. Every one knows the effect that certain callings, or habits of life, have on the *physique* and on the face of those that follow them. The horsy man, the drunkard, are known by gait, physiognomy. How many of us have ever paused, or dared to pause, upon the serious fact that in the streets and public buildings, in the friend-circle, we can, in a moment, tell the unmarried women, if they are beyond a certain age which lively writers call, with a delicate irony peculiarly their own, 'uncertain'? But we cannot tell a man that is unmarried from one that is wedded. Before the question that arises out of this fact is asked, let us call to mind the terrible proportion of women that are unmarried. For example, in England, in the year 1870, 42 per cent of the women were in this condition. The question to which all this leads is a plain one, a legitimate one, and is only an unpleasant one because of the answer that must be given. How is it that our sisters bear upon their brows this stamp of lost instincts, stifled affections, a nature in part murdered? How is it that their 'more fortunate brothers' bear no such mark? Here, assuredly, no 'natural law' obtains. This licence for the man, this prevention of legions of noble and holy unions that does not affect him, but falls heavily on her, are the inevitable outcome of our economic system. Our marriages, like our morals, are based upon commercialism. Not to be able to meet one's business engagements is a greater sin than the slander of a friend, and our weddings are business transactions.

6 The time is come to act

George Jacob Holyoake (1817–1906) started work in a foundry at the age of nine. At seventeen he attended the Birmingham Mechanics' Institute (with the help of W. J. Fox, W. H. Ashurst, and the Mills) and the young man became a powerful writer and public lecturer (several female figures of Victorian feminism attended his meetings regularly). Holyoake warmed to Robert Owen's ideas of co-operation and rational religion, and was devoted to Auguste Comte, whose Religion of Humanity contributed to the shaping of Secularism. He published *The History of the Rochdale Pioneers* (1857), *The History of Co-operation in England* (1875), *The Co-operative Movement of To-day* (1891) and *Origin and Nature of Secularism* (1896). An indefatigable activist, he founded several newspapers to promote his freethinking views: the *Movement* (1843–1845); the popular and enduring working-class *Reasoner and Theological Examiner* (1846–61), dedicated 'to instructive criticism rather than subordinate to the task of pleasing' (it sold five thousand copies a week in 1852); the *Secular Review* (1876–1907). He edited the overtly atheist *Oracle of Reason* (1841–1843), and the co-operative *English Leader* (1864–1867). Holyoake was tried for atheism in 1842, and spent six months in prison. A lover of justice and freedom, he agitated for many causes, the first suffrage reform in 1832, the freedom of the press (a fight he related in his *Life and Character of Richard Carlile*, 1849), Chartism (by the side of William Lovett), and Secularism. Although he was not opposed to birth control, he disagreed with Charles Bradlaugh and Annie Besant over their decision to launch themselves into a highly public trial [IV, 4], and dissociated himself from Bradlaugh's National Secular Society by creating the British Secular Union with Kate Watts and Harriet Law. His deep admiration for his mother, a 'self-acting managing mistress', undoubtedly lay at the root of his support of the cause of women. During his election campaign for

(1903.)

1 George Jacob Holyoake

Tower Hamlets in 1857, he circulated four thousand copies of Harriet Taylor's 1851 pamphlet 'Are Women Fit for Politics? Are Politics Fit for Women?', and publicly defended the independent right of women to property and earnings. His support of the female vote, 'Woman Suffrage:

A Suggestion', was published in the *Independent Review* in 1906. He also opposed the marriage laws, promoted divorce and free unions in the *Reasoner*, even if he never cautioned the libertarianism of Drysdale, and eulogistically prefaced young Florence Dixie's *Isola; Or the Disinherited. A Revolt for Woman and All the Disinherited* (1904). In 1848, he was proud to attend the first women's rights convention (Seneca Falls) in New York, a year after calling women to arms in the press (see below). Holyoake relentlessly encouraged women to fight for themselves, bringing to fruition a debate started by the Owenite John Finch in 1838 in the *New Moral World*.[21] Interestingly, women did not always view unilateral action as appropriate: Geraldine Jewsbury or Mary Leman Grimstone considered that the onus of the task fell upon males: 'Men it is who must begin ... before women can break through',[22] a view shared by D. W. Jerrold, or John Cowrie.[23] However Holyoake successfully persuaded Bessie Rayner Parkes and Barbara Leigh Smith Bodichon (both brought up in Unitarian circles and displaying freethinking sympathies) to launch the first woman's journal in 1858.[24] His enthusiastic presumption that 'the arguments of Mary Wollstonecraft and Madame de Staël, the splendid political capacity Harriet Martineau displayed, must issue in action' (p. 225) ended up galvanizing women, giving them the confidence to start a movement of their own.

George Holyoake, *Sixty Years of an Agitator's Life*, 2 vols (London: T. Fisher Unwin, 1892), vol. I, pp. 222–4

In 1840 there were no signs of an agitation for the civil rights of women. Only a small number of women knew how few the rights of their sex were, or had any desire to increase them. The majority did not know, in any intelligent way, whether they had any civil rights at all. Women had no journal of their own. Ladies' newspapers there were, but they were edited by gentlemen. The public tongue of women was in the mouth

---

21 In 'Ralahine Letter XII', the *New Moral World*, 4:194 (1838), 299, he wrote: 'Women of England! Arouse yourselves "they that would be free, have only to will it!"'.
22 Jewsbury, 'How Agnes Worral Was Taught to Be Respectable', *Douglas Jerrold's Shilling Magazine*, 5 (January–June 1847), 258.
23 Cowrie, 'Noble Sentiments on the Influence of Women', *Howitt's Journal*, 1:11 (1847).
24 Founded with the help of G. W. Hastings. The first and short-lived London weekly *Isis* (February–December 1832) was edited by Eliza Sharples [IV, 1].

of men. Among social reformers, Mrs. Chappell Smith, Mrs. Emma Martin, and one or two others were public advocates of social rights. Only in that quarter of society were women speakers seen upon the platform; they were counted willful and presuming, and it was thought that they would be better employed at home. At a later period a lady known as Mrs. Clara Lucas Balfour appeared as a lecturer on uncontested subjects before religious and literary societies. She was a lady of goodly presence, whose husband was the littlest man ever seen about the House of Commons. He had an appointment in the Private Bills office. He had fought on the *Bellerophon* and it was put down to his sailor's daredevilism that he allowed his wife to speak in public.

Seeing how much faster political and social amendment would proceed were the quick discernment and decision of women engaged in public affairs, I often spoke of it in lectures. The fine scorn of women for delay in doing what can be done and ought to be done was much wanted in politics, where men who declare an evil to be intolerable will desist from abating it on the appearance of the first fool who tells them 'the time is not come' to act against it. Women, being one-half of society, suffered greatly by the intolerance and ignorance of men in matters which did not concern men. Still the women who well knew this, and wrote eloquently against it, had no idea of combining against it.

In 1847, I wrote in the *Free Press* printed in the Isle of Man for the advantage of free postal circulation in England, the following passages: –

'Women have no *esprit de corps*. The language of Lord Grey, when he said, "I shall stand by my order", is scarcely understood by them. We have a race of women, but no order of women. ... Reputable and intelligent women were deputed in America to attend a conference of the Peace Society in London. They crossed the Atlantic on this public mission, and when they arrived in London they were refused the privilege of sitting in the conference because they were women. Yet this insult was never resented.

'The police courts of the metropolis are satiated with complaints of half-murdered women against brutal husbands who escape with comparative immunity. But where are the women out of court who remonstrate? Why have they not formed a society for their own protection? Women desire a share in the suffrage. They are taxed, and therefore they claim a right to vote. But where are women's political unions – self-originated and self-sustained? If they want political rights, why do they not themselves ask for them? If it is unwomanly to ask for them, it will be unwomanly to exercise them when granted – in short, unwomanly to have them. Women, like peers, should "stand by their order" – should have societies of their own. The impunity with which women are despoiled of property, liberty, and even of their children, at the caprice of their husbands, as some melancholy instances in our law courts have lately shown, is an imputation more powerful than any conceivable argument upon the womanly spirit of this nation. Let them take their own affairs into their own hands, as Sir Robert Peel once advised the men of this country to do.

'Let them draw up a list of their legal disabilities, and take the usual constitutional modes of obtaining redress. Let them have societies and public meetings of their own. Let all the offices be filled by women – let the audiences be of women entirely. Let the womanly mind come into action as a separate element of reform – as a "Fifth Estate". It is no use to talk about fitness; it must be proved – the question is not one of theory, but of practice. If women have capacity for public affairs, let it be demonstrated. Familiar as women now are with literature, we have not one periodical, magazine, or newspaper conducted by women. In America the *Lowell Offering* was produced by Lowell factory-girls, but in England we have nothing of the kind. The *Lady's Newspaper* is not conducted by women. We ought to have a *Woman's Journal* – edited by women, contributed to by women, and in every sense an exponent of womanly thought and an advocate of women's rights. Hints and suggestions might be accepted from men, but no interference, no dictation, no direction. For well or ill, skillfully or unskillfully, the act should be their own in every sense.'

I suggested this to several intelligent women without inducing one to follow it out. Those who saw the importance were not prepared to act upon it, and those who were able wanted the spirit of enterprise. 'Propose it to Margaret Fuller,' said one, when that lady was in this country. But it was not good taste to press upon an American lady a task that ought to be undertaken by an English one. I further urged that 'an enterprising woman of wise will, who would undertake such a task, and would train her unpractised sisters in the art of self-emancipation, would be more of a practical benefactor than the authoress of twenty volumes in favour of their rights. When women begin to conduct their own affairs – to generate an *esprit de corps* among themselves, to discuss their own questions in public – there will be blunderings committed, weaknesses displayed, exaggerations perpetrated; but let them remember that men blundered, erred, and exaggerated times without number before they arrived at their present facility. Failure must be ventured or efficiency will never be won. Were women to attempt to legislate for men, and exclude them from their Parliament while doing it, and suffer no information of the rights or claims of men to come before them save through their wives – what an outcry there would be from men against what they would call "one-sided, ignorant, blundering, unjust, insolent, feminine legislation!"'

7 'Woman ... cast aside the chains'

Among the Protestant radical movements that developed in the eighteenth century in the wake of the Reformation, the Baptists (with John Rogers) and the Quakers (with Richard Farnworth) always showed themselves amenable to the recognition of spiritual equality between the sexes, and open to women's public preaching.[25] John Wesley, originally an Anglican divine, more concerned about the pulpit than the altar, founded in 1739 the Methodist Society, which distinguished itself from the Anglican Church by a search after personal holiness, religious discipline, and a strong evangelistic missionary impulse. Wesley, an indefatigable outdoor preacher (he delivered more than forty thousand sermons), opposed women's submissiveness and was the first to authorize a woman to preach in 1761.[26] Female travelling evangelism, encouraged by Hugh Bourne (*Remarks on the Ministry of Women*, 1808), knew its heyday in the 1820s and 1830s, and thrived again in the 1860s (Lloyd, 2009). Methodist itinerant preachers were actively involved in the social issues of their days, particularly in the fight against poverty and ignorance: they campaigned for prison reform and the abolition of slavery, and contributed to the creation of day and Sunday schools and charities. Robert Percival Downes (1842–1924) was instructed in the theological interpretations of Wesley and Adam Clarke by Samuel Coley (a seasoned field preacher who remained his mentor). After his ordination in 1865, Downes proved a most fervent Methodist and became renowned

---

25 Seventeenth-century Puritanism emphasized the importance of individual freedom of conscience, and personal relationship with Christ. Drawing from St Paul's biblical verse to the Galatians ('ye are all one in Jesus Christ'), it established the spiritual equality of men and women in the Church – which did not preclude a strong sense of sexual difference.

26 It was banned in 1803, although the Primitive Methodists kept the tradition alive. The Evangelical revival gave female preaching a tremendous fillip in the 1860s. The first Female Friendly Society, founded by the Methodist Rev. David Simpson in York in 1778, gave women expertise in running their own political unions, and provided a model for future female associations, including the Chartist ones.

for his commanding personality. Widely read in the feminist writings of
his times, he cherished the ambition to bring his contribution to the
emancipation movement, by writing a book 'that the woman who reads
it may be led to say: "It helped me to a light of which before I did not
dream"' (p. 8). That is why the introduction exhorted the female reader
to 'not be discouraged by the unjust things which have been said of her
by men' (p. 16). Downes was also inspired by the formidable and most
revered educationalist J. H. Rigg.[27] He appears genuinely supportive
of women's claims to enter the professions and speak in the churches
(including ordination). His chapter on the rights of woman (pp. 258–61)
definitely marks him as a progressive and a humanist, in spite of some
more conservative views on women's mission as philanthropists, and of
his disapproval of the New Woman (perhaps due to his blind admiration
for John Ruskin). Downes's justification for remedying injustices against
woman, improving her education and widening her sphere was a belief
in 'equality in difference' (p. 21).[28] His opinion that 'it is no more the
exclusive vocation of a woman to be a wife and a mother, than it is
the exclusive destiny of a man to become a husband and a father' (p.
228) led him, remarkably, to praise 'old maids' as 'the very salt of the
earth' (p. 235). His awareness and reproval of women's treatment as
'animated dolls' (p. 47), of 'shallow thinkers who regard woman merely
as the property of man' (p. 228), undoubtedly reflected a desire to redress
'the wrongs of woman'. By urging women to 'cast aside the chains of
false traditions, marring womanhood' (p. 52),[29] Downes encouraged a
dynamic image of women and a new code of social manners which
would allow them to become more independent beings. The book ran
into eight editions. Compared by the journalist George J. H. Northcroft
to a modern Samuel Smiles, Downes was celebrated for many other
works (*John Ruskin*, 1890; *The Pillars of Our Faith*, 1893; *Pure Pleasures*, 1894;
The Art of Noble Living, 1902; *Samuel Coley, the Illustrative Preacher*, 1907; or
Thoughts on Living Subjects, 1909). He is remembered for editing a one-

27 He was Principal of Westminster College, a mixed teachers' training college
founded in 1851 (followed by a women teachers' training college, Southlands,
in 1872).
28 See also [II, 4; IV, 7]. The view was 'the common sense of the English middle
class' (Davidoff and Hall, 2002: 149). For the Chartist William Lovett or the
Evangelical John Angell James (*Female Piety: Or the Young Woman's Friend and
Guide Through Life to Immortality*, 1852) the complementary roles and differen-
tial contributions of both sexes were of equal social value.
29 Poetry was Downes's second passion: the verses are his.

penny weekly compendium, *Great Thoughts from Masterminds* (1884–1937) – an occupation to which he exclusively dedicated himself from 1885 to 1914. In keeping with the Wesleyan tradition of using literature as a weapon of the gospel, Downes's intention in founding the journal was to provide valuable and instructive reading for the voiceless masses. Its influence was far-reaching at home (circulation figures oscillated between fifty thousand and a hundred thousand) and throughout the Empire. The paper contained extracts from literary works and scientific articles, as well as topics aimed at a female readership. It launched the career of countless men and women journalists: Florence Bone, Dorothy Una Ratcliff, and the botanist and suffragette Edith Gray Wheelwright were regular contributors.

Robert Percival Downes, *Woman: Her Charm and Power* (London: C. H. Kelly, 1900), pp. 45–50

The 'stern old king' in Tennyson's 'Princess' correctly states the opinion of the past where he says, with an absoluteness which defies criticism and silences appeal –

> This is fixt
>   As are the posts of earth and base of all;
> Man for the field, and woman for the hearth;
>   Man for the sword, and for the needle she;
> Man with the head and woman with the heart;
>   Man to command and woman to obey.
> All else confusion.

The revolt of woman

Woman has now revolted from this arbitrary standard. Every step of social progress in later years has been marked by a softening of the tyranny of man and a lifting of the position of woman, – an approximation towards an equal companionship. First the tool of his will, next the toy of his pleasure, then the minister of his vanity, she is at last to become the free sharer of his life, the friend of his mind and heart.

This healthy and necessary change has been brought about chiefly through the realisation by woman of her own individual value. She has learnt the glory, the beauty, and the significance of her own existence. She has risen to the true conception of her position as the equal and the fitting complement of man. She claims an equal right with him to the use of every means of self-development in the fulfilment of her destiny. She rises to the possession of her own soul.

Improved methods of education have also done much for the social and intellectual advancement of woman. The female education of fifty years ago was superficial, trifling, and babyish. Girls were not half developed. Their minds did not exhibit one-half of their native strength and beauty. They were robbed of much of their natural vigour. Their education differed not only in degree, but in kind, from that of their brothers, being confined to a smattering of modern languages and a few elegant accomplishments. Neither were their natural aptitudes sufficiently considered. Girls were doomed to practise on the piano for an hour a day who had no idea of tune; to whom, indeed, the whole exercise was a mere slavery. Others were condemned to draw and paint, who had no innate perception of form and colour. To study botany without seeing a flower, astronomy without looking at a star, geology without handling a clod or a stone; write half a dozen compositions on friendship, love, or home; cram into the brain a few dates of history and a few names of kings; daub a little in oils or watercolours. This was female education – without an object, without an ambition, without a definite purpose of any kind. In place of drawing out the mental fineness and tender glory of womanhood, this kind of education left her merely a prey to frivolous excitement, gave her a taste for no other form of literature than that of the novel, and doomed her to the life of an animated doll.

Frances Power Cobbe wittily says that the attitude of many men in the last decade with regard to the question of the higher education of woman might be summed up as follows: 'Woman, beware! beware!! You are on the brink of destruction. You have hitherto been engaged only in crushing your waists; now you are attempting to cultivate your minds! You have been merely dancing all night in the foul air of ball-rooms; now you are beginning to spend your mornings in study. You have been incessantly stimulating your emotions with concerts and operas, with French plays and French novels; now you are exerting your understanding to learn Greek and solve propositions in Euclid! Beware, oh, beware! Science pronounces that the woman who *studi*es – is lost.'

When a Chinese mandarin in California was told that the women of England and America were all taught to read and write, he shook his head thoughtfully, and, with a foreboding sigh, replied, 'If he readee, writee, by'n-by he lickee all the men.'

But, regardless of these foolish objections, in these later years the decree has gone forth that our maidens should have a more vigorous, practical, and useful education, – one that should develop strength of character, power of will, and efficiency of life. It has been demanded that they should be trained with something of the same freedom as their brothers – to know their own powers, to understand their own duties; to mark out their own course in life; and, if needful, to earn their own living.

The results of this social change have been beneficial beyond expectation. One important result is, that with development of mind there has followed improvement of physique. 'The health of woman generally,' says Dr. Richardson, 'is improving under the change; there is amongst women generally less bloodlessness, less of what the old fiction-writers called swooning; less of lassitude, less of nervousness, less of hysteria, and much less of that general debility to which, for want of a better term, the words "*malaise*" and "languor" have been applied. Woman, in a word, is stronger than she was in the olden time. With this increase of strength woman has gained in development of body and of limb. She has become less distortioned. The curved back, the pigeon-shaped chest, the disproportioned limb, the narrow feeble trunk, the small and often distorted eyeball, the myopic eye, and puny ill-shaped external ear, – all these parts are becoming of better and more natural *contour*. The muscles are also becoming more equally and more fully developed, and with these improvements there are growing up amongst women models who may, in due time, vie with the best models that old Greek culture has left for us to study in its undying art.'

The old idea that helplessness is feminine and beautiful, and helpfulness is unwomanly and unbecoming is exploded. Knowledge, reason, strength, and thoroughness are no longer rated masculine; while half-knowledge, unreasoning impulse, weakness, and superficiality are rated feminine. The frivolous, fickle, ignorant woman, incapable of all studious pursuits and of all consecutive attention, is being gradually supplanted by the intelligent, judicious woman, capable of sustained thought, and well versed in everything which it is useful for her to know as a mother, as the mistress of a household, or as a citizen of the world.

Woman has cast aside her old timidities and gained a new freedom. She has achieved intellectual emancipation, and is well-nigh as conspicuous as man in every branch of intellectual achievement. The avenues of work open to her have broadened and multiplied. Her capacity for business has been amply attested. Her skill in organisation and in executive have been forced upon the notice of the world, while, at the same time, she has retained the virtues which have made her in all ages the creator and the guardian of society.

8 Banding together in the fight for human liberty

The creation of the Church League for Women's Suffrage (1909–1919) by the Rev. Claude Hinscliff, with the backing of dignitaries such as the Bishop of Lincoln, the Bishop of Hereford, the Rev. Charles Gore, Scott Holland, and Cosmo Gordon Lang, belies Elisabeth Cady Stanton's verdict that 'the most bitter and outspoken enemies of woman are found among clergyman and bishops of the Protestant religion'.[30] A pioneer in the involvement of the Church in suffrage campaigns, the League set out to remodel public opinion by organizing hundreds of meetings throughout the country, preaching from the pulpit and the public platform, and picketing the Commons; in 1914 it counted 103 branches. Its *Monthly Paper* (1912–1917) sold 96,000 copies soon after its launch. Its editorial manifesto professed an egalitarian catechism (the establishment of 'absolute equality of rights and opportunities between the sexes'), and its intention to rally 'people of every shade of opinion'. The magazine was no flash in the pan. After 1918 it was renamed *The Church Militant*, and continued to display a genuine dedication to the cause, particularly regarding equal pay, universal suffrage, and the question of women's presence in church assemblies and synods. Dr William Moore Ede (1849–1935) shared with his suffragist wife Sarah, a member of the League, a strong belief in the equality of the sexes. An active campaigner for women's votes, he signed a letter to *The Times* in 1909 to advertise male support, and spoke at suffrage meetings. He also engaged in the critical interpretation of the Book of Genesis and of the Pauline Epistles (whose influence on suffrage support can be measured in the passage below). Before becoming Dean of Worcester (1908–1934), William had held several curacies in populous and industrial parishes. Very concerned by the welfare of the working class, Ede, known as 'the busy Dean', had involved himself indefatigably in the life of his community and made himself a reputation as a social crusader. He vice-chaired education and health committees on Tyneside, promoted old-age pensions, and 'homes for aged miners', while fighting for world peace throughout the First World War (he had been a militant of the Peace Society international committee since 1896). Ede also lectured in the university extension movement at Cambridge (where he had brilliantly graduated in the Moral Sciences Tripos). His interest for social

---

30 *The Woman's Bible* (New York: European Publishing Co., 1895), Introduction. A list of suffragist churchmen is available in *Opinions of Leaders of Religious Thought on Women's Suffrage* (Women's Suffrage Committees, 1895).

reform led him to write several books on the subject: *National Insurance Necessary and Possible* (1889); *The Attitude of the Church to Some of the Social Problems of Town Life* (1896), and *The Educational Needs of Democracy* (1927). But it was his conception of the temporal role of the clergy, following the example of Christ himself, that prompted him to become one of the champions of justice and redress women's wrongs (*The Clergy and Social Service*, 1909, and *The New Man in Christ*, 1932). The League and its magazine proved inspirational to suffragist Maud Royden, first chair of the League and author of *Women and the Church of England* (1911), and fertilized the contemporary debate on women's place in the Church.

The Dean of Worcester, 'A Sermon'. Preached at St. George's, Bloomsbury, on Tuesday, December 10th, 1912, *The Church League for Women's Suffrage* (January, 1913), pp. 152–3

When we turn to the records of the life of the Head of the Church, our Lord Jesus Christ, and endeavour to ascertain what He would have us learn from His treatment of women, we can hardly fail to be struck with the way in which He treated women as spiritual entities, and talked to Martha and Mary as He talked to Peter and John. Nowhere in the whole of the New Testament is there any indication of His speaking of women, or to women, as if they were in any way different from, or inferior to, men. This is all the more remarkable when we consider the current ideas about women at the time throughout the world and among his own countrymen the Jews; for the Jew regarded woman as an inferior being, and thanked God every Sabbath that he was not born a woman. The Jews had no ceremony by which a woman was admitted into Church membership, did not allow women to take part in public worship on the same terms as men, but relegated them to the seclusion of a gallery. It is little wonder, then, that the disciples should marvel when they saw our Lord talking to a woman as He sat by the side of a well. Still greater would have been their surprise if they had realized that He talked to the woman about the water of life which will satisfy the soul, and about sin and repentance. Talked to her about spiritual things just as He talked to a man. Thought it worth while to teach her religion.

Nowhere in the recorded sayings of Jesus can one find any indication which would imply that Jesus considered He had one gospel, one religious message, for men and another for women; one code of duty for men, and another for women.

Nowhere in the teaching of Christ is there any support to be obtained for the view that there is one code of morals for men and another for women. When they brought to Him the woman taken in adultery, in the very act, His words, 'Let him that is without sin among you cast the first stone,' hits the unclean man as hard as the impure woman. Everywhere our Lord in His dealings with women recognizes them as spiritual entities, alike in their relationship to God, and though having different duties in the community, as precious in the sight of the Father and as dear to Him as men.

The disciples, though they marvelled at first, did learn from the action of their Lord to place women on an equality with men, and it is a remarkable fact that in the upper room at Jerusalem the women were not consigned to the gallery, but worshipped on terms of equality with the men, joining in prayer. 'They all continued with one accord in prayer and supplication with the women, and Mary the mother of Jesus, and with His brethren.' And on the day of Pentecost the Holy Ghost descended on the women of the company just as He did on the men.

It is because of these things that both sexes are admitted into Church membership by the same rite of baptism – both are received as children of God, taught to regard themselves as children of God. No favoured position is conferred on the male. Woman is in the Church regarded as in every way as much a child of God as man is, possessing the same spiritual nature – equally with man a spiritual being, a soul.

St. Paul enunciated the principle which for the Church is fundamental when he said that in the Christian Church 'there is neither Jew nor Greek, there is neither bond nor free, there is neither male nor female.' No recognition of distinction of race, none of social status, none of sex. The Kingdom cannot come, cannot be fully realized on earth, till these principles are embodied in practice.

It is because of these things we believe that Women's Suffrage is the logical and necessary outcome of principles which the Church recognizes and teaches. Two objections may be and are raised.

That the Church has not been consistent, because it has retained authority in the hands of men; and that the time for applying the principle in the political sphere has not arrived, and may never arrive. We must admit that the Church to-day, in excluding women from control in Church matters, has been inconsistent. It has treated women as politicians do. Has asked them to give their labour and do much of the work, but retained the power in the hands of men. This is not peculiar to our day, but has prevailed throughout, even in Apostolic times, and St. Paul, notwithstanding what he said about there being no distinction of sex, insisted on women being veiled, deprecated women speaking in Church, and evidently regarded the husband as head over the wife.

That is all true, but we need to bear in mind that it takes a long time for people to recognize all the applications of a new social principle; old prejudices die hard, and even men like St. Paul, who grasp a new principle, find it difficult to free themselves from the customs and ideas in which they have been brought up. In some respects St. Paul, however much he may have recognized the equality of the sexes in the Church, was influenced by contemporary custom as regards the dress of women. If he had encouraged women to go unveiled, it would, in view of the prejudices of that age, have created a scandal, and caused people to regard the Christian Church as encouraging licence instead of standing for a higher moral ideal.

It must be borne in mind that as a germ needs suitable conditions before it can develop, so a social principle needs suitable environment before it can be applied.

When St. Paul said that in the Church of Christ there was neither bond not free, he laid down the principle of human liberty; but in a world in which the whole economic structure rested on slavery it was impossible at once to carry that principle to its logical consequences. And we not only find St. Paul sending back a runaway slave, but we fail to find in his writings any attack on the slave system. But the principle being recognized, it acted as a solvent: first mitigated the worst evils of slavery, and then undermined the system; first, of white enslaving white, and then of white enslaving black, and the only influence in the world to-day which is fighting against the enslavement of the weaker races is the conviction of Christians – of those who believe that God cares for every individual, and that there should be no such distinction as that expressed by bond and free.

It was the same with the equality of the sexes. There was the principle – neither male nor female in Christ Jesus. Woman equally with man a spiritual being, having access to God on the same conditions as man.

9 What is feminism?

The son of British citizens, educated in Germany and France, Walter Lionel George (1882–1926) retired from a successful career as a journalist in London to write twenty-eight novels and essays. George's works,

2 Walter Lionel George

particularly *The Second Blooming* (1920), won him international acclaim. He befriended many literati and was also acquainted with prominent women like Marie Stopes, Sasha Kropotkin Lebedeff, the daughter of the revolutionary anarchist, and Sheila Kaye Smith, whose talent he celebrated in *A Novelist on Novels*. In 1905 he moved to London and made himself famous as a social and political essayist committed to pacifism, labourism and feminism (*Labour and Housing at Port Sunlight*, 1900, *Engines of Social Progress*, 1907, *France in the Twentieth Century*, 1908). A lover of America, George observed its mores by travelling widely across the country in the 1920s, and contributed several articles to *Harper's Magazine* on social and political subjects. His sympathetic writings on woman's condition date back to his first novel, *A Bed of Roses* (1911), depicting a woman's descent into prostitution, which caused quite a stir and was banned by several libraries. *Woman and To-morrow* (1912) was followed in 1916 by a thought-provoking series of seven essays, *The Intelligence of Woman*. In 1925, *The Story of Woman*, based on George's extensive knowledge of the lives of women revolutionaries, contained an enthusiastic historical analysis of the 1890s – 'a period of magnificent intellectual activity, when it was possible at last to pronounce the words "free love" or "socialism", without being excluded from human society'.[31] George, however, disapproved of the New Woman movement which, to his eyes, had retarded female emancipation, but he was a great admirer of the Women's Social and Political Union. Married three times, avowedly 'feminist', self-described as 'conservative English radical' in *Hail Columbia!* (1921), George never stopped fighting injustice and gender prejudices. Unhesitatingly provocative in *Woman and To-morrow* – 'I do not believe that women are fit to have a vote. That is why I want them to have it' (p. 27) – he took up the cudgels for sex equality in all chapters. Marriage was described as a vastly overrated institution (George pleaded for divorce and freedom of choice), and the home as 'the enemy of woman' (p. 57); women's inadequate education was judged responsible for women's 'faults'. Hailed indeed as excellent and inspiring by *Votes for Women* (8 November 1912), the book was however judged too dogmatic because of the 'demarcation' it made between feminism and suffragism (whose aims George criticized as too narrow). It was humorously reprobated for being advertised by the publisher as 'the book that women have been waiting for'. George deserves however to be rediscovered, if only for his call for a gender-neutral society – 'Since the intellectual life of the world began … the works of women have not been judged as works, but as the works of women, and that spirit is the one we wish to destroy' (p. 10) – and his plea for reconstructing masculinities: 'Only if man will readjust his views, expel *vir* and enthrone *homo*, can women cease to appear before him as a rival and a foe' (p. 93).

---

31 No place, no publisher, p. 231. It has also a chapter on women's male allies.

Walter Lionel George, *Woman and To-morrow* (London: Herbert Jenkins, 1913), pp. 3–9

Feminism can be defined broadly as a furthering of the interests of women, more specifically as the social and political emancipation of woman, and philosophically as the levelling of the sexes. The three definitions have their value, especially their application value, especially their application values, for they enable the exponent, in a Jesuitical spirit, to convert with the one formula persons to whom the other two would mean nothing. The first is, however, somewhat dishonest; the second is sound but theoretic; the third embodies our immediate aims. To further woman's happiness or interests may indeed be taken in different ways. A number of white men are still imbued with the harem idea. They have, it is true, called it 'home,' taken a hare and baptised it 'carp'; they have relaxed the harem regulations, but in the main they still believe in 'woman's sphere.' They do not confine women by means of bars and bolts, but still attempt to limit their activities, to throw them back on their household, their household gods and the household god – the husband. Naturally this does not appeal to us, who consider that '*Homo sum: humani nihil a me alienum putto*' should include woman together with man. Those men who wish to exclude woman from certain occupations, to discourage the exercise of her discretion in the choice of friends and pleasures, to maintain her in a state of favoured subjection, may love woman very deeply, but much as they love their dog. Their attitude is that of the Victorian sentimentalist who never laid his hand upon woman save in the way of patronage. For this reason the definition is inadequate.

The social and political emancipation of woman corresponds far better to the true meaning of Feminists; it includes Suffragism, but is not limited by it. Indeed, Feminists look upon Suffragism as no more than a part of their programme; they invest its obtention and its use with no sacred quality. It is for them but one of the steps which should be taken, and it is not proven that Feminism cannot succeed unless women have votes. The development of Syndicalism, of which we know little save the early stages, tends to show how greatly overrated is political pressure, how much swifter and more drastic action can be when it is freed from the childish formalities of procedure. The sex-Syndicalism to which Feminists may yet resort should be a far more efficient weapon than the more or less purchasable polling-slip men have for so many generations dropped into the Lethe of the ballot-box. We wish to establish that the intellectual capacities of the two sexes, though different, are not unequal. We do not contend that a woman will make a good soldier, sailor, judge, foreign minister, railway guard, or horse slaughterer, but we do contend that she should not be debarred by law or by custom from competing for these more or less valuable offices. We ask that woman should be allowed to enter the lists, and that she should not receive a handicap. At present male society either favours women or hampers them: it is unable to look upon them as rivals or equals, but must consider them as humble collaborators or as gracious queens. The Feminist claim is that they should be considered merely as human beings.

It will be seen in the chapters that follow in what directions emancipation is required. The suffrage agitation has cast so lurid a light upon many of these that it will not be necessary to dilate upon them. The material sex-disabilities, such as the exclusion of women from the legal profession, their partial exclusion from priestcraft, the quasi-inaccessibility of the Honours List, the denial of a vote and of the faculty to sit in Parliament (even when they possess a barony in their own right), their ineligibility to Freemasonry – these are not in the Feminist view the vital grievances of women. Feminist action is directed against attitudes rather than against situations; its desire is to abolish in men a state of mind which it considers evil, suicidal and cruel. Briefly it aims at a mental rather than at a material adjustment of relations. It is essentially philosophic.

I do not suggest that sex-disabilities must not be removed. They must and they will be removed, as they have been to a greater or lesser degree in certain States; but this again is but part of the Feminist programme. It is not enough that New Zealand should give women votes; it does not even satisfy us that Norway allows women to sit in Parliament. We want a mental recognition of status, for there is no true status without a mental recognition. The removal of sex disabilities does not of itself alter the status of woman; being a product of public opinion, the status of woman can be modified solely by the result upon men's minds of the equalising of sex-conditions. The levelling tendencies of Feminism are best understood if we resort to a simple illustration. I cannot trace the exact date when women began to smoke cigarettes; I imagine that the practice followed upon the great stiff-collar-and-bloomer movement of the eighties, but that is not important. What is important is that, at the inception, a woman who smoked cigarettes was regarded as loose; then, and little by little, she was allowed to smoke in public, until to-day, in all save the most *collet-monté* circles, no protest arises when a woman takes a cigarette from her case. So far that is what the Suffragists would call a victory: the prohibition has been removed. But the Feminists go further. They find that, in certain circles, a woman need no longer smoke covertly, apologetically, or archly; she merely smokes, and a man will offer her a cigarette as casually as he would to another man. Therein lies the difference of degree between Suffragism and Feminism: we do not attach much importance to the removal of the disability, but we attach immense importance to the fact that some men have forgotten that there ever was a disability. *It is not what women may do that matters, but the taking for granted of what they may do.*

It appears at once that Feminism is infinitely more greedy than Suffragism. We are not content with the more or less sterile products of the ballot-box; we wish to arrive at a state when the differences between men and women will be reduced to sexual differences, because those alone are natural.

II

Provisions to be made for the education of women

> The true measure of a woman's right to knowledge
> is her capacity for receiving it.
> Joshua Fitch

1 The cultivation of a woman's understanding

The Rev. Sydney Smith (1771–1845), an Anglican clergyman of humble origin, was one of the greatest English wits. Impressed by his intellectual talents, the squire of his parish, Michael Hicks Beach, hired him as a tutor for his eldest son in Edinburgh, while Smith studied moral philosophy under Dugald Stewart, the renowned scholar of the Scottish Enlightenment. He rapidly made himself a name by preaching powerful sermons in Charlotte Street chapel. With two Whig friends, Francis Horner, a political economist, and Francis Jeffrey, a literary critic, he founded the *Edinburgh Review* in 1801, and wrote more than eighty articles for the journal (later collected in several editions in Britain and America). Smith defended unpopular causes, such as the emancipation of the Catholics (*Peter Plymley's Letters*, 1807), and the abolition of the slave trade ('Catteau, Tableau des Etats Danois', *Edinburgh Review*, 1803), with great conviction and audacity. His reputation for piquant remarks rapidly spread and he was received in London with acclaim: not only did his sermons attracted large audiences but he became a hugely popular figure in high society where he was in constant demand. He became one of the prominent fixtures of Holland House[1] where he rubbed shoulders with eminent

---

[1] Lord Holland's House served as a place for Whig meetings. The Third Baron, a sceptic in religion, who married Elisabeth Vassall, a divorcee and a freethinker, was the recognized keeper of the Foxite conscience in the party.

3 Sydney Smith

politicians and writers. Smith was born with an extremely sharp mind but also with a kind heart. His dedication to the fight against poverty never flagged, from the days when he was a simple curate to the final canonry at St Paul's.[2] Remarkably too, Smith was a devoted father (he supervised his daughter Saba's lessons with great care), and an unconventional husband, revelling in domesticity. Smith had shown an early concern over the shortage and inadequacy of provisions for women's education when he set up a Sunday school for girls in his parish. He was saddened by the ignorance and 'the trifling pursuits to which they are condemned' (p. 231). The publication of Thomas Broadhurst's *Advice to Young Ladies on the Improvement of the Mind* (1808), which Smith originally reviewed in the *Edinburgh Review* (15, October 1809 – January 1810), was an opportunity for him to state his case on an educational system that allowed 'half the talent in the universe' to run to waste (p. 249). Smith took pleasure in deriding the opponents of the 'cultivation of women's faculties' and turning their objections on their heads: 'Can any thing, for example, be more perfectly absurd than to suppose that the care and perpetual solicitude which a mother feels for her children, depends upon her ignorance of Greek and Mathematics'? (p. 235). His plea for an improvement of the educational system, in spite of conservative aspects, was quite distinctive, for it stemmed not from purely practical reasons but from a desire to increase women's personal development and economic independence. Smith denied the idea of any original difference of capacity between the sexes as 'fanciful' (p. 231); he was convinced 'that the happiness of a woman will be materially increased in proportion as education has given to her the habit and the means of drawing her resources to herself' (p. 241). An ardent believer in freedom and progress, he contributed throughout his life to the spread of libertarian thought.

The Rev. Sydney Smith, 'Female Education', *The Works of the Rev. Sydney Smith*, 3 vols (London: Longman, Orme, Brown, Green, and Longmans, 1839), vol. 1, pp. 242–6

We know women are to be compassionate; but they cannot be compassionate from eight o'clock in the morning till twelve at night: – and what are they to do in the interval? This is the only question we have been

---

2 At Foston, Smith acquired a reputation for philanthropy. He acted as 'village parson, village doctor, village comforter, village magistrate', *A Memoir of the Reverend Sydney Smith by His Daughter Lady Holland* (New York: Harper & Brothers, 1855), vol. 1, p. 146.

putting all along, and is all that can be meant by literary education.

Then, again, as to the notoriety which is incurred by literature. – The cultivation of knowledge is a very distinct thing from its publication; nor does it follow that a woman is to become an author merely because she has talent enough for it. We do not wish a lady to write books, – to defend and reply, – to squabble about the tomb of Achilles, or the plain of Troy, – any more than we wish her to dance at the opera, to play at a public concert, or to put pictures in the exhibition, because she has learned music, dancing and drawing. The great use of her knowledge will be that it contributes to her private happiness. She may make it public: but it is not the principal object which the friends of female education have in view. Among men, the few who write bear no comparison to the many who read. We hear most of the former, indeed, because they are, in general, the most ostentatious part of literary men; but there are innumerable persons who, without ever laying themselves before the public, have made use of literature to add to the strength of their understandings, and to improve the happiness of their lives. After all, it may be an evil for ladies to be talked of: but we really think those ladies who are talked of only as Mrs. Marcet, Mrs. Somerville, and Miss Martineau are talked of, may bear their misfortunes with a great degree of Christian patience.

Their exemption from all the necessary business of life is one of the most powerful motives for the improvement of education in women. Lawyers and physicians have in their professions a constant motive to exertion; if you neglect their education, they must in a certain degree educate themselves by their commerce with the world: they must learn caution, accuracy, and judgment, because they must incur responsibility. But if you neglect to educate the mind of a woman, by the speculative difficulties which occur in literature, it can never be educated at all: if you do not effectually rouse it by education, it must remain for ever languid. Uneducated men may escape intellectual degradation; uneducated women cannot. They have nothing to do; and if they come untaught from the schools of education, they will never be instructed in the school of events.

Women have not their livelihood to gain by knowledge; and that is one motive for relaxing all those efforts which are made in the education of men. They certainly have not; but they have happiness to gain, to which knowledge leads as probably as it does to profit; and that is a reason against mistaken indulgence. Besides, we conceive the labour and fatigue of accomplishments to be quite equal to the labour and fatigue of knowledge; and that it takes quite as many years to be charming as it does to be learned.

Another difference of the sexes is, that women are attended to, and men attend. All acts of courtesy and politeness originate from the one sex, and are received by the other. We can see no sort of reason, in this diversity of condition, for giving to women a trifling and insignificant education; but we see in it a very powerful reason for strengthening their judgment, and inspiring them with the habit of employing time usefully. We admit many striking differences in the situation of the two sexes, and many striking differences of understanding, proceeding from the different circumstances in which they are placed: but there is not a single difference of this kind which does not afford a new argument for making the education of women better than it is. They have nothing serious to do; – is that a reason why they should be brought up to do nothing but what is trifling? They are exposed to greater dangers; – is that a reason why their faculties are to be purposely and industriously weakened? They are to form the characters of future men; – is that a cause why their own characters are to be broken and frittered down as they now are? In short, there is not a single trait in that diversity of circumstances, in which the two sexes are placed, that does not decidedly prove the magnitude of the error we commit in neglecting (as we do neglect) the education of women.

If the objections against the better education of women could be overruled, one of the great advantages that would ensue would be the extinction of innumerable follies. A decided and prevailing taste for one or another mode of education there must be. A century past, it was for housewifery – now it is for accomplishments. The object now is, to make women artists, – to give them an excellence in drawing, music, painting and dancing, – of which, persons who make these pursuits the occupation of their lives, and derive from them their subsistence, need not be ashamed. Now, one great evil of this is, that it does not last. If the whole of life were an Olympic game, – if we could go on feasting and dancing to the end, – this might do; but it is in truth merely a provision for the little interval between coming into life, and settling in it; while it leaves a long and dreary expanse behind, devoid both of dignity and cheerfulness. No mother, no woman who has passed over to the few first years of life, sings, or dances, or draws, or plays upon musical instruments. These are merely means for displaying the grace and vivacity of youth, which every woman gives up, as she gives up the dress and manners of eighteen: she has no wish to retain them; or, if she has, she is driven out of them by diameter and derision. The system of female education, as it now stands, aims only at embellishing a few years of life, which are in themselves so full of grace and happiness, that they hardly want it; and then leaves the rest of existence a miserable prey to idle insignificance.

2 What is learnt from teaching girls

F. D. Maurice (1805–1872) is best remembered for *The Kingdom of Christ* (1838), which laid the basis of Christian Socialism. Maurice believed that the coming of God's Kingdom to Earth would eventually replace a competitive, unjust society with a co-operative and egalitarian order. He was deeply troubled by social unrest resulting from industrial misery, and recommended that Church and State should work in closer relationship towards the improvement of social arrangements. As the linchpin of Queen's College in London, a college for girls founded in 1848, where, with other professors from King's, he lectured for many years, he features high amongst the pioneers of female education. Created with a view to improving the general education of ladies and the training of governesses, the institution was the first of its kind in England, and significantly counted amongst its pupils Dorothea Beale (who tutored there until 1856, and later became the principal of Cheltenham Ladies' College), Frances Mary Buss, founder of the North London Collegiate School for Girls, and Katherine Mansfield. Maurice's personal expertise in pedagogy (he instructed his own sisters at home) probably developed thanks to his father's connection with the natural philosopher Joseph Priestley, himself a promoter of women's education, and to his admiration for Robert Owen's ideas which he spread in his short-lived *Educational Magazine* (1839 to 1841). Maurice always prided himself on independent thought, an unmistakable characteristic of the forty (often controversial) volumes that he authored. The son of a Unitarian minister, he first refused his degree at Cambridge rather than subscribe to the Anglican Thirty-Nine Articles, but after his Oxford years he was finally ordained deacon in 1834. He became a respected Professor of English Literature and History at King's College, but lost the post following the publication of his unorthodox *Theological Essays* (1853). Maurice was also an active member of the Society for the Promotion of Social Science, and involved in a number of important social initiatives (such as co-operative associations and Friendly Societies, the opening of a girls' home in Portland Place, London, and of the Working Men's College in 1854, to which he appointed Octavia Hill to be secretary of the women's classes in 1856). His letter written to *The Spectator* in support of women's votes became subsequently a standard of suffrage literature, and several of his disciples joined the campaigns for married women's property rights. Maurice died before the launching of the Working Women's College which he contributed to establishing. The extract below echoes a quarrel at Queen's with Miss Beale, who preferred female rather than male instructors for girls.[3] Interestingly Maurice breaks free from gender stereotypes when he recommends equal instruction for both sexes: 'The difference in the capacities of boys and girls does not the least involve a necessity for a difference in their studies[4] ... if the studies were exactly the same the peculiar strength and weakness of the two sexes would undoubtedly reveal themselves in the manner in which they received the lessons that were imparted to them' (p. 270). Perhaps he was not as conservative as it would seem ...

The Rev. F. D. Maurice, '"The Education of Girls", What Better Provision Ought to Be Made for the Education of Girls of the Upper and Middle Classes?', in G. W. Hastings (ed.), *Transactions of the National Association for the Promotion of Social Science*, Sheffield Meeting, 1865 (London: Longman, Green, Longman, Roberts, and Green, 1866), pp. 268–70

My belief that male instruction – formal, methodical male instruction – is needed for girls, is certainly not derived from any apprehension that female lessons are likely to be more frivolous or insincere than those which we impart. Those words sound almost impious when one remembers the testimonies which the most earnest thinkers and doers in the world have borne to the influence of their mothers, in saving them from frivolity and insincerity, in making them steady and conscientious in their study and their work. I should suppose that men of science and men of business have owed the habit of observing facts – the preservation from

3 Another divisive issue, the question of special examinations for girls, was predicated on 'differences of kind, not of degree' between the sexes by its partisans, Joshua Fitch for instance, or Canon J. P. Norris ('The Education of Girls', *Transactions of the National Association for the Promotion of Social Science*, York, September 1864). On the debates see Kamm (2010: 184–98). Two men were particularly helpful in canvassing for the Cambridge Locals for girls (1865): the lawyer and ex-Cambridge man H. R. Tomkinson, and Sir Thomas Dyke Acland, himself the pioneer of the system for boys in Oxford in the 1850s.
4 The same premise underpins *The Education of Girls; and, The Employment of Women of the Upper Classes Educationally Considered* (1869) by the Scottish educational reformer W. B. Hodgson.

mere dreaminess and flights of fancy – very much indeed to the counsels of their mothers, still more to the examples of minute and steady diligence which they have afforded. And if we consider the women who have done most for their own sex and for ours, especially on the subject of education, we shall find that there is nothing for which they have laboured more than to cultivate an honest and truthful temper – to banish whatever they thought was likely to interfere with it. Miss Edgeworth is an obvious instance. Whatever defects we may find in her scheme of education,[5] or in the remarkable series of books which illustrates it, the last complaint any reasonable person can make of her is that she exalts the fancy too highly, that she does not encourage the most profound reverence for fact. If any man starts with the notion that this reverence does not exist as strongly in the other sex as in his own, if he supposes that to inculcate it is his peculiar vocation, I suspect he will misunderstand his pupils, and will never give them the help which he might give them. It has always seemed to me that I acquire more of this blessing from my female pupils than I can impart to them.

Precisely because I have this conviction, I think that it is in our power to give them a kind of aid which they could not ordinarily obtain, even from women far more accomplished than we are. In trying to teach them a little modern history, I am continually reminded of a tendency in my own mind to generalize. I see how dreary my lessons become to them if I give way to that tendency: what a demand there is in them for acts and characters, for living deeds and living persona. That which is especially our masculine infirmity is discovered and rebuked whenever we seek to hold any serious intercourse with them. But it may also be cured. Our temptation is to seek for laws apart from facts: theirs is to seek facts apart from laws. If they compel us always to connect our grand enunciation of laws with their lively apprehension of particular facts, we may be saved from much vagueness and pedantry – from building on mere hypotheses – from describing circles when we suppose we are making progress. On the other hand, they may be saved from that passion for petty details, which characterises some of the female writers, in many respects highly instructive and useful, who have dealt with history. They may be saved from the still more dangerous habit of supplying the want of principles by exaggerations of the fancy.

5 *Practical Education* (1798), written by Anglo-Irish Maria Edgeworth in collaboration with her father, advocated Rousseau's principle that education should be practical and accommodate itself to the child.

The temptation to do this arises from no indifference to reality. One may see in the most outrageously sensational novel, written by a female pen, what a desire there is to dwell on all the little points which convey the sense of reality and minister to the craving for it. But the powerlessness to group the separate facts and the different personages, to find out some living and intelligible connection between them, suggests desperate experiments for making them cohere. By fair means or foul, human life, and every one's own life, must be contemplated as a whole. If we are desirous that the means shall be fair and not foul, that there shall be some discovery of the actual relation between acts and the doers of acts, we must not confide the education of girls exclusively even to those who would most faithfully impress them with the superiority of the smallest fact to the most elaborate fiction. We must put them in communication with those who have, even to excess, the habit of referring all particular cases to some principle: at any rate who are always in search of some principle to which they may be referred. I have admitted fully, that as much is taken by the instructor as he gives; that the action and reaction exactly correspond; that just so far as he is profited by that disposition of an attentive pupil in which she differs from him, just so far she will gain by what he tells her.

If this be a true statement, it may go some way towards settling certain questions which occasionally trouble us more perhaps than is necessary. Controversies about the relative capacities of men and women may be discussed, it seems to me, for ever, with very little result, whilst we repeat the phrases 'equality' or 'inequality' and make the decision turn upon them. The necessity of each sex to the other may be surely taken for granted as a preliminary. And if it is taken for granted, the inference would at least be probable à priori, were it not established by evidence, that each had capacities which the other did not possess,[6] and which could only be unfolded through the help of the other; that each had defects answering to these capacities, which can only be remedied by the same help. I am ashamed to utter such truisms; but since they are often overlooked, and much precious time is wasted from the neglect of them, some one or other must recal attention to them.

---

6 The belief in the sexes having different skills did not entail that women should be denied equal opportunities to develop their specific talents.

3 'The highest aim of any true system of education'

Richard Whately Cooke Taylor (1842–1918) was the son of the Irish historian and staunch free trader William Cooke Taylor. An avid reader of the liberal economists, he was himself an ardent defender of industrial capitalism, which he associated with the progress of civilization. In *The Modern Factory System* (1891), he wrote: 'The capitalist is above all things the friend of labour'.[7] As one of H.M. Inspectors of Factories, he reported widely on the subject (*Introduction to a History of the Factory System*, 1886; *The Factory System and the Factory Acts*, 1894). But, unlike his father, he was aware of, and preoccupied with, the poor intellectual and physical conditions of factory operatives: 'The enormous inequalities of modern industrial life are not necessarily permanent, any more than were the atrocious cruelties of the early factory system, or the heavy burdens of serfdom and slavery. They can be, and therefore should be remedied' (*The Modern Factory System*, p. 447). He admired George Holyoake, and Robert Owen, whose exemplary mills in New Lanark he valued as model of 'humane administration' (*The Modern Factory System*, p. 206). A progressive reformer, he contributed actively to the major debates of his times, and supported Lord Ashley's factory legislation (*The Modern Factory System*, pp. 391, 447, 467). From 1858 to 1885 he was a council member of the National Association for the Promotion of Social Science. When serving as one of the secretaries of its Education department, he recommended the teaching of Social Science in elementary schools as a way of remedying poverty (*Transactions of the National Society for the Promotion of Social Science*, London meeting, 1872). He promoted women's access to higher education (he particularly approved of Emily Davies's project of a college for ladies), and the opening of new employments to women, particularly in the Civil Service (see *Transactions*, Plymouth and Devonport Meeting, 1873, pp. 274–5). Unsurprisingly, he sympathized with the liberal view that the chief end of education was the development of 'self-reliance, industry, prudence and effort'. Taylor has been reviled by feminist critics for opposing restrictions on the employment of mothers in factories. His position was an unconditional vindication of women's individual choice to work, and he justified it on the contrary as the defence of a right: 'Might it not rather seem that a simpler and more certain way of checking infant mortality would be to make some provision for infants not otherwise provided for, to offer some support to their

---

7 *The Modern Factory System* (London: Kegan Paul, 1891), p. 39.

mothers instead of depriving them of all and to encourage them to look on maternity as a high and proud privilege, instead of a disqualification and offence?' (*Transactions*, Glasgow meeting, 1874, pp. 574–5). Taylor resented the philanthropists' zeal to shut women out of the labour market, supposedly for the sake of their children's welfare. For him 'most intimate domestic family affairs' should never be 'a matter of public concern and penal enactment'. 'I raise my voice', he explained, 'against this tyrannical interference with the freedom of private life, however humble, this intolerable Government meddling with individual liberty, personal dignity and social propriety' (*Ibid.*, p. 574). His vision of woman's sphere in the extract below is strangely reminiscent of Harriet Taylor's opinion that 'the proper sphere for all human beings is the largest and highest which they are able to attain to' ('The Enfranchisement of Women', *Westminster Review*, July 1851).

Whately Cooke Taylor, 'On Indirect Sources of Advanced Female Education', in Andrew Edgar (ed.), *Transactions of the National Society for the Promotion of Social Science*, Birmingham Meeting, 1868 (London: Longmans, Green, Reader, and Dyer, 1869), pp. 404–6

I wish to suggest for the consideration of this meeting, certain measures by which I think the higher education of women would be fostered.

The first necessary step to the education of our faculties is evidently their employment. Now, from what sources can this employment be supplied? We know of a great many. Instruction is one; instruction in the Arts, in the Sciences, in the history of other countries and our own – in the laws, language, and literature of various nations. The cultivation of the imagination is another; the leading forth, by whatever means, the higher and holier faculties of our nature. So also the development of the affections, and the moral and social qualities, by arousing the passions of love, ambition, patriotism, &c. All that supplies motive to the employment of these are sources of education, properly so called. In like manner the social and material qualities – the qualities of industry, frugality, forethought, self-reliance;—whatever circumstances favour the growth of these, foster education in that degree. All occupations, then, which have for their object the attainment of material prosperity, of independence, of eminence or renown, are indirect sources of education.

Surveying now this extensive prospect in connection with our subject, we are painfully struck by the number of indirect sources of education, which are permanently closed to women. What motives does our system of civilization supply to women for educing the political, social, and material virtues, rightly esteemed the greatest educators of men? It supplies little, or perhaps none. Until recently, indeed, it did not recognise their claims to the possession of such, and it is still somewhat sceptical on that head. It has left this side of their character altogether unwrought, and that notwithstanding the manifold, and even singular marks of capacity in these directions which the female mind has from time to time exhibited. In the matter of the imagination and the affections we have been more generous. The Christian religion, and the civilization founded upon it, does not, like the Mohammedan, preach the eternal inferiority of women; it teaches (I suppose) only their temporary degradation; I am not quite sure that it teaches even that! To their imaginations and affections, then, we have permitted them, at all events in theory, to give as free a rein as we have permitted to ourselves, and they share with us in common the great motives which investigate to the employment of these. They, as well as we, may hope and strive for life eternal, may range at will throughout the realms of fancy, and love and worship as their hearts dictate. But all the rest we have closed to them. The privilege of benefiting their fellows in the practical concerns of legislation and of life, the privilege to labour when they choose, how they choose, and for what they choose, to earn their livelihoods in this various world through whatsoever channels they think fit – this we have denied; and the consequence has been, that the sources of their education dried up here, the others have too often filled up all their life, and then with effrontery unparalleled we turn and say: – 'See here; you are not fit for the work that men do; you're too impulsive, and too sensitive, and know too little of the world.' Having denied them the means of a completed education, we cast on them the shame of our success! 'You bring up,' says Ruskin, 'your girls as if they were meant for sideboard ornaments, and then complain of their frivolity.'

What, then, are the fostering circumstances that I am prepared to recommend as means for advancing the education of women? They are the opening to them more freely the various channels through which men attain independence, and social and intellectual eminence. This is strictly within the compass of our will. If usage and law can withhold from one sex the opportunities which they accord to the other, so also can they certainly abstain from withholding them if so minded. Independence is the highest aim of any true system of education, for the individual as well as for the nation. It pre-supposes, in a well-constituted state, almost all the other virtues; it is a guarantee for the enjoyment of almost all its possible advantages. Regarded solely then from an educational standpoint, for with no other have I any present concern, I look to the increased employment of woman in the various occupations of life now mainly monopolised by man, as the most hopeful source of her further intellectual development.

I am here haunted by a portentous phantom! The awful spectre of the 'woman's rights' question rises before me! Have I been all this time unconsciously drifting towards that, and to that have I come? I think not. I disclaim any such intention. I profess to know of no 'woman's rights,' or 'man's rights' in particular. I am aware of no natural right in the actual possession of any human creature. I know of what is called expediency in human affairs, and of the faculties through which we are permitted to form our own opinions of what is expedient and what is not. Mine have taught me that it is expedient that the field of woman's employment should be extended, that thereby those qualities might be educed in which she is now notably deficient. Searching about me for means of advancing her education, it has struck me that here is a mighty one. Neither let me be misunderstood as advocating the identity of the male and female intellects. Such is far from my thought. I do not believe in 'the two sexes of man,' nor in the natural superiority or inferiority of either; rather do I prefer to cast in my opinion with that of our greatest living poet, that –

> 'Woman is not lesser man,
> But diverse.'
> 'Not like to like, but like in difference.'

Of 'woman's mission' I am profoundly ignorant. Doubtless, there is a high sense in which it may be said we have all our missions to fulfill in this world, but in no instance has the particular mission of any person or class been revealed to me. What I suppose to be the mission of every one is the career which they carve out for themselves, and the ends which, in the long run, they compass. It seems to me but folly to decide beforehand for what sphere any man or woman is fitted, for that fitness is best proved by the event. Many, I believe, never find their proper sphere, and often only for want of opportunity, and for that reason I cannot but think it just that, in so far as in us lies, we should give to all a fair start. But I cannot take it upon myself to say that it is a right.

4 A system of public education for girls

The Evangelical Charles Kingsley (1819–1875) was with F. D. Maurice [II, 2] one of the most eminent propounders of Christian Socialism. His energetic life, instanced by a walk from Cambridge to London in his youth, embodies the type of 'muscular Christianity' he cared to define in his sermon, 'David's Weakness' (1866).[8] Throughout his clerical career (from priest in 1842 to canon of Westminster in 1873, including being private tutor to the Prince of Wales in 1861), Kingsley remained inspired by Maurice's belief that physical activity must complement spirituality. The high-hearted style of his novels on the condition of England question won him international acclaim (*Alton Locke, Tailor and Poet*, 1850; *Yeast; A Problem*, 1851; the popular *Westward Ho!*, 1855, and *The Water-Babies*, 1863). His critical sermons against liberal economics and Malthus's theories caused sensation and controversy. In the 1840s Kingsley had supported Chartism,[9] but his socialism had been of a moral and educational rather than political nature. He never viewed the preaching of the Gospel as an end in itself, and was more concerned about its practical success on morality; he regarded the Bible as 'the true Reformer's Guide'. A convinced evolutionist and Darwin's friend, Kingsley became passionate about two issues, sanitary and educational reform (see *Health and Education*, 1874; 'Nausicaa in London; Or the Lower Education of Women', in *Social and Sanitary Essays*, 1880; or his articles in the *Christian Socialist* and *Politics for the People*). He pleaded for State schools rather than denominational ones, and relentlessly promoted the teaching of science and hygiene in the curriculum. Remarkably, the great advocate of masculinity had 'a vein of almost feminine tenderness in him'.[10] He was a very loving father, preoccupied well ahead of his times with the well-being and happiness of all schoolchildren. An admirer of prominent women activists (in particular Elisabeth Fry, the prison reformer, but also Catherine Marsh, who preached among navvies, the nurse Florence Nightingale, or the social purity crusader Josephine Butler), he

---

8 Leslie Stephen is credited with the origin of the expression. The creed was anti-theological, but presented itself as common-sense Christianity. It taught a practical morality which involved the culture of athleticism, Spartan habits and discipline, stoicism and a repression of sentimental impulses (also at the heart of T. Carlyle's philosophy).
9 His definition of Chartism was at odds with that of its official leaders, though.
10 *Charles Kingsley, His Letters and Memories of His Life Edited by His Wife* (London: Macmillan, 1895), vol. 1, p. 289.

proved very supportive of the cause of women, regarding the right to vote, work, and most of all to study as men: 'On every side the conviction seems growing (a conviction which any man might have arrived at for himself long ago, if he would have taken the trouble to compare the powers of his own daughters with those of his sons), that there is no difference in kind, and probably none in degree, between the intellect of a woman and that of a man'.[11] Following the reports of the Taunton commission on the failings of girls' schooling (1868), Kingsley, as president of the education section of the 1869 Social Science Congress in Bristol, delivered a sensational address (extracted below) with a view to influencing the recently appointed Endowed Schools Commissioners (particularly to persuade them to share endowments equally between the sexes). His imperious demand that a system of public education for girls of the middle and upper class 'must arise, and arise soon' reflected a national apprehension: 'For a people like our own, so rapidly increasing in mere material wealth, and, let me say it, brute prosperity, can only be preserved ... by instilling a true and lofty civilisation into its sisters, wives, and mothers of every class' (p. 56). Kingsley also campaigned with Elisabeth Blackwell for securing women's medical degrees; he taught in F. D. Maurice's Working Men's College, and held the chair of Literature at women's Queen's College in 1842. Interestingly, in the passage below, Kingsley, like Hobhouse [III, 4], showed a real concern over the plight of *un*married women (admittedly an issue far less contentious than the economic rights of spouses), but the real originality of his discourse lay in the unusual praise of childless females, often denounced by his contemporaries as 'failures': 'A very large proportion of the spinsters of England, so far from being, as silly boys and wicked old men fancy, the refuse of their sex, are the very *elite* thereof; those who have either sacrificed themselves for their kindred, or have refused to sacrifice themselves to that longing to marry at all risks of which women are so often and so unmanly accused' (*Women and Politics*, p. 24).

Charles Kingsley, 'An Address on Education', in Edwin Pears (ed.), *Transactions of the National Association for the Promotion of Social Science*, Bristol Meeting, 1869 (London: Longmans, Green, Reader and Dyer, 1870), pp. 54–6

I turn now to a subject of equal importance, and one which is exciting increased interest among thoughtful women and men; I mean the better

11 *Women and Politics* (London: Spottiswoode & Co, 1869), p. 8.

education of girls. That something must be done, and done on a large and generous scale, in this direction is becoming, thank God, clear to many an able head and noble heart. But let me remind you, first, that while you are devising plans for educating and civilising the so-called dangerous classes, you must not forget that the most dangerous class of all – far more dangerous than the street Arabs or thieves, is composed, alas, of women; and that the causes which keep that class continually recruited are not so much poverty, as emptiness of brain and heart; want of education, whether intellectual or moral, which leaves too many a fair savage (and too many not only of our lowest, but of our lower middle class, are nothing else) with no rational or profitable occupation, no sense of duty or responsibility, no intellectual exercise, if she can read, save the perusal or silly and exciting novels; and no ideal life, save one which will give fullest scope to vanity, luxury, and passion. On behalf of these, the most pitiable of all the victims of ignorance, I urge earnestly on every man, and yet more on every woman in this room, the duty of offering girls some education which will teach them what vast numbers of middle-class girls are not now taught, that there are higher objects in life than finery and amusement; that they are responsible to themselves, to the State, and to God, for the precious gift of womanhood. And if I urge the higher education of women for the sake of such as these foolish butterflies, how much more for the wise working bees of the human hive; for the two and a half millions of women who in this land at this moment have to earn their own bread, and often the bread of children and relatives beside; and who, for want of due education, are too often unable to compete in the labour market against the better taught male sex, and are, therefore, too often beaten down to starvation wages – from the widow who, as a last resource, takes to her needle, to the gentle-woman who, as a last resource, turns governess, both, too often, equally unskilled in the occupation which need has forced upon them. If the vast and steadily-increasing number of women who must earn their own bread in these days are to be aught but a source of misery to themselves, and of confusion to society in ways which I foresee but shall not particularise here, then we must offer to them an education which will at least enable them to get their own bread.

And is not the necessity for some higher, and for that reason more practicable, education of women just as needful in the case of those who will hereafter become wives and mothers, who will have the training of children, the management of a household; who may be, and should be, helpmates for their husbands, and not mere costly playthings? I can conceive few objects, if any, more important to a well-ordered State than the education of its women; for that will, in the long run, educate the men. The public opinion of pure, prudent, cultivated, pious women is a moral power which, as history shows us again and again, the men of a State cannot resist. 'If one only of the parents of a child,' says a wise man on this matter, 'could be sensibly and well-educated, it would be most for the public good that it should be the mother.' Who doubts it? Or rather, I meant to say, who would doubt it if he would use his common sense? For as yet so little has this, to me self-evident, truth been acted on, that while boys of the middle class everywhere in these islands have rich advantages in Grammar schools, Public schools, Universities, Scholarships, Fellowships, girls have – to speak roughly – none. The wealthy fathers of England have taken good care to see that they and their sons were freely and well-educated. The mothers of England, to whom the men of England will in each generation owe their earliest, and therefore deepest impressions in all that relates not only to God and to virtue, to duty, but to the outward world, and man's relation to it – the mothers of England, I say, are to be educated any how, or not at all. Even where the generosity of our ancestors has endowed foundations for girls as well as boys, the boys have been allowed, again and again, to appropriate the whole, or nearly the whole, of the endowments, till we have cases like the otherwise noble institution of Christ's Hospital, which, founded originally for girls as well as boys, now educates (I quote from the Report of the Schools Inquiry Commission) 1192 boys and 18 girls. Why not? Those who will be only wives and mothers need, forsooth, no endowed schools and colleges to teach them, if not Latin and Greek, if not philosophy, or political economy, or the history of their own land, at least a little of the laws of life and health, a little of the laws of the human mind, a little of the right method of preserving the body and the soul of their own babes. What need to teach them that? Let it come by chance or not come at all, if the learning of it is to rob the girls' brother of any of his rightful schooling. Ah! how many a young mother, looking on the face of her first-born, cries, with poor Margaret Fuller Ossoli,[12] 'God be merciful to me a sinner! I am the mother of a human being!' and then adds in her heart, bewildered, reproachful – 'And why is it that I have been no more taught what to do with the treasure which has been confided to me, than if it had dropt

---

12 Ossoli was an American journalist and women's rights advocate, the author of *Woman in the Nineteenth Century* (1843).

by miracle from another planet?' I trust that I need not, in the present temper of the most highly educated persons – both men and women – I trust, I say, that I need not invite discussion on the question of the better education of girls. I know that there are in this room ladies who have set before themselves, as the duty which lies nearest them, the thing to be done just now, with all their heart, and soul, and strength; and gentlemen likewise who, like many of the most able and highly cultivated men of the University of Cambridge, have thrown their talents freely into what seems to be, and what is indeed, a new quest of chivalry – of chivalry sound and rational, because founded not on mere sentiment, but on justice itself.

5 'They will not be unsexed by education'

Sir Alexander Grant, Tenth Baronet (1826–1884), graduated at Oxford with a particular interest in philosophy and study methods (*The Ethics of Aristotle*, 1857). In later life he continued to show the zeal, enthusiasm, and dedication for the improvement of educational standards that had made his reputation at Balliol. He was successively public examiner and schools inspector before accepting a post in India in 1860 as part of Charles Trevelyan's plan to extend public education there. He held the first chair of History and Political Economy at the University of Bombay before being appointed Principal and later Vice-Chancellor. In 1868, as head of the University of Edinburgh he never spared his efforts contribute to its development and repute. Grant was favourable to women's admission to classes within his University walls, but his vision of female nature, inspired by Tennyson's – 'woman not undevelopt man, but diverse' – led him to disapprove of mixed classes, and to believe that the 'Woman's University of the future' – an idea he personally welcomed – 'should probably be one cast on different lines from the present University system for men'.[13] He had been a supporter of Queen's College and Girton, and had fully endorsed 'the solid education of girls' promoted by the Edinburgh Local Examinations. However, he was rather apprehensive of dramatic changes, and particularly wary of the consequences of female suffrage. Grant has been attacked for his conservatism, and held responsible for the University refusal in

---

13 *The Story of the University of Edinburgh during Its First Three Hundred Years* (London: Longmans, Green & Co, 1884) p. 159.

1876 to create medical lectures for women,[14] after Sophia Jex-Blake (who in 1869 had been admitted to attend some classes in the medical faculty as an 'experiment') expressed her wish to continue for a medical degree. But, understandably, he was himself up against the mood of his times, 'remunerative' questions, and most of all the faculty's 'jealousy, trades-unionism, fear of the rivalry of women' (*Story of the University of Edinburgh*, p. 160). In the address he was invited to deliver at the sixth session of the Edinburgh Ladies' Educational Association (which had been campaigning for the opening of universities to women since 1867), Grant promoted the lectures in general cultivation given by Edinburgh professors to the women of the Association.[15] But as a true educationalist, and confident that the feminine intellect would benefit from them, he also recommended more specialized courses of studies, in particular the teaching of the classics, Latin, Mathematics, Geometry, Algebra, Philosophy, History. He also appealed to directors of schools to found more scholarships for girls. Revolted by what he called the 'violation in girls' schools of the laws of mental progress', barring them from 'bread-winning opportunities',[16] Grant pleaded for the creation of 'a system of proper secondary education' which would suitably prepare them for higher education. Like Smith [II, 1], remarkably, Grant believed that by having greater advantages of intellectual culture women might individually gain in 'happiness for themselves'.

Alexander Grant, 'Happiness and Utility as Promoted by the Higher Education of Women', *Speech to the Local Ladies' Educational Association* (Edinburgh: Edmonston & Douglas, 1872), pp. 10–14

Just as no improvements in schools and colleges can be expected to produce greater individual minds, in their different spheres, than the great men of history, so no improved educational systems will give us in the female sex anything more admirable than the noble women who, in all ages, have adorned society, and whose names, in the great majority

14 The MPs William Francis Cowper-Temple and Russell Gurney were favourable to the admission of women in medical schools. Passed against much opposition, Gurney's Enabling Act (1876) gave medical examining bodies the option to test women for a medical degree.
15 Professor Henry Morley also lectured on behalf of the Association, and conducted a vigorous campaign from 1865 with W. P. Ker to get women admitted to London University. He taught at Queen's and Bedford College for Women.
16 'Reform of Women's Education', *Princeton Review*, 1 (1880), 346; 358.

of cases, have never been known to history or to fame at all.

But, as we do our best to improve our boys' schools, without any hope that by so doing we shall produce minds to eclipse Aristotle and Newton, so we may well aim at reforming, and, if necessary, at remodelling from the foundation, the education of women, though we distinctly disavow any intention to supersede the feminine ideal of past times. As Mrs Fawcett very well remarked at Brighton, 'Nature is quite strong enough to take care of herself in this matter.' Women will not, through improved education, become individually superior to the noblest women who have yet lived, and whose school has been life and its vicissitudes; but, on the other hand, they will not be unsexed by education; they will retain, unless society loses its good sense, those feminine characteristics which I for one consider above price in this world; and, at the same time, by having greater advantages of intellectual culture afforded to them, the general level of the sex may be raised, and women may individually gain much both in happiness for themselves and in usefulness to their fellow-creatures. And this I conceive to be the aim of the Association, namely, to help women, as the poet expresses it, –

> 'To live, and learn, and be
> All that not harms distinctive womanhood.'

The system of female education hitherto in vogue has grown up out of accidental custom in absence of all theory. But now the time has come when a theory is demanded. The whole subject must be reconsidered, and unless the old methods can be justified on theory, they must certainly be revised and modified. But to justify the old plan, a theory would be required to the effect, that women are in no case intended, when grown up, to follow intellectual pursuits. And who could allow such a proposition as this to be maintained? Yet the present system implies this assumption, for it gives no preparation of the mind in early life for subsequent intellectual pursuits. A system which provides only primary instruction *plus* accomplishments, must necessarily place even the most gifted minds under some disqualification for after development. It leaves the rudiments of higher studies to be acquired by voluntary, late, and painful effort, after the school days are over. The effort *then* can hardly be otherwise than painful, just because it comes at an unnatural time, for particular kinds of study belong to different times of life, and grounding in the rudiments belongs to childhood, so that there is something naturally repugnant in going to school over again, in order to learn the rudiments after one is grown up. This effort has often gallantly been gone through with, but in other cases it has been found too deterrent, and the result has then been, a sense of powers unevoked, and capacities that could never find their proper object. Hence have arisen voices of complaint, and the cry that the present system of education is an injustice to women. If it be so, it has been a wrong inflicted in unconsciousness and ignorance by society as a whole on half of its numbers, and, doubtless, has been avenged on society itself, for, as Aristotle said long ago, 'Those nations must be considered only half prosperous in which the arrangements concerning women are not good.' The mere statement of such an injustice, if it be done, is sure to bring about efforts at its abolition, so soon as public attention is thoroughly and earnestly directed to the subject, which now, perhaps for the first time, appears about to be the case.

As a contribution to the question, we may do well to observe for a moment the strong contrast which exists between the secondary education of boys and that of girls, in respect both of aim and method. Look at the grammar schools of England. I say this, because in Scotland secondary education even for boys has been undeveloped; but look at the English grammar-schools for boys, and see what they have done. For a long period they have aimed almost exclusively at thoroughness of grounding in the classical languages. They comparatively ignored everything else, and the reproach against them was, that they spent too much time in digging the foundations. They taught as if boys were going to live to the age of Methusaleh, and were to spend their first hundred years at least, at school or college.

With girls throughout Great Britain the exactly opposite plan was adopted. Having learned to read and write, they were taught French as an accomplishment, not as a study, and the result, in most cases, was that with very little cultivation of the mind they got a sort of courier's facility of using this and perhaps other modern languages. Not only language, but also art and science, were turned into accomplishments. Music was made mechanical, and was taught to the fingers rather than to the mind. Drawing became a trick of copying other people's copies of nature. Science was robbed of all that was scientific, and was handed over in the shape of a collection of facts, to be acquired by the memory. Thus, girls' education, while covering a much wider field than that attempted in boys' schools, and aiming at a much more immediate and practical preparation for life, unfortunately eliminated all that is really intellectual out of teaching, and thus debilitated the mind of the pupil, whom it often turned out greatly incapacitated for further acquisitions of knowledge. The boy, on the other hand, if he had really worked hard at his Latin and Greek, and especially if he had had the good fortune to be taught some mathematics beside, commenced life exceedingly ignorant of many subjects which it was desirable for him to know, and yet somehow he was a cultivated man, and was found to possess a faculty of acquiring afterwards almost any subject to which he might have the energy to apply himself.

From this contrast of two extreme systems, it would naturally suggest itself to enquire whether some compromise might not be made between them. The question for us is, Whether the education of girls, at home and at school, cannot borrow some of the features which experience has proved to be valuable in the secondary education of boys? I have heard it suggested as a maxim, and until it be experimentally disproved, I do not see why this maxim should not be adopted – that Whatever study is good for the mind of a man, must also be good for the mind of a woman.

6 Admission of women to university degrees

William Forsyth (1812–1899), a talented classical scholar and successful lawyer appointed QC in 1857, was for fifty years one of the most distinguished intellectuals of the exclusive Athenaeum Club in London. He authored several books and legal treatises, contributed articles to the major reviews of his times, and from 1842 to 1868 was editor of the *Annual Register*. He was also a philanthropist. Widely travelled, he developed a keen interest in politics, particularly concerning prison reform and education. A friend of Lord Brougham, he was one of the twenty-eight founding members of the Social Science Association. On his return to Parliament as a Conservative MP for Marylebone (1874–80), he proved not only an enlightened reformer but also a genuine defender of the cause of women. His *Treatise on the Law Relating to the Custody of Infants in Case of Difference between Parents or Guardians* (1850) was openly critical of a father's absolute right over his offspring. In 1875, he agreed to take charge of the woman suffrage campaign at Westminster, in the wake of J. S. Mill and Jacob Bright. Although he insisted that the Bill should explicitly exclude married women (a point which notoriously divided the suffragist societies), Forsyth regarded the vote as a weapon for women to advance issues specific to their sex. He persuaded Disraeli's government to allow time for the second reading of the Women's Disability Removal Bill until it was finally talked out in 1877. Forsyth was however opposed to giving women seats in the House. Like many of his contemporaries (of both sexes), he remained attached to the separation of spheres, but he publicly asserted that women were intellectually equal to men (as evidenced by the passage below). A great believer in legislation as a means of redressing wrongs and promoting social progress, Forsyth did not mince his words when denouncing the subordination of women, and the 'social tyranny' which oppressed them, whether their unjust absence of rights as mothers or the 'shameful' neglect of their education (see the parliamentary debates of 26 April 1876). With great courage and in the face of much hostility he supported the admission of women to university degrees, eventually awarded in 1878 by the University of London. Although the Scottish universities admitted female students, they refused to follow suit until 1892. Oxford and Cambridge did so only, in 1920 and 1948 respectively.

William Forsyth, Universities (Scotland) (Degrees to Women) Bill, Second reading, 3 March 1875, *Hansard*, third series, vol. 222, cols 1141–4

Mr FORSYTH said,[17] that the hon. Gentleman had referred to Mr. John Stuart Mill and Mr. Ruskin as not distinguished for their commonsense. The Universities of Scotland Act provided that the University Courts should make improvements, provided they obtained the consent of the Council and the Chancellor. Therefore, the whole Governing Body of the Universities had to give their assent before any steps could be taken. What was the interpretation that had been put upon the Act by the Courts of Scotland? In 1869, five ladies entered a University in Scotland. They went through their examinations, and had every reason to believe that they would be admitted to take their degrees. But some time afterwards 'a change came o'er the spirit of their dream,' for a resolution was come to which practically stopped them from taking their degrees. An appeal was made to a Court of Law which supported the views of the University authorities. The ladies felt, however, that it was a great hardship that they should be prevented from taking a degree by an accidental barrier arising out of the construction of an Act of Parliament. Aberdeen and St. Andrews might be in favour of the admission of women. Edinburgh and Glasgow might be opposed to it. Was it not a hard thing that those Universities which were willing to make

17 Until 1909 Hansard was not a verbatim report. It was copied from newspaper reports.

arrangements should be debarred from doing so, simply because Edinburgh and Glasgow objected? It was perfectly well known that arrangements could be made for separate classes, especially in the medical department, so as not to mix young men and women together. In the opinion of the lecturers of the University of Edinburgh, there was no reason, in justice or expediency, why women should be refused to practise medicine, especially among their own sex. [Mr. LYON PLAYFAIR: Not the University.] It was the lecturers in the School of Medicine in Edinburgh. There was the Petition of 27 Professors of the University – including among them Professors of Rhetoric, Moral Philosophy, Public Law, History, and Mathematics – which said there was a general and growing opinion throughout the community that women who desired to have scientific education ought to have the way open to them, and ought to be encouraged rather than discouraged in their honourable pursuit. He might rest his case in favour of the measure on the fact that this was an enabling Bill, and not a compulsory one. It left things as they were, and merely took away an artificial barrier. If the authorities of the Universities did not wish to admit ladies, they need not do so; but the Bill gave the authorities power to admit them if they thought fit. Although the Bill, if passed, would open the University examinations generally to female students, permitting them to take all degrees – and he was quite prepared to go that length – he believed they would confine themselves almost exclusively to the study of medicine, and the only arguments that could be maintained against their being allowed to do so must be based either on their intellectual unfitness, or disability on the score of sex. With reference to the first argument, he would only say it reminded him of the argument of the sophist that there was no such thing as motion, and his challenge to the philosopher to prove it. The answer of the philosopher was *solvitur ambulando*. They had only to look to the Continent of Europe to find that in most European countries – notably in Italy, France, Switzerland, Saxony, Sweden, and Russia – women were admitted to the practice of the medical profession, and many of them had attained to great eminence. Similar instances – few, unhappily, in number – were to be found in this country; but he did not think Englishwomen were so far behind the women of the Continent that they could not practise with equal ability? Take the case of Mrs. Garrett Anderson and Miss Blackwell, whose names had been put on the register, and who had a large and extensive practice. It was surely a narrow and bigoted view to take of any question like the present that England and Scotland should refrain from taking a forward movement, until they had received an example and an impetus from foreign countries. In reference to the argument of sex, he said that women constituted the majority of the population, and that in many diseases they shrank from the attendance of a male doctor. In that view, who were more fitting attendants on women than women themselves, if they were properly qualified? The object of the Bill was to enable them to get the best education the Universities could supply with regard to medicine to enable them to practise. If they were fitted intellectually, and not unfitted by sex, what reason could be urged why they should not practise? We lived in times when it was very often most difficult even for an educated man to obtain a livelihood. Nothing could be more painful than to see that when a place, with a very small salary, the duties of which a man of education could perform, was advertised, an immense number applied for that place. But if the competition was intense with regard to posts that men could fill, what was it with regard to women? They formed, as he had said, a majority of the whole population. What were the careers open to women of education? He was not talking of women employed in shops or in factories. He was talking of women of education, who had faculties which God had given them, and which might be employed in a useful and honourable career. We all knew what miserable salaries were paid generally to governesses and schoolmistresses. It might be said that authorship was open to women of education, but a man or a woman that was not a successful writer could not live by authorship. One of the greatest writers of modern times (Sir Walter Scott) said – 'Never regard authorship as a crutch, but only as a staff to lean your hand upon.' If women of education could earn a livelihood in an honourable and useful career, he thought it was a cruel injustice that that career should not be open to them. For those reasons he would vote most assuredly for the second reading of the Bill.

7 Progress in the cause of women's higher education

The Rev. John Llewelyn Davies (1826–1916) distinguished himself as a brilliant Cambridge scholar before becoming a Fellow of Trinity in 1851. Davies was renowned not only for his celebrated translation of Plato's *Republic*, which went through many editions, but for being one of Queen Victoria's chaplains in 1876 (which was no deterrent from inveighing against imperialism when preaching at Windsor). A disciple of F. D. Maurice, Davies was a theologian of unorthodox views, one of the many Liberal Anglican clerics who regarded the Church as an instrument for combating the ills of industrial society – to which he employed himself, whether as a vicar in London for forty-three years, or as Rector at Kirkby Lonsdale. He authored several theological treatises. His radical opinions on current political affairs often appeared in the *Contemporary Review*, the *Guardian* or *The Times*. Independent, charitable, he enjoyed a happy family life for many years, and was devoted to his wife, Mary Crompton (although she made a point of never attending any of his sermons). The conversion of his vicarage in Cumbria into headquarters for his daughter's political campaigns was a test of his commitment to women's votes: Margaret, a former pupil of Girton College, founded by Davies's own sister Emily, was one of the first female suffragists and a fervent women's rights activist; she became the mainstay of the Women's Co-operative Guild. Himself a convinced trades unionist, Davies promoted working-class associations and co-operatives. His collection of essays, *Social Question from the Point of View of Christian Theology* (1886), contains several addresses on the Woman Question. While respectful of gender hierarchy, he denounced the assumption 'that woman is permanently and in all respects the weaker vessel', and contended that 'the bearing of the original Christian teaching on the advance of women has not been rightly understood, and that it is more favourable to it than has commonly been supposed' (*Social Question*, pp. 351–3). The book includes a chapter on 'the advancement of women', which recommends a historical approach to revelation, and a radical proposal for legal reforms: 'No law or custom should be maintained which tempts man to lord it over woman, or which is unfavourable to the complete development of woman's nature' (*Social Question*, p. 117). Davies supported women's education (including their training for the medical profession), as well as the rights of married women to their property, and child custody rights. He lectured at the Working Men's College which he had helped set up (*The Working Men's College, 1854–1904; Records of Its History and Its Work for Fifty Years*, 1904). He was one of the ardent upholders of Maurice's educational principles, and, while principal of Queen's College (1873–1875, and again 1879–1886), organized teaching for the University of London matriculation and BA examinations.

The Rev. J. Llewelyn Davies, *Thirty Years' Progress in Female Education: An Address to the Students of Queen's College and Their Friends* (London: Ballantyne, Hanson & Co., 1879), pp. 8–10

I am not sure whether I ought to call the Cheltenham College a school; but the large institutions in Camden Town, under Miss Buss's direction, and the vigorous schools planted throughout the country by the Girls' Day School Company, expressly aim to be for girls what our older public schools are for boys. A step of another kind was taken, when the Cambridge Local Examinations were opened to girls. This was done tentatively at first. There was a good deal of trepidation in many minds, as to what might happen if girls were examined by University Examiners. It was feared that they might faint and be made ill, or that the domestic bloom would be rubbed off their minds. By a private and personal arrangement, a certain number of girls were examined by friendly Cambridge Examiners in just the same way as the boys, until experience showed that such an examination was a safe and innocuous process. The University of Cambridge, thereupon, with little hesitation, undertook to put no difference between girls and boys in respect of its Local Examinations. I am proud of the generosity manifested throughout this whole movement by my own University. I remember Mr. Maurice telling me, after he had gone to reside at Cambridge as Professor of Moral Philosophy, that there was nothing about which he found the younger graduates more zealous, than in endeavouring to put every academical advantage at the service of women. It is impossible to say for how much this cause is indebted to the sympathy and courage of a number of Cambridge men. The experimental examination which I have just mentioned was the beginning of a long series of helpful acts, which only wait now to be crowned by the formal admission of women to Cambridge University degrees. I say their formal admission, because – as you may know – they are virtually admitted to them already through the kind offices of friendly Examiners. It was a distinct step in advance when what is now Girton College was opened in 1869, at Hitchin. This was an uncompromising attempt to create for women a College, not like Queen's or Bedford, but of the same type as the Cambridge Colleges. And the attempt has prospered. This College has made gradual assured progress, and is still lengthening its cords and strengthening its stakes. In the same year an association was formed to organise Lectures for women at Cambridge; and as a place of residence for the students who were drawn to the town for the sake of attending these Lectures, a boarding-house was opened, which has developed into Newnham Hall and Norwich House and many lodgings under the same supervision. Oxford, as it has done throughout this movement, is following in the wake of Cambridge. A similar association has been formed there, and two Halls are about to be opened, one of them bearing the honoured name of Mrs. Somerville, for the reception of student. In London,

University College some years ago gave encouragement and hospitality to a Ladies' Association, which made arrangements for the voluntary instruction of classes by Professors of that College, and it has now gone on to open most of its Lecture-rooms, I believe, to women and men indiscriminately. More recently, King's College, not to be behind its rival, planted an offshoot for women in Kensington, which sprang at once into flourishing prosperity. And lastly, to change the metaphor, the edifice was crowned, when the University of London, which had already opened its Matriculation Examination to young women, was induced in 1878 to know no distinction of sex in examining for, and admitting to, any of its degrees. It was to the determined attempt to open the medical profession to women that this last success was due. And I might well include, amongst the most important achievements for the promotion of female education, the establishment of the London School of Medicine for women, which is now training female medical students on exactly the same level as that of the Hospital Schools for men.

Well, in this concession of the University of London women have received all that they can ask from a University. In Girton College, as a home of academical study, and in these London University Degrees, the tide of which we have been noticing the advance has reached high-water mark. A girl has now the chance of attending a good public School, of sharing Collegiate life and training, and of winning a University Degree – just as if she were a boy.

I have intimated already that this attainment of equality with the other sex, is only the form which circumstances have imposed upon the great effort of the last thirty years, and does not represent the ultimate desire in the hearts of those who have taken part in it. It must be considered a distinct advantage, indeed, that the two sexes should have such a fellowship of studies and knowledge as may enrich and exalt the communion between them. It is surely an injury and not a gain to the companionship of domestic and conjugal life, that the woman should be unable to enter fully into the intellectual interests of the man. And for this reason it might be rightly desired that girls and boys, young women and young men, should have similar opportunities of education. But what is most important is, that either sex should have the teaching and the training which will do the most for it, and bring it forward to its highest possible life. It would be an unworthy aim, that we should be struggling to get for a girl just what a boy has, without considering whether it is good in itself, and good for her, or not. Such an aim we of Queen's College decisively repudiate. If we prescribe to our girls that they shall learn Latin as well as French or German or Italian, it is not simply because boys learn it, but because we are convinced that the learning of Latin is a most desirable element in a girl's education.

8 Are women's brains inferior to men's?

David George Ritchie (1853–1903), the son of a Church of Scotland dignitary, was born into a family of scholars. In 1869 he graduated brilliantly in the classics at Edinburgh University, where he took a particular interest in the study of moral philosophy. From 1878 to 1886, while a fellow at Oxford, mainly under the influence of his teacher T. H. Green, and of Arnold Toynbee, he came to question the application of laissez-faire to the social question, proclaiming on the contrary that 'the business of the State is to regulate'. In 1894, Ritchie taught Logic and Metaphysics at St Andrews University. He was a very popular lecturer: strong-willed, unbowing to conventions, he attracted a wide circle of student followers. He contributed regularly to various journals of ethics and philosophy, and published several acclaimed essays: *The Principles of State Interference* (1891); *Darwin and Hegel* (1893); *Natural Rights* (1895), which was considered as inspirational in the development of New Liberalism; and *Studies in Political and Social Ethics* and *Plato* (1902). Close to the Fabians, and representative of the New Liberal approach which sought to provide liberalism with a social conscience, Ritchie had a passionate interest in practical politics which led him to address the consequences of evolutionist theories on society. *Darwinism and Ethics* (1889), permeated by an acute awareness of social inequalities, expressed a profound desire for reform, and a concern for a true 'social evolution' and progress (which would include self-realization and common good). Ritchie was unsurprisingly labelled an 'Idealist evolutionist', although he described himself as a 'socialist'. If he shared the socialists' belief that the relations between the sexes could not change 'till the whole economic structure of society ... [was] altered',[18] he lambasted them for opposing birth control – which he viewed as the best means to that end. *Darwinism and Ethics* was a vehement disapproval of crude individualism and of the ruthless application of the struggle for existence to social ethics. Ritchie attempted to exorcise the devil of biological determinism by showing that Darwin's theories had been misused. He inveighed against the 'biological politi-

18 Robert Latta (ed.), *Philosophical Studies* (London: Macmillan, 1905), p. 47.

cians' and contemporary 'sociologists' who opposed State intervention – particularly Herbert Spencer's influential *Man versus the State*, 1884):[19] 'In the name of Evolution and on behalf of the survival of the fittest Mr Herbert Spencer cries out against "the Sins of the Legislators" in interfering with the beneficent operation of the pitiless discipline which kills off the unsuccessful members of society, and against "The Coming Slavery" of socialistic attempts to diminish the misery of the world' (p. 11). The book also protested against the prescriptive ideals of femininity. The chapter dedicated to the improvement of 'The Position of Women' is a plea for the demise of the fossilized customs which impeded progress by keeping women in subjection: 'Those societies which have exaggerated the patriarchal type and built all their civilization upon it, seem to be incapable of advancing further' (p. 90). Ritchie denied the 'scientific' claim that women's higher education could be damaging to the race, and, contrary to those who warned against the dangers of women's mental exertion (owing to sexual differences in brain structure and fibres, and typified in Dr Henry Maudsley's *Sex, Mind and Education*, 1874), set to demonstrate that the biological arguments concerning women's inferiority were meaningless.[20]

D. G. Ritchie, *Darwinism and Politics* (London: Swan Sonnenschein & Co., 1889), pp. 77–83

(2) The claim of women to an equal share with men in the advantages and responsibilities of education and citizenship is very frequently met by the objection that to grant this claim is to fly in the face of nature. And the objection, when it comes from the evolutionist, has a certain plausibility. He points out, perhaps, how advance in organic life goes along with increasing differentiation of sex – a rash assertion in biology, but I have heard it made by a biologist. And so, it is asked, are not the advocates of women's rights trying to reverse all that, and to produce a morally asexual being? Again, if we limit ourselves to human society, it is urged that 'the difference between the sexes, as regards the cranial cavity,

19 Spencer is the father of Social Darwinism, i.e., the application of the law of natural selection to individuals, races, nations, and economic competition.
20 'With regard to the argument from nature generally ... it must be insisted that *difference* is not the same thing as *inequality* (though the two are very apt to be confounded), and that the very difference between the sexes is a reason why the State should not disregard the opinions and the feelings of half ... the population' (p. 84).

increases with the development of the race, so that the male European excels much more the female, than the negro the negress' (quoted from Vogt[21] by Darwin, *Descent of Man*, p. 566n.; but it is admitted that more observations are yet requisite before the fact can be positively asserted). It is argued from this fact, *if such it be*, that the progress of society has brought with it a still greater differentiation of sex, and, this having proved beneficial for the human race, it is folly to seek to reverse it. Let us take the last argument first. Because a certain method has led us up to a certain point, it does not follow that the same method continued will carry us on further. Races that have reached a certain stage may be hindered by extreme conservatism from making any further progress – like the Chinese. Again, at what degree of differentiation between the habits and lives of the sexes are we to draw the line? Englishmen, Frenchmen, Turks would draw it very differently. And the Turk ought to please the biological Conservative best, because he has pushed the differentiation of the sexes to a logical issue. The persons who use this kind of argument fancy that they are influenced by scientific considerations, but they are really influenced by what they happen to have grown accustomed to. Thirdly, *if* there is this greater difference between the cranial cavities of savage and civilised men than between those of savage and civilised women, to what must it be due?

(a) Those who believe that acquired characteristics (*i.e.* characteristics produced by agencies external to the organism) are transmitted, must explain this difference by the difference in institutions, laws and customs. Well, then – what these have done before in one direction they may do again in another. And the *same* education and the *same* responsibilities will, in course of time, put the average woman on the same level with the average man. (b) If use and disuse are not allowed as explanations, then this alleged brain inferiority of women must be due either to natural or to sexual selection. (α) If to natural selection, this would mean that in the struggle for existence those races or tribes have succeeded best in which the males have on the average had better brains than the females. And this *may* have been so in times when constant fighting was necessary for existence, though in such a case it would be the greater superiority of the male and not the greater inferiority of the female that had been the real

---

21 August Christoph Carl Vogt (1817–1895) was a Swiss professor of zoology; he provided a preface for *The Descent of Man* in 1873. His *Lectures on Man: His Place in Creation, and in the History of the Earth* were published in London in 1864.

cause of success. But this affords no argument that, when many other conditions of success than fighting power become necessary, the process of natural selection will continue to act in the same way. A people, *all* whose members become superior in mental qualities, will have the advantage over those peoples in which the development is partial and one sided; for, certainly, it could not be argued that the (alleged) relatively greater inferiority of the civilised female brain[22] had gone along with an increased capacity for the purely physical functions of maternity, as compared with what is found among savage races. (/3) If, on the other hand, the alleged difference is due to sexual selection, this must mean, not merely that men as a rule have preferred women with inferior brain power to their own (which is likely enough), but women whose female children were also on the average inferior in this respect to their male children. Supposing such a kind of selection to be possible (one can only admit it for the sake of argument), then, if men's ideas about women come to be altered, sexual selection will work in an opposite manner. With a new ideal of woman, the clever would be preferred to the stupid, and the mother of clever daughters to the mother of stupid daughters. Thus, *even if* the assertion of Carl Vogt were true, it offers no conclusive argument against the political and social equalization of the sexes; because this equalization would on *any* recognised principles of evolution, bring about ultimately a natural equality. On the whole, however, one may fairly retain the suspicion that this alleged difference is not a fact, and that the greater average eminence (in the past) of men than of women in intellectual pursuits is entirely due (as on any theory it must be mostly due) to the effect of institutions and customs and ideas operating within the lifetime of the individual, and not to differences physically inherited. Little girls are certainly not on the average stupider than little boys: and, if on the average men *show* more intellectual ability than women, may not this be due to the way in which the two sexes are respectively treated in the interval?

But, even if there were an *average* mental superiority in men due to sex-differentiation becoming greater with the attainment of maturity (we have really no right to make definite assertions on the subject, because women have never yet had a fair chance of showing their capacities on a sufficiently large scale), Plato's argument still hold that, though there

---

22 Phrenological studies and ethnographic data had been used by Owenites in the 1830s to show that differences in skull topology were a result of education (Taylor, 1983: 26–8).

may be a general superiority of men, yet there are many women superior to many men, and it is a pity that the State should lose the advantage of their services.

9 'The moral benefits of co-education'

The Rev. Cecil Grant (1870–1946), a theologian endowed with a fiery and innovative personality, and more inclined to lecture on Kant and Hegel than on Anglican orthodoxy, was one of the pioneers of co-education in Britain (with J. H. Badley, the founder of Bedales School in 1893). Grant's feminist readings, particularly those of Mary Wollstonecraft, testify to a keen interest in women's rights.[23] Grant was a personal friend of Maria Montessori, but his approach to education drew also upon the works of several prominent educationalists – Herbert Spencer's theory that education should be pleasurable (*Essay on Education*, 1861) and Charlotte Mason's original experiments, but also J. H. Pestalozzi's practical methods, and Friedrich Froebel's play-based kindergarten. Grant started his career as headmaster of Keswick School, Cumbria (1898–1907), and made his mark by re-establishing it as a co-educational boarding school. Increasingly frustrated by the criticism levelled against his unique experiment, he 'migrated' to Harpenden, with part of his staff and pupils, to found St George's, where he served as headmaster from 1907 to his retirement in 1936. The school, popular with the middle-class intelligentsia, rapidly outgrew its original buildings, and never stopped expanding. From 1917 it implemented Montessori pedagogy. Grant appealed to the editor of *The Times* to raise funds in order to acquire the freehold of the St George's estate. His dedication to the enterprise attracted a good deal of interest (as well as polemic), particularly in eugenics quarters. *English Education and Dr Montessori* (1913) had a preface by C. W. Saleeby, who regarded education as 'the provision of a special environment' and rejoiced that 'the nature of education as a biological instrument is beginning to be understood'.[24] Grant was asked to write special reports for the Board of Education. His observations were widely publicized in *The Times Educational Supplement* or in his essays, *A School's Life* (1903) and *The*

---

23 See the chapter 'The Woman's Movement' in *The Case for Co-Education* (London: Grant Richards, 1913).
24 Significantly Havelock Ellis also hailed co-education as a form of eugenics (*The Task of Social Hygiene*, p. 58) [IV, 9].

Case for Co-education (1913), written with Norman Hodgson (a scholar of Queen's College). For Grant the most invaluable gains of the experiment were better mutual knowledge, greater respect, and a 'natural community of feelings' between the sexes – the living proof that 'the divergence of interests which the sex distinction makes between boy and girl has been much exaggerated'.[25] Grant was confident it would forge equal gender relations, as well as teach men and women to 'know and to appreciate each other better, and to make fuller use of each other, whether they be partners in marriage or in the work of the world'.[26] By 1919, out of 1,080 maintained or recognized secondary schools 224 were co-educational. The extract below is from the paper he was invited to read at the International Moral Education Congress held at the University of London on 25 September 1908.

The Rev. Cecil Grant, 'The Relative Failure of the English Public Schools: The Moral Benefits of Co-education', in M. E. Sadler (ed.), *Moral Instruction and Training in Schools: Report of an International Inquiry*, 2 vols (London, New York, Bombay, and Calcutta: Longmans, Green, and Co., 1908), vol. 1, The United Kingdom, pp. 247–50

In addition to what I have already said under this head, I should add that my staff and myself believe that the right direction of feeling should always be assisted by full use of such subjects as music, poetry and art. At the same time practical and manual work is also of the utmost use, especially when associated with freedom of choice and time. We have found much good resulting from two experiments:

(a) An afternoon devoted to 'hobbies' on one or other of which every member of the staff is engaged.
(b) A rule that every boy and girl should devote a certain amount of his spare time every week to some employment useful to the school.

The average time thus spent last term was three hours by each child each week, and employments varied from carving for the chapel to picking up paper.

Similarly, too, much good can result from the existence of a School Mission among the poor, provided it is wholly free from any sense of patronage. There is no limit to the interest and enthusiasm and self-sacrifice which may be called forth in this way not from a few children

---

25 *The Case for Co-education* (London: Grant Richards, 1913), pp. 214–16.
26 *Ibid.*, p. 145.

only, but from practically every child in a school. At the same time they must be allowed to grow naturally amongst the children themselves. I would never ask for a penny directly or have a collection unless asked by the children to do so. All mission work is absolutely useless and unreal unless intimately associated with the religious life of the school.

4. *Our Public School system, to be fully efficient, should educate both sexes together from childhood up to university age.*
Our Public Schools have been fatally handicapped by the unnatural conditions caused by the separation of boys and girls which tend to produce and foster an unnatural vice. It is this which has brought down a school with an otherwise true system almost to the level of the rest, so that, as Arnold confesses, one is bound to ask, 'What good can be ascribed to the system itself; for there seems to be no sure improvement in it, but that it is at best a passive thing, presenting a good aspect when the individuals who belong to it happen to be good, but being in itself without any power to make them good or keep them so'.

Take away the unnatural conditions and the system *has* the power both to make them good and to keep them so.

It has been the experience of my staff and myself for eight or nine years that co-education has no disadvantages at any age. It would be as reasonable to speak of the disadvantages of having both boys and girls in a family. Its advantages being with the earliest school years, but they are naturally greatest during adolescence and the succeeding years. For it is then that separate schools experience in their worst form those evils against which co-education, properly conducted, is a complete safeguard. I do not believe that in a school of boys alone or of girls alone all risk of immorality can by any means be avoided. For separate education defies Nature and renders it impossible to teach sex-reverence. I do not believe that in a co-educational school, properly conducted, there need be any fear of immorality whatever. On the contrary, I am convinced that if a wise system of co-education were universal in England, sexual immorality among young or grown-up people would become as extinct as hydrophobia now is. Yet natural differences of sex would remain and the healthy instincts which make possible the preservation and renewing of the race.

I say wise co-education because I have scant sympathy with mixed schools[27] at any age where co-education existing for economic rather

27 Tentative experiments had existed since the 1850s, and more mixed schools

than moral ends is given but a half-hearted trial, or where, as in America, women teachers are in excess and discipline tends to be lax. It is obviously unfair to judge co-education by the products of such a bastard system.

At Keswick and at Harpenden we have found the following points vital:

(*a*) The school has been of such a size that the head-master could treat each boy or girl as a distinct and separate problem.

(*b*) Men teachers and women teachers have been in equal proportions, and, though at times the boys have tended to exceed the girls, a fair balance has been preserved.

(*c*) We have found immense benefit accrue from the adoption of the prefect system as it exists in the ordinary Public School, though the authority of boy prefects has been confined to the boys and that of girl prefects to the girls.

(*d*) A very considerable proportion of the school have been boarders. At Harpenden, moreover, all day scholars have been day boarders. Unless efficient supervision is in this way guaranteed, co-education can only be a partial success.

(*e*) Boys and girls only share in games so far as is natural.

Among the marked advantages to both sexes has been a complete absence of unnatural vice in any shape or form, a complete absence of impure talk of any kind, an immense improvement in the manners of both boys and girls, and a pleasing absence of that gloom which in a greater or less degree pervades all monastic institutions. Association with their brothers and their brothers' friends has rendered the girls less self-conscious than the ordinary school girl, has given them wider interests and a sense of *esprit de corps*. Association with the opposite sex has taught our boys, on the other hand, to be more painstaking and industrious, and has deprived them of that tendency towards vindictiveness and cruelty which is so marked in the monastically educated boy: while they have not lost, but gained, in manliness and true chivalry. There has been no tendency either of girls to become tomboys or of boys to become effeminate.

---

were established after the 1869 Act, in particular thanks to the recommendations of the Nonconformist MP Henry Winterbotham (who wanted the principle to be applied to Third Grade Schools at least, i.e., schools with a leaving age of fifteen), Jacob Bright, or Whately Cooke Taylor (Fletcher, 1982).

III

The vindication of women's civil rights

Women are not made for man at all, but are made for themselves.
George Dawson

1 A proposal to make marriage a civil contract

William Bridges Adams (1797–1872) was born in a prosperous family of coach and carriage builders. He made a career as an inventive railway engineer, celebrated for his thirty-two patents (*English Pleasure Carriages*, 1837; *Railways and Permanent Way*, 1854; *Roads and Rails*, 1862). Unlike his father, William, a member of the London Corresponding Society (1796), one of the numerous radical debating clubs dedicated to increasing the political knowledge of the working class,[1] Adams did not immediately get involved in politics. He lived in Valparaiso in the 1820s, with his first wife Elisabeth, Francis Place's daughter, until she died in childbirth. After travelling widely in South America, he returned to London in 1826, and wedded Sarah Flower, a talented poet close to the Mills and daughter of the radical publisher Benjamin Flower.[2] His social concerns for the housing conditions of the poor operatives and their animal-like lives in manufacturing towns led him to write *The Producing Man's Companion; An Essay on the Present State of Society, Moral, Political, and Physical, in England* (1833), first published under the title *The Rights of Morality* (1832), which

---

1 A Jacobin society that demanded manhood suffrage, equal representation, annual parliaments and payment of MPs; in 1838 it drew up the People's Charter with the help of Francis Place, who was on its general committee. One of its leaders, Thomas Spence, began to commit to women's rights in the 1790s, and advertised Mary Wollstonecraft's *Vindication*.
2 Flower was one of the intellectual figures of the Craven Hill circle.

was greeted as original and inspirational by the press. Adams soon made himself a name as a polemicist by writing more than three hundred pages on controversial topics in W. J. Fox's *Monthly Repository*, under the name 'Junius Redivivus' (1832–1836). His views 'On the Condition of Women in England' (1833) – the article described wives as 'sensual toys' and 'inmates of a Turkish haram', opposed marriage as a form of prostitution (a popular equation in radical circles), and pleaded for divorce – were so iconoclastic for the times that they split the Unitarian congregation. Even Harriet Martineau's radical stance on women's roles did not stretch that far, and she subsequently stopped writing for the journal in disapproval of Adams's positions (which, incidentally, Harriet Taylor considered largely as the expression of her own views). In 'Coriolanus, No Aristocrat' (*Monthly Repository*, 8, 1834) he was equally critical of women's bondage. Confident that machinery would free women from domestic chores (and increase their domestic efficiency), Adams promoted associated housing schemes with communal kitchens and laundries, which became popular in the 1840s with the radical intelligentsia ('Housebuilding and Housekeeping', *Monthly Repository*, 8, 1834). He published his own short-lived rationalist journal, *Common Sense*, in 1841. Like all Unitarians, Adams had faith in the regeneration of society through the liberation of the mind for both sexes: '*Woman must be made morally the equal of man* ... The only remedy for all these evils is to make her free, to make her a responsible agent' (p. 227).

Junius Redivivus (William Bridges Adams), 'On the condition of women in England', *Monthly Repository*, new series, 7 (1833), 228–9

Whatever it may be in effect, marriage is in legal form a bargain, a covenant, in which one of the principal stipulations is the observance of personal fidelity on both sides. No one will deny that chastity is a good thing, and in the case of the female, the penalty of transgression is rigidly exacted. But is it so with the male? Does he not stray about the world and sin with impunity, and is not the honour of the female impugned if she does but step across the threshold of her lord? Is it not the essence of a bargain, that there be two parties to it, and if one transgress, is not the other absolved? Legally, it is so. But what is the morality of the matter? That in the male the breach of this covenant is scarcely considered an offence, and in the female, it is visited with remorseless and unsparing severity. Is not this a most base and unmanly act of oppression? All the answer which will be given by the males is, 'We, having the power, have thus decreed it.'

To make woman what she ought to be, and might be, marriage should be rendered a civil contract,[3] capable of being dissolved like any other contract, with provisions to meet all results, whether of children or otherwise. The examples of murder, and other abhorrent things, springing from unequal marriages, would then disappear. The human affections cannot on all occasions be controlled; in some cases it is not desirable they should. Those who are disappointed in their expectations with a human being, who has not proved to them what they could wish, ought not to be doomed to misery for a whole existence. I am aware that the proposal to make marriage a civil contract, dissoluble like any other contract, by the mutual agreement of the parties, will possibly shock the feelings of many well-meaning persons, who, not accustomed to think deeply on the subject, will be apt to think that the possibility of procuring a divorce would act like an epidemic, and that all married couples would instantly take advantage of it, merely for the sake of the experiment, just as all the world flocks to an unknown sight. I will not advert to the fact that divorces are to be procured at present, because, on account of the heavy expense attendant on them, they may be regarded merely in the light of an expensive indulgence for the very rich, like the bulls of the ancient Catholic church, by which all who could afford to pay, might procure absolution for any darling vice they might choose to indulge in, while the poor were left to get over the matter as they could, and possibly fared as well as their masters after all. But I would ask, does the difficulty of divorce actually oblige persons who disagree with each other to live together even now? Are there no such things as separations? Are deeds for that purpose utterly unknown in lawyers' offices? And, if not unknown, what are they but a species of illegal divorce? Do the parties after that lead chaste lives? If they afterwards become attached to new connexions, is it not the mischievous, the immoral law, which forces them to live in a state of scandal? To contemplate the annihilation of human passions by an edict, is a monstrous absurdity. St. Paul says, 'If they cannot contain, let them marry;' but our sapient English law

---

3 The idea can be traced back to 1653, when the Barebones Parliament declared marriage to be a civil contract. For radical Unitarians like Adams and Fox ('The Dissenting Marriage Question', *Monthly Repository*, 7, 1833), this was the solution to the problem of prostitution: men trapped in unsatisfactory marriages looked for sexual solace elsewhere. In 1836, the Dissenters' Marriage Bill legalized civil marriages and created civil registers, putting an end to the Anglican monopoly in the registering of births, marriages, and deaths.

forbids them to marry, and nature forbids them to contain. There was a law existing formerly, that the widows of officers in the army and navy should lose their pensions upon marrying again. The pension was useful, but the penalty of single life was deemed a hardship, and it became a desirable thing to solve the problem, how the advantages of the pension and the comforts of marriage might be united. It was soon found out that the mere omission of the marriage ceremony was all that the government required, and I have heard it stated, that some three thousand fair widows at one period had taken their lovers' words as a sufficient security. Amongst those classes of the community who have no dealings with lawyers, and cannot afford to pay for 'separations,' is it found in practice that those who disagree live together, unless obliged by the circumstance of poverty rendering them chargeable to the parish? Have we no examples of the practical divorces of the poor, in the mock sales of wives with a halter round their necks in the public market? Are not these brutal acts the consequence of the mischief produced by the law of marriage as it at present stands? And, still worse, have we not many examples on record in which murder has been resorted to for the purpose of dissolving a connexion nothing else could dissolve? Surely any alteration of the law would be desirable, which might prevent the possibility of such things recurring. Let me not be misunderstood. I am no advocate of light love, or changing affections. I believe that constancy between the sexes is more productive of human happiness than any other condition, and it is only because I would ensure, as far as possible, that constancy, that I would wish to sever the unnatural unions whose only result is misery, both to parents and offspring. I would ask those who believe that universal divorce would be the result of attaining the power of divorce, what it is that restrains separations at present, in so many cases, where the father and mother dislike each other? What but moral power, the sense of duty to offspring, and deference to public opinion? There exists no legal preventive against separation, therefore the only restraint must assuredly be a moral one. And can it be imagined that this moral check would cease to exist, if divorce were legally attainable? Surely not.

2 'Talents merely to fold in a napkin?'

William Johnson Fox (1786–1864), originally a bank clerk, was one of the leaders of the radical vanguard of the first half of the Victorian age. Educated as a Calvinist, he was attracted to the branch of the Unitarian church (1774) under the influence of Joseph Priestley, characterized by an ethos of absolute freedom of thought and a historicist approach to the Bible. In the late 1820s, the Unitarians, though a small denomination, were particularly militant in political affairs, close to socialist movements and Chartism (they fought in particular for electoral reform and the religious rights of Dissenters and Catholics alike), and held very advanced ideas on womanhood.[4] On becoming a Unitarian minister, Fox became one of the most charismatic and prolific preachers of the congregation.[5] In 1824, he founded South Place chapel, London, which for thirty years was the magnet of an eclectic coterie of progressive intellectuals, and in 1831 bought *The Monthly Repository*, which became the mouthpiece of the Unitarian movement [III, 1]. Until 1836 his paper was to be a platform for social reform and feminist discussion, reflecting the South Place debates on the cultural conditioning of girls, new family roles, prostitution and marital relationships (see his contributions in the *Monthly Repository* on the question, 'A Political and Social Anomaly' (1832); 'The Dissenting Marriage Question' (1833); 'The Victim' (1833)). Although it was of limited circulation (1,200 copies), the paper's polemical articles against the marriage law caused heated controversy and alienated prominent Unitarians (such as Russell Lant Carpenter, Robert Aspland, and William Turner). Unhappy in his own marriage, Fox created more scandal by setting up with the musician Eliza Flower, and ended up breaking from his church (1835). The couple held a lively salon in Craven Hill, considered as the hotbed of the feminist movement, which attracted prominent radical literati.[6] He continued to write for Liberal papers including Dickens's *Daily News* and the *Weekly Dispatch* ('Women's Right to Property', 1856; 'Education of Woman', 1858). A Liberal MP (1847–1862), Fox campaigned for the education of the working classes and defended the Bill on the rights of married women in 1856 (he had previously supported the legal action taken by Caroline Norton against her tyrannical husband in 'Politics of the Common Pleas', *Monthly Repository*, 1836). He served as auditor of the nascent *English Woman's Journal*. He was never at a loss for arguments in the defence of women's rights. In spite of the raging opposition to female work (the Evangelicals, the Chartists,

---

4 Minister J. P. Estlin called Unitarianism 'the religion of females'. Many women reformers came from their ranks.
5 In 1819 Fox defended Richard Carlile [see IV, 1] in 'The Duties of Christian towards Deists: A Sermon'.
6 His daughter Eliza, 'Tottie Fox', was one of its figures.

the Unitarians were particularly hostile to the employment of married women in mines and factories, which they considered as detrimental to domestic bliss), Fox held fast to the principle as a right, and exposed the objection as spurious: no 'branch of trade suited to her station and sex, take[s] a woman out of her family more than dissipation, fashionable accomplishments, and the opportunities sought and made for their exhibition' (p. 496). In the article below, he makes out a case for the opening of more professions to women which he thought would provide an outlet for their talents and energies. In 1869 a magnificent plea was made along the same lines by the Liberal lawyer John Boyd-Kinnear.[7]

W. J. Fox, 'On Female Education and Occupations', *Monthly Repository*, new series, 7 (1833), 496–8

Every woman has not a domestic establishment to occupy her, every woman has not a family to nurse and train, every woman has not a husband able to maintain her and that family. The greatest benefits conferred upon society have been in general by the agency of men unconnected with, undisturbed by family cares. It is not necessary that every one should marry; in populous states, under expensive governments, prudence keeps many in celibacy. This, if it is an evil, is now likely to be increased: various channels are open to single men, into which to divert their energies and render them honourable to themselves and useful to their fellow-citizens. But what has been the fate of unmarried women? If not wealthy, and large fortunes rarely devolve to women, if not endowed with a strength of mind and character that falls to the lot of few, the situations into which the majority of them sink, when unsupported and unprotected by male relatives (and even by these they are often plundered and oppressed,) is indeed pitiable; and even for their very misfortunes instead of sympathy they meet with insult. And why is this? Because they are allowed no reputable productive means in which they might employ their time and talents, and by independence enforce respect. If created merely to blossom, to fade, and to be trampled under feet, why has Nature, that does nothing in vain, endowed them with reason, with capacities and powers similar to those of man? Has Providence given them talents merely to fold in a napkin? Are they unaccountable and unresponsible for their use or abuse of such talents? Can they benefit society in no other way than by increasing its numbers? Are

---

7 'The Social Position of Women in the Present Age', in Butler (ed.), *Woman's Work and Woman's Culture* (London: Macmillan, 1869), pp. 331–67.

they, because less corporeally robust than man, incapable of any productive labour, of any useful exercise of the intellectual powers? This will not be affirmed, because experience has proved the contrary.

Why then not lay open to female exertion and industry more liberal sources, more various and respectable modes of occupation? If woman must be accomplished in the arts, for which by her taste and sensibility she is eminently fitted, why fritter away her time and talents by exacting from her a smattering of *all*, instead of inciting her to pay attention to *one only*, and thus by concentrating her powers to invigorate and render them really productive? Woman wants only opportunity and encouragement to rival man in every elegant, in every useful art; but she is rarely, if ever, trained as a professor, but merely as an amateur. Where nature has denied genius to reach to eminence in art, yet a steady undiverted attention to *one* pursuit will rarely fail of producing some degree of excellence. How many male artists procure a respectable provision for themselves and families by instructing youth in their art. Why should not female youth be taught exclusively or chiefly by females? Surely, both in schools and private families, they are the more proper instructors? Not as governesses, having a smattering of every branch of knowledge or of art, and a proficiency in none: but let them, as do the other sex, maintaining an independent home, instruct their pupils at their own houses, or in the several schools in which they may be placed by their friends. By women so prepared and trained, men would soon be superseded, as they ought to be, in the education of females.

Many branches of trade and commerce should also be thrown open to women in a manner that should render them respectable. Several of the bazaars have set an excellent example, by employing only females: in the shops of milliners, haberdashers, retail linen-drapers, &c. it is disgusting to see men officiate. The married woman who has been thus taught and trained in the middling class of life, would be able to assist in providing for her family and house, she would not be a useless burthen on the industry of her husband, and would thus ensure his respect with his love. The unmarried would, by the professions or trades which they exercised, keep a rank in society, and maintain the respect due to that rank: they would no longer feel the humiliation of having no social consequence but through the men, and their characters would acquire dignity and strength.

Before reason and justice can maintain their rights over mankind, all odious distinctions and prejudices, whether sexual or feudal, must be done away. If woman is inferior to man, it is not in nature but in degree, reason and virtue must be the same in both; if their duties are different in some respects, they are still human duties, and their foundation and end must be the same. Virtue can only be depended upon that has its foundation on principle and truth. The wisdom, the happiness of succeeding generations must depend upon the instruction and impressions they receive during childhood and youth. Every system of education, whether male or female, calls aloud for examination and reform. Men, I repeat, cannot reap wheat where tares only are sown, or from thistles expect to gather grapes.

3 A law to protect married women's property

Henry Peter Brougham, First Baron Brougham and Vaux (1778–1868) was a very active participant in the intellectual ferment of his times. He was raised twice to the peerage for services rendered to the nation. Brougham was one of the founders of the *Edinburgh Review*, and a prolific and versatile writer on subjects as diverse as religion,[8] politics, the arts, and science, in which he had developed a keen interest. Brougham, originally a lawyer, had been a commanding, but independent and controversial Whig MP from 1810 (and was always deemed too radical by his party), until he had to sit in the Upper House as a result of his position as Lord Chancellor (1830). But he made his mark as a passionate reformer, renowned for his outstanding oratorical skills. His support of the 1832 Reform Act, which he piloted through the Lords, and the 1833 Slavery Abolition Act for which he had campaigned intensively, branded him as a true liberal (although he was a Whig), attached to the principles of individual freedom and responsibility. Brougham also gained a reputation for advocating the legal redress of women's wrongs. His first remarkable involvement with the cause started in 1812, when he successfully took on the defence of Caroline of Brunswick on trial for adultery by her husband, George IV. Although the king was himself notorious for his own extravagance, and mistreatment of his wife, he was intent on divorcing the Queen and on depriving her of her royal title. The trial marked a turn in public attitudes to marriage, and brought Lord Brougham to the zenith of his national popularity. He was, however, no dangerous radical and had no wish to destroy the essential fabric of British legal and political institutions, in particular 'the character of the

---

8 *A Discourse of Natural Theology* (1835) branded him as an unorthodox Anglican.

institution of marriage'. Caroline's legal action to see her two sons was for him a step too far: although he acknowledged the inequity of the law against mothers, he voted against Thomas Talfourd's Custody of Infants Bill (1838), arguing: 'Could anything be more harsh or cruel than that the wife's goods and chattels should be at the mercy of the husband ...?' (*Hansard*, House of Lords, 30 July 1838, vol. 44, col. 781). His attitude exemplifies that of many legislators (rationally) anxious to accommodate the legitimate claims of women, while (emotionally) desirous to preserve the framework of male authority.[9] Brougham's next feat of courage was shown in the debates on the married women's property and divorce law. In 1851, his commitment to legal equality had led him to found the Law Amendment Society (1844). Amongst a variety of reforms,[10] it suggested the fusion of the two courts of law in order to put paid to what he considered an unfair set of rules, the court of common law and the court of equity (the latter allowed married women, generally of aristocratic birth, to enjoy their wealth under the management of a trustee, if it had been designated as separate by the latter). Brougham defended the first version of the Married Women's Property bill[11] in the Lords. It proposed to abolish the doctrine of spousal unity and apply the rule of equity to all. But the view of marriage as the union of two separate individuals with the same legal rights (embodied by the separate use of their income) was revolutionary for the times,[12] and, unsurprisingly the law was not amended until 1870.[13] Until his death Brougham remained president of the National Association for the Promotion of Social Science and encouraged women to voice their claims at its annual meetings.

9 Particularly regarding the father's right to a child's religious education (Griffin, 2014: 143–50).
10 The 'Brougham's Act' (1850) for instance specified that the word 'man' in all legislation should be taken as including women unless specified otherwise; it triggered off the first (Sheffield) suffrage petition the following year, presented to the Lords by Liberal George Howard (Seventh Earl of Carlisle).
11 It had been presented in the Commons by Sir Erskine Perry in 1856, following a petition of 26,000 signatures.
12 The view of women as free and responsible moral agents was however shared by Liberals like A. Hobhouse, G. W. Hastings, and F. W. H. Myers, all members of the National Association for the Promotion of Social Science.
13 In May 1857, Perry introduced another version. It was dropped, following the enactment of Lord Lyndhurst's Divorce Bill: although it did not affect the marriage law, the Act protected injured women in the most extreme circumstances, which put an end to the debates until the late 1860s.

Lord Brougham, Speech in the House of Lords, 13 February 1857 (Property of Married Women, first reading), *Hansard*, series 3, vol. 144, cols 607–9

It may be in the recollection of your Lordships that I last Session presented a petition, with which I had the honour to be intrusted, from two thousand and upwards of our fellow countrywomen of all classes; some supporting themselves by the wages of their daily labour; some having property bestowed upon them by the kindness of friends, or the testamentary bounty of persons deceased; others earning gains to a considerable, even to a large amount by their industry and their talents, not a few even by their genius in letters and in the arts, as authoresses, as painters, and as sculptors; and the names of several of these adorned the list of signatures to the petition, while they gave weight to its prayer. Now it must be remembered that all such earnings, whether the gains of the ordinary labourer who toils for the daily, the scanty supply of her own and her children's wants, or the Linwoods whose needle rivals the pencil of the Kaufmans [*sic*] – and all such gains are only in name theirs of whose toil and whose skill they are the produce. All in reality belong by our law's decrees to the husband, all are vested in him by right, and he may at his own good pleasure vest them also in possession; nay never having in the least degree helped their production, he may without the delay, the respite of an instant, or one word of notice or warning, or even demand, seize upon the whole, sweep all away, and leave her who created the whole stript of them to the very last farthing. He may squander them upon his pleasures, lavish them on his paramour, employ them to support his spurious progeny, and there exists not the possibility of his being in any the very least degree either controlled or even called to account for the heartless cruelty of his robbery, or his profligate use of its fruits.

Such is the law of England, and of this law we complain. But I have the greater confidence in my prospect of obtaining the concurrence of this House in our views, because your Lordships and your connections are not those on whom its pressure weighs so heavily. In your fortunate position, with the protection which settlements and the interposition of trustees afford,[14] the grievance is felt, but it is comparatively slight; above all the worst part of the evil can hardly be felt in any way, for that refers to the earnings of labour and of skill, for the exertion of which for their

14 The properties of the wives of the wealthy were placed in trusts, a system which did not endanger the husband's authority over his spouse.

support your wives are happily relieved. It is not upon the families of those whom I now address, or of persons generally in the upper ranks of society, but upon the middle classes and the humbler order of our fellow citizens that the evil falls, to crush their most deserving members, while it protects and even encourages the worst in their idleness or their profligacy.[15] The instances which I have once and again given in this place, to show how certainly the fact corresponds to whatever might have been most confidently expected beforehand to follow from the state of the law, I need not now repeat; they were truly heart-rending, and I gladly spare your feelings with my own the pain of their rehearsal. An instance or two may suffice, and I select the least painful of purpose. My noble Friend opposite (the Marquess of Lansdowne) stated one of them in his place. It was that of an industrious and honest woman who had married a good-for-nothing husband; he deserted her and went to live with another. The wife took to the occupation of a ladies' shoemaker and earned a pittance for her own support: when the husband found that she was thriving by her successful labour he returned to her, but for the moment only; he seized the little fund she had scraped together, collected the money due from the customers, sold her furniture, and went back to his paramour, leaving her as helpless as before, except for the resources of her own industry. – Another case came to my own knowledge, at least I saw the party and took pains to inquire into the truth of the statement. Here the parties were of higher rank. A gentlewoman had been deserted by her husband, who went with another woman to Australia upon a speculation of a mining kind. The wife, a well-educated person, most meritoriously took to school keeping for her support rather than throw herself upon the bounty of her relations; she was eminently successful in forming an establishment, and had been able to lay by some portion of her gains. The husband's speculation proved unsuccessful, and he could barely find the means of returning home. Home he came, and at once rushed upon the mine which his wife's labour, prudence, and accomplishments had created; seized the whole, collected the debts due, sold the furniture and the lease of the premises, and returned to enjoy the fruits of her toil, if enjoyment, such a thing in such circumstances, can be called – but his

15 Protecting women 'from the combined fraud and violence of the idle or dissolute husband' (col. 609) was part of the attempt to reform the morals of the poor. However the Divorce Court (1857) revealed that domestic abuse went largely beyond the confines of the working classes, as evidenced by Brougham's remark, and from then on was increasingly identified as a larger social problem.

perverted taste might so feel it – at any rate he returned to squander the proceeds of his spoliation upon his mistress.

I freely admit, however, that though the recital of such outrages upon all right feelings as upon common honesty be serviceable by way of example, in showing what the state of the law may lead to, yet they may possibly be treated as exceptions, as extreme cases, and it may be alleged that in the great number of married persons, some such instances of profligacy are likely to occur, and may be deemed singular and only possible. I therefore go at once to what cannot fall within the scope of such an observation. I go to the manufacturing districts, from which our information is as precise as it is striking. From persons intimately acquainted with one of these resorts of labour, persons residing on the spot, we learn (and the case is the same with all the Lancashire country) the operation of the law upon the comfort and the morals of the working classes. You have only, it is said, to approach the premises of any of the manufacturers upon the Saturday night and observe the crowd of men that surround the door from whence issue the workwomen after receiving their week's wages at the pay-table; all who have husbands are seized by the hand, and with what in many instances proves anything rather than a soft violence, a gentle pressure, compelled to surrender their gains.

---

4 'The remnant of an old barbarous law'

Arthur Hobhouse (1819–1904), made First Baron Hobhouse of Hadspen, is a perfect instance of men who played a part in the evolution of women's legal rights, but whose name history seems to have forgotten. Inspired from an early age by a father imbued with a deep sense of public duty (he was Permanent Under-Secretary at the Home Office), Arthur was determined to rise to the task: 'There is no more noble or useful life than one spent in honest and zealous devotion to those things'. 'The work brings in no money, and reputation', he added, 'but such men are the very cement of the society in which they live'.[16] Hobhouse's remarkable capacity for Aristotelian analyses earned him the reputation of an 'ideal' judge. He enjoyed an extensive career, well until his eighties, as QC, bencher of Lincoln's Inn, lawyer of the Governor-

---

16 L. T. Hobhouse and J. L. Hammond, *Lord Hobhouse: A Memoir* (London: E. Arnold, 1905), p. 2.

4 Arthur Hobhouse

General's council in India, and member of the judicial committee of the Privy Council (where he accepted to work without pay). Hobhouse was an advanced Liberal, an uncompromising lover of justice, a man of great sensitivity and strong opinions, which he defended fearlessly in the face of opposition, always faithful to his principles, even if they clashed with his personal ambition. Since his Oxford days he had been deeply preoccupied by the issue of poverty and the general welfare of society. His desire of social improvement never flagged, and he left his mark on a number of legal reforms. A vestryman in London in the 1880s, he was one of the most efficient artisans of the creation of a single and representative government for the metropolis. On becoming a Charity Commissioner in 1874 (he was an former Endowed Schools Commissioner), he threw himself into the reorganizing of the educational system, and launched a fierce attack on the regulations of outmoded charities (*The Dead Hand. Addresses on the Subject of Endowments and Settlements of Property*, 1880). Hobhouse supported women's higher education, and helped create Somerville College at Oxford. He delivered powerful comprehensive papers at the annual congresses of the National Association for the Promotion of Social Science. His speech against the forfeiture of property by married women, delivered at the Birmingham meeting in 1868, was especially reprinted for the use of the Married Women's Property Committee that examined the 1870 Bill.[17] Hobhouse's arguments reflected a growing public awareness of, and sensitivity to, violent household conflicts and neglectful or abusive husbands, a phenomenon which lay at the heart of the gradual erosion of the Victorian ideals of domesticity and masculinity.[18] Hobhouse also contributed to the recognition of mental cruelty in divorce cases, following a judgement of Appeal rendered in the House of Lords. In contrast with Brougham, seemingly less concerned with women's rights *per se* than with the moral reform of the working classes, Hobhouse appears as one of women's 'advocates of freedom', passionately desirous to free them from 'the shackles of paternal government', and to enable them to deal with their own money (Appendix to *On the Forfeiture* ...).

17 The Bill provided that women who married subsequently to the Act should be as capable of holding property as single ones. The measure was stopped in the House of Lords on the ground that its provisions required further consideration. The 1870 Act was severely amended to allow (essentially poor) women to own their earnings. It did not repeal the system of trusts. Rich and poor continued to be governed by two different systems until 1882, when the new Act extended the rules of equity to all married women (Shanley, 1989). But they had to wait until 1935 for full equal rights with men. However, allowing women to control their property theoretically removed the constitutional argument against granting them parliamentary franchise, itself based on property.
18 Following the Susanna Palmer trial in 1868 (a case of domestic violence and abuse), Russell Gurney presented her cause to Parliament asking for the protection of married women's property. In 1869, two equally powerful cases were made out by the historian Charles Henry Pearson, 'On Some Historical Aspects of Family Life' (in Butler, ed., *Woman's Work and Woman's Culture*, pp. 152–85), and Herbert Newman Mozley, 'The Property Disabilities of a Married Woman and the Legal Effect of Marriage' (*Ibid.*, pp. 186–246).

Arthur Hobhouse, *On the Forfeiture of Property by Married Women* (Manchester: A. Ireland & Co, 1870), pp. 6-8 [Reprint from the *Fortnightly Review*, Feb. 1870]

It is not my object now to discuss the provisions of the Bill in detail. Indeed I have throughout confined myself to discussing principles. It is because there were some, though uncertain, indications in both Houses that alterations might be proposed, which, though in the form of details, would really defeat the whole measure, that I am anxious to recall attention to the previous stages of the discussion, and to add some observations on the threatened danger. And I am the more anxious to do this, because the alterations in question seem to find favour not only with those who, consenting to change merely because the advocates of change are too strong for them, really hate the Bill, and will substitute a changeling for it if they can, but with some who are sincerely convinced of the evils of the present system, and wish to see a remedy applied to them. Neither do I propose to amplify or add to the arguments contained in the Birmingham paper. It is there stated that I had not the advantage of seeing any detailed or methodical statement of the objections to altering the law. Neither have I now; and I may fairly assume in so contentious a matter, that arguments asked for but not yet adduced do not exist; and that those which have been adduced for the change, and have not been answered, are unanswerable. I wish now to address myself solely to the suggestions, that the necessities of the case will be met by extending the remedies of wives under the Divorce Act, and that it would be for their advantage to tie up their property for themselves and their children.

At the present time, if a wife is deserted by her husband she may apply to a magistrate, who may grant her an order of protection, the effect of which, to use popular language, is to place her as regards ownership of property in the position of a single woman. It is suggested that these powers of magistrates might be largely extended, so largely in fact as to give to wives all the protection they need. I have never seen any statement of the mode in which it is proposed to do this, and I shall be surprised if any can be put into definite words and not forthwith break down by its own weakness. But the proposal is so faulty in principle, that on principle it ought to be decided, and we ought never to arrive at the stage of discussing specific provisions for this purpose.

In the first place I would ask, For what reason is a change desirable at all? and then would ask Whether that reason is satisfied by facilitating protection orders?

It must be remembered that I am addressing myself to those who are convinced that, for some reason or other, probably one or more of those contained in the Birmingham paper, a change is necessary. Is it on account of the abstract justice of the case? Then what justice is there in providing that a husband's property shall be secured to him by the simple operation of the law without any misconduct on the wife's part, but that a wife's shall be taken away from her unless her husband ill-treats her and she has the courage to embark in a litigation and the luck to emerge successfully from it?

Is it because good laws ought to harmonise with the arrangements which people make for themselves when they have knowledge and power enough to act for themselves! Then follow those arrangements, so far as they are applicable to the subject matter you are handling, and make the property of wives theirs by direct right, and not merely on condition that a magistrate thinks they have suffered ill-treatment enough to claim it back from their husbands.

Is it because there ought not to be two contradictory laws – one for the rich and one for the poor?[19] Why, such a measure would make the contradiction more sharply defined, more glaring than ever. I would ask any advocate of such a measure, Would you be content to mete it out to your own daughter? If she marries, will you consent to abstain from securing to her any property of her own, in consideration of her getting more favourable opportunities of appearing in a police office?

Is it on account of the lessons afforded by Transatlantic experience?[20] Then that experience teaches us to make married women owners of property, not to give them greater facilities of prosecuting quarrels with their husbands.

Is it because you are convinced that giving one consort's property to the other is no proper part of the contract of marriage – is only the remnant of an old barbarous law and is not necessary to preserve harmony or due subordination in families? Then such a gift should not be made by the law at all, and its existence should not depend on the chance of the parties remaining in more or less friendly relations with one another.

Or is it simply because you are struck with remorse at hearing evidence of the shocking cruelties which spring from the present law?

19 See [III, 3].
20 In Canada and parts of the USA, women had been given equal property rights, a practice used as evidence in the support of reform.

Then look at the evidence again, and you will find that many even of the evils brought to light are such as it is most difficult to remedy through a court of justice. And depend upon it that where, in a delicate and painful matter, so much comes to light, much more remains in darkness, and that for one case that could be reached by the action of a magistrate, scores, or even hundreds, would be reached by a simple change of the principle of law. Those who contend that the principle of the law is not bad are bound to give some satisfactory explanation of the phenomena, to tell us why sufferings are so frequent among those who remain subject to it, and why all who can escape from it, do so. No such explanation has ever been attempted. The principle then is bad.

5 A question of justice

Henry Fawcett (1833–1884) features among the most popular and respected intellectuals of his times. A self-classified radical, but described as an 'advanced Liberal' in the Bentham–Mill tradition (which considered that the government's task was to help people to help themselves by encouraging fair competition), he found himself frequently in conflict with Gladstone's policies. He flirted with republicanism in the 1870s, but his interest in reform always stopped short of socialism. His feminism developed from an early age, partly as the result of his admiration for his mentor John Stuart Mill, but also for Thomas Hughes. Hughes's androgynous vision of manliness, popularized in *The Manliness of Christ* (1879), contributed to creating a new emotional climate which made it more acceptable for men to be both manly and feminine.[21] Fawcett had a curious natural attraction for women activists: he proposed marriage to three prominent figures of the movement before being finally accepted by Millicent Garrett (1867). The union was blessed by similarity of temperament and convictions. In 'perfect intellectual sympathy' with his wife, he

---

21 The book was written in protest against 'muscular Christianity' [II, 4]; it placed courage, i.e., loyalty to the truth, at the root of manliness. Hughes's definition embraced tenderness and thoughtfulness for others, which unsurprisingly included women: 'One of the most searching of all trials of courage and manliness', he wrote, is 'when a man or woman is called to stand by what approves itself to their consciences as true, and to protest for it through evil report and good report, against all discouragement and opposition from those they love or respect', *The Manliness of Christ* (London: Macmillan & Co., 1879), p. 36.

taught her in classical economics, and encouraged her to lead her own political career (she headed the National Union for Women Suffrage from 1897). Fawcett consistently campaigned for women suffrage from his return to Parliament in 1865 until his death (he joined Mill in the presentation of Barbara Bodichon's petition for woman franchise in 1866). Like many academic radicals in the 1860s, he promoted university reform (undenominational education and equal opportunities between all sects and creeds). The project to create Newnham College was discussed in his Cambridge drawing room in 1869. Fawcett supported the movement to open the Cambridge Local Examinations to girls, and urged that women be admitted to study for degrees at Oxford and Cambridge. He was a recognized authority on political economy, which he taught at Cambridge for thirty years, and served as President of the Department of Economy and Trade (1859–1868) in the National Association for the Promotion of Social Science. Fawcett authored several inspiring books. *Manual of Political Economy* (1863), his magnus opus, went into six editions. *Pauperism: Its Causes and Remedies* (1871) proved sympathetic to the opening of more employments to women. *Essays and Lectures on Social and Political Subjects* (1872), and *State Socialism and the Nationalisation of Land* (1883) were published jointly with his wife. Fawcett, at first in favour of regulating the working conditions of women, opposed the special protection of women under the Factory Acts when he realized that the trade unionists' goal was to restrict the competition of women's labour (see his intervention in the discussion of 'Employment of Females', *Social Science Association*, Birmingham meeting, 1868, p. 611; or his speech on 30 July 1873 against the Nine Hours Bill in the Commons, *Hansard*, 3rd ser., vol. 217, col. 1298). While occupying the post of Postmaster General (1880–1884), he opened positions in the Post Office to women.

Henry Fawcett, Speech in the House of Commons, 30 April 1873 (second reading of the Women's Disabilities Bill), *Hansard*, vol. 215, cols 1240–3

I must confess that the Home Secretary astonished me very considerably by going into an historical argument, in which he seemed to think that he had discovered, as a reason why women should not have votes, that it was men who had always defended the country, and that it was the barons who obtained the Magna Charta from King John. If this argument is worth anything it certainly amounts to this, that no one should have votes except barons and soldiers. Repeating the argument of the right hon. Gentleman the Member for Kilmarnock (Mr. Bouverie), the Home Secretary said, the great argument against the Bill of my hon. Friend was that if it were carried it would ultimately lead to the giving of votes to married women and to women taking seats in this House. Before I reply to that argument let me say that it is an old one. Never was there a great change proposed, or a great measure of reform brought forward, but that some 'bogey' was immediately called up to alarm and terrify us. When Catholic emancipation was proposed, and it was advocated that Catholics should have seats in this House, one of the favourite arguments of the opponents of the proposal was, that if the Catholics were admitted to this House there was no reason why a Catholic should not sit upon the throne. One of the favourite arguments used by the opponents of household suffrage was that if household suffrage were granted there was only one other step, and that was manhood suffrage. We have not been intimidated or frightened by arguments such as this, but it seems to me that the Home Secretary and the right hon. Member for Kilmarnock are indulging in doctrines which are dangerous, when they assume to think that property is no longer to be the basis of the qualification for a vote in this country. The right hon. Member for Kilmarnock quoted with commendation a saying of the democratic Benjamin Franklin, that it is idle to suppose that property possesses the exclusive right to the franchise. Without presuming too confidently to predict what will happen, I have no hesitation in saying that these words of the right hon. Gentleman the Member for Kilmarnock, will next Easter Monday be quoted with rapturous applause, when 60,000 men gather together on the Town Moor at Newcastle to demand manhood suffrage. There is no logical reason why married women should not have votes if you demand manhood suffrage. But we who support this Bill do not wish to declare that we desire that the franchise should be based upon any other condition than it is based upon at the present moment – namely, property. Unless a woman can obtain a vote by property we do not wish to do anything either to admit her or to exclude her. It is therefore you who, if you throw this argument of property aside, will be lending an assistance to the agitation in favour of manhood suffrage which I believe you will heartily repent. I wish now, as briefly as possible, to go through the leading arguments which have been advanced in the debate upon this Bill. The reasons in its favour have been stated so often, and I am anxious to occupy as little as possible of the time of the House, that it appears to me to be the fairer course to deal with the arguments against rather than those in favour of the Bill. The first argument is that the majority of women do not ask for this Bill, and that a great number of them are opposed to it. If this Bill contemplated making a woman vote who did not wish to vote, it would not find a more resolute opponent in this House than myself. But when you say that a majority of women are opposed to it, I say that it is impossible to prove it; and I say further, that the same argument, in an analogous case, you did not accept as complete. I remember perfectly well, when I first came into this House, that I heard it stated again and again that the majority of the working classes of this country were not in favour of the extension of the suffrage. It was said that it was only the active politicians among them, just as it is now said that it is only the active women agitators who are in favour of this Bill. Now, what do we observe? No doubt it never could be proved that a majority of the working classes were in favour of the extension of the suffrage, and [*sic*] more than it can be proved now that a majority of the agricultural labourers are in favour of household suffrage in counties; and yet it was again and again stated that the majority of the working classes were in favour of household suffrage. The House soon after that recognized the justice of the claim for an extension of the suffrage to the artizan class, by having once recognized the abstract justice of the plea. But the argument which no doubt produced the most influence on the House is this, that at the present time the interests of women are far better looked after by men than they would be looked after by themselves; and it was said by the Home Secretary that if you could only prove to him that women's questions of a vitally interesting nature were treated with injustice in this House, it would be a conclusive argument in favour of voting for the Bill. Nothing could be further from my mind than to accuse this House of consciously doing anything which is unjust or wrong to women, but women and men may have very different views of what is best for women, and our position is this, that according to the principles of representative Government it is only fair that women should be able to give expression to their wishes on measures likely to affect their interests.

6 A eugenicist point of view on the marriage question

Karl Pearson (1857–1936), born into a Quaker family, is mostly known as the mathematician who, in 1911, founded the first Department of Applied Statistics in the world. A man of brilliant intellect and eclectic tastes, Pearson embraced freethought and socialism, consorted with the

Fabians, the anarchists and the Theosophists, and became a passionate proponent of Eugenics, a science invented by the man who became his mentor (and to whom he paid tribute to in a most comprehensive biography, *Life, Letters, and Labours of Francis Galton*, published between 1914 and 1930). Pearson has often been misrepresented as an 'antifeminist', a view challenged by 'The Woman Question', a speech delivered at the inaugural meeting of the Men's and Women's Club, which exposed an acute awareness of men's fault in women's subordination: 'How often do men take to heart the too obvious fact that they are to a great extent responsible for the way in which the life of the subject-sex has been moulded?' (p. 392). Founded by Pearson in 1885 with the conviction that the combination of Eugenics and Socialism would bring about a new and more moral society, the club attracted radical and freethinking intellectuals of both sexes,[22] purposely enrolled in equal numbers to debate on all questions related to gender relations. Although short-lived (1885–1889), this adventure gave women an opportunity for presenting challenging papers and subverting received ideas, notably the assumption that women had weak physical appetites. In his address to club members, Pearson blamed 'women's presumed mental inferiority' on their poor education (p. 376), arguing for an equality of intellect between the sexes: 'What women can do when they compete with men intellectually has been well brought out by their recent university and college successes' (p. 376). He proved an egalitarian when it came to marriage (he advocated free unions), education ('what man *may* read, woman *must* read'), or employment. He was very critical of kept women described as 'dolls', and considered it was vital for women to be 'absolutely independent in matters of economy'. But Pearson's main preoccupation was the improvement of public health – and its corollary, 'race permanence', a means of securing of Britain's supremacy in the world, to which he believed the emancipation of women must remain subordinate: 'Women's rights are after all, only a vague description of what may be the fittest position for her, the sphere of her maximum usefulness in the developed society of the future' (p. 371). Throughout his life Pearson cultivated close friendships with unconventional female figures, such as Elisabeth Cobb, Olive Schreiner, Eleanor Marx, Emma Brooke and the Fabian turned anarchist Charlotte Wilson. Impressed by Florence Nightingale's valuable statistical work, Pearson recruited in his

---

22 Jane Hume Clapperton, Maria Sharpe, Mona Caird and Charlotte M. Wilson were members.

laboratory women mathematicians and biometricians, such as the Cave-Brown-Cave sisters, Alice Lee, or Cicely Fawcett. Although he thought 'the only remedy' against prostitution was 'to pass through anarchy, i.e., dynamite the present social arrangements and society generally', he did not oppose the Contagious Diseases Acts. Pearson viewed strong and healthy mothers as the key to national progress. His proposal of a state-endowed motherhood scheme ('Socialism and Sex', 1886), and his desire to convert the Woman Question from 'the cry of the unmarried for equality of opportunity to the cry of the married for the reconciliation of maternity with the power of self-determination' ('Woman and Labour', 1894) convinced many activists to adopt a eugenicist perspective. Perhaps in an attempt to temper the necessity of the sacrifice, or because he anticipated criticisms, Pearson reminded his contemporaries that both sexes were equally restrained by the imperatives of national interest: 'There will be little hope of real reforms unless men and women know one another's aims and views in detail, and then accept to some degree the same standard, the same ideal for the community. We must not, however, for a moment forget that the woman question is essentially also a man's question' (p. 393).

Karl Pearson, 'The Woman Question' (printed for private circulation in 1885), reprinted in *The Ethic of Free Thought. A Selection of Essays and Lectures* (London: T. Fisher Unwin, 1888), pp. 383–6

It will be asked whether the binding of man and woman together for life be either expedient or necessary – whether it may not be a real hindrance to progress, and this in more respects than one? Whether marriage, after all, be not the last, and therefore the greatest, the least-recognised superstition which past barbarism has handed down to the present? We shall have to search for the real social grounds upon which the institution may be defended. Can we argue that because monogamic lifelong union exists among certain Christian peoples, whom we are accustomed to look upon as in the van of civilisation, therefore it must be a needful condition of progress? Might not the same argument have been used at one time for slavery, at another for the Holy Catholic Church, and even now be used for prostitution? Is not this last as much a social institution of our Christian civilisation as marriage? It will not do to translate the law of 'survival of the fittest' into 'whatever is surviving *is* fittest.' Fittest for the age in which it exists, but may not that age be passing away? Will or will not the independence of woman shake this institution? I merely suggest the problem; this is not the time to attempt, were it possible, any solution. I would only add that, personally, I see no reason why two persons, who may be in no way responsible to a third, should be bound together for life, whether they will or no. The birth of a child undoubtedly makes them responsible to a third being, and may be a strong social reason for making marriage permanent, at least till the child has reached its majority. If we except the case, where young children might suffer, may not the question be raised whether marriage should not be a socially recognised but far more easily dissoluble union? Can marriage, lasting when the sympathy which led to it has died out, do ought but make two lives miserable? The life-long tie may be needful so long as society casts a slur on a woman who is separated from her husband, so long as woman is not in as good as an economic position as man – that is, so long as separation would cast her helpless on the world, or so long as she is a mere plaything with no individual activity. But let us put the case of equal education, of equal power to earn a livelihood, of equal social weight; what woman, under these circumstances, would desire to continue a union which had become distasteful to either party? The union enforced in such cases by our present system is surely a nightmare which even Goethe's *Wahlverwandtschaften* fails to paint. On the other hand, so long as marriage is entered upon without any study of character, upon the bidding of some slight sexual inclination or fancied sympathy – as so frequently happens at the present day – any relaxation of the marriage tie would certainly lead to an anti-social spread of sexual irregularity. How will the self-dependent women of the future regard this problem? What line have such women taken in the past? With the past to guide us it seems not improbable that, when woman is truly educated and equally developed with man, she will hold that the highest relationship of man and woman is akin to that of Lewis [*sic*] and George Eliot, of Mary Wollstonecraft and Godwin; that the highest ideal of marriage is perfectly free, and yet, generally, lifelong union. May it not be that such a union is the only one in which a woman can preserve her independence, can be a wife and yet retain her individual liberty? I suggest no solution to these problems, but I believe that without facing them we cannot fully grasp whither the emancipation of woman is likely to lead us.

Taking marriage as it is, we may ask how far it necessarily cramps a woman's growth? This is not a question we can lightly answer. There are many women who affirm that it distinctly does. Admitted this is true in the present state of subjection, will it be possible to remedy the evil in any state so long as the wife is a child-bearer? Can such a woman ever hope to equal intellectually the single woman? If not, how will it be possible for her to meet the average man with an equal mental force, and so preserve her individuality? The possibility of woman's individual development after marriage is important; all the more so, as certain ardent advocates of woman's higher education have put forward as a plea for it, the happiness which would arise if woman were only educated so as to understand her husband's ideas and enter into his pursuits. A baser argument for woman's education it is hard to conceive. It denies her an individuality, even as the Mohammedan denies her a soul.

But there is another problem of marriage, which is all-important, and which the advocates for emancipation are called upon to face. How will it ever be possible for the child-bearing woman to retain individual freedom? She cannot during child-bearing and rearing preserve, except in special cases, her economic independence; she must become dependent on the man for support, and this must connote a limitation of her freedom, a subjection to his will. How is this to be met, or does the very fact of child-bearing inevitably produce the subjection of women? The happiness of any human being is commensurate with the sphere of its individual activity, of its freedom to will; how infinitely narrowed this sphere is for woman in the average marriage is obvious enough. How far this can be changed by a truer education of both sexes is a very complex problem. By such means a more social tone might be introduced into men's and women's conceptions of their mutual relations and duties, into their respect for the individual's sphere of freedom. Perfect legal and political equality might strengthen this respect in the family, but I fail to see how, without perfect *economic* equality, the freedom of woman can ever be absolutely maintained. Yet without a complete reorganisation of society how can there be economic independence for the child-bearer? Here again the emancipation of woman seems to call into question the economic basis of existing society.

It is not only the *form* of marriage, but the feelings and objects with which it is entered upon, that are likely to be questioned and remoulded by the woman's movement. Protestantism cannot be said to have formed an elevated conception of the conjugal relation, [*Footnote*: See *A Sketch of the Sex Relations in Primitive and Medieval Germany* for some account of the nature of Luther's teaching.] and there can be little doubt that the cultivated woman of the future will find herself compelled to reject its doctrines on this point.

7 'A sanatorium with female attendants'

Henry Nevinson (1856–1941), born into a staunch Evangelical family, received a classical education at Oxford, where he became acquainted with the Christian Socialists. He worked at Toynbee Hall, the first university settlement (where Charles Booth wrote his survey of poverty in 1889), where he acquired first-hand experience of the living conditions of the poor in the East End of London (*Neighbours of Ours*, 1895). A friend of Kropotkin and Carpenter, in 1889 he joined the Social Democratic Federation for a while, and later became a member of the Labour Party. From 1897, Nevinson spent most of his life travelling around the world as a war correspondent for the *Daily Chronicle*. A fine journalist and an acute observer of the transformations of the twentieth century, he wrote for the liberal *Daily News*, the *Manchester Guardian*, and H. W. Massingham's *Nation*, a paper influential in the shaping of New Liberalism. A champion of liberty, he remained however a free (liberal) spirit throughout his life. He published thirty books (the best known significantly titled *Essays in Freedom*, 1909, and *Essays in Rebellion*, 1913). Never indifferent to the terrible atrocities he witnessed in Africa and Russia (he was himself wounded at Gallipoli), deeply committed to social justice, he exposed the illegal slave trade in Portuguese Angola (*A Modern Slavery*, 1906). Interestingly, and paradoxically, his interest *in* women's rights allied with his interest *for* women. His first marriage to childhood friend, suffragist Margaret Wynne Jones, was an unhappy one, and Henry had multiple passionate affairs with intelligent, highly politicized women activists; in particular he entertained a remarkable thirty-year liaison with the suffragette and writer Evelyn Sharp (who married him in 1933 after Margaret's death). Her wit and eloquence, her rebellion against inequity fascinated him. They never lived together, but were kindred spirits in intellectual and political pursuits, reading and influencing each other's works. Nevinson's support of militancy never flagged, as evidenced by *More Changes, More Chances* (1925), an account of his involvement in suffragism. A member of the National Union of Women's Suffrage Society, of the Women's Social and Political Union (which he supported financially), and of the first male association, the Men's League for Women Suffrage (1907), he wrote several articles in support of militancy in *Votes for Women*. Nevinson never hesitated to join demonstrations. When he allied forces with Victor Duval in the Men's Political Union (1910), he took part in the deputation that confronted Lloyd George in Oxford on the issue on 28 November 1913. His pamphlet 'Women's Vote and Men', excerpted below, reflected many of Mill's ideas: Nevinson rested his case for suffrage on the conviction that 'the assertion of self ... is the final object of life' (p. 10). The achievement of sex equality was a means of increasing the general good (including the improvement of men's souls (p. 5) – an echo to his combat for 'equality of opportunity, for all men and women, independent of their inheritance, birth, or surroundings'.[23] More than the handsome chivalrous 'fearless knight' he is known to have been,[24] Nevinson typifies the tensions inherent in the definition of Victorian masculinity, if only because, while supporting suffrage on humane and rational grounds, he still associates the male social status with protecting women. His resignation from the *Daily News* in 1909, after the paper refused to condemn the force feeding of the suffragettes on hunger strike, is an undeniable testimony of his sincerity.[25] On 6 February 1918, he waited in the Commons for the passing of the Franchise Bill – the triumph of a cause that cost him a position he had found so fulfilling.

Henry W. Nevinson, *Women's Vote and Men* (London: The Woman's Press, 1910, reprinted from *The English Review*, October 1909), pp. 6–9

It is said that the evil effect of this doctrine of women's inferiority, decreed by heaven and inculcated by nursemaids, has long been mitigated by the usages of chivalry, and if women are granted political equality, the blessings they receive from chivalry will be lost. I recognise the beauty of the chivalrous ideal as much as anybody. The conception of the courtly knight killing dragons without fear, and honouring women without reproach, is always attractive, and it makes a far better training for Sunday schools than the older doctrine of woman as a spare rib. But when people begin to talk about the loss of chivalry owing to the vote, I have the same sense of sickness as when they talk about the

23 *The Growth of Freedom* (London: T. C. & E. C. Jack, 1912), p. 89.
24 His chivalry evokes gallantry, a refinement of manners praised in the Enlightenment by David Hume as '*generous*' and '*natural* in the highest degree', *Essays: Moral Political and Literary* (London: Miller, 1777), p. 132. In the nineteenth century, manliness and gentlemanliness went hand in hand in the upper classes. Griffin argues that chivalry was a way for men to meet the slur of effeminacy when supporting women's rights (2014: 185).
25 Henry Brailsford, a Methodist turned radical socialist who worked for the same paper, also lost his job in protest against A. G. Gardiner's refusal to disavow the treatment of women prisoners. He established the Conciliation Committee in 1910, and acted as unpaid secretary for it.

loss of womanliness and about woman's weakness being her strength. I much prefer to remember the definition given by a young curate in Whitechapel when he was taking a party of working people round the picture gallery. Coming to a picture representing a knight heavily clad in armour releasing a beautiful woman bound to a tree and not at all heavily clad in anything, he became conscious, perhaps, of the shock to the habitual decency of the poor, for he hurriedly exclaimed: 'That, my friends, represents the glorious days of chivalry, when knights rode about the country rescuing fair damsels from other people's castles, and carrying them off to their own!'

Though rapidly conceived, it is the best definition of chivalry I know. I remember it with satisfaction whenever I see the men in the Tube spring up to offer their seats to pretty and well-dressed women, but remain profoundly occupied with the politics of their paper while a worn-out and draggled creature with a baby and a roll of butter sways from the straps against their knees. I see no reason why this chivalry should ever become extinct, vote or no vote. For there will always be plenty of well-bred men who can rise to that pitch of heroism and politeness, provided the vote does not have the effect of making all women hideous, which is against likelihood and the experience of our Colonies.

Chivalry would be safe even though Mr. Asquith, in a fit of repentance, proposed plural votes for women. What serious people mean by chivalry is, I suppose, the special courtesy and consideration due to all women as such, because they are in some respects physically weaker, in some respects more sensitive, and surrounded with the halo of danger and pain from actual or possible motherhood. 'We honour them for that, just as we like an old soldier for his medals and a young one for his uniform. But the idea that true chivalry will decline seems to spring from the notion that a vote will make women, not only equal to men, but the same. You might as well say that a poplar is the same as a church because it is equally high. All the old-fashioned attempts to prove that women are the same as men, and should have the vote for that reason, were beside the mark. It is just because they are different that the votes of men cannot represent them.

Chivalry has become a mawkish word, but the honourable idea still lingering in it will remain; and so will good manners, and the natural attraction between men and women. It is a fine old saying that 'the King's Government must be carried on.' But Nature has a much more important thing to carry on than the King's Government, and we may be quite sure she will go through with it, not suffering the country to be depopulated because women obtain the right of walking to a polling station once in five years. For us men, I think the standard of manners towards women will even be raised, and our efforts to win approval will become more strenuous. Suffragists who carry sandwich boards and sell their paper in the streets tell me that already the manners of the working people towards them show a visible and audible improvement. The poor are always more sensitive and quicker to politeness than shop assistants, Liberal stewards, and others of the middle classes, because they are nearer to suffering and less trammeled by snobbery; but the improvement due to women's claim for equal rights will gradually spread upward. The complacent sense of natural and legalised superiority, so bad for us all, whether we are dukes or only men, will be shaken when the law and constitution refuse to recognise it. This alone will make us men more agreeable, besides increasing our chance of heaven, and in every class throughout the country a finer respect will be paid to every woman when she is no longer debarred from equal citizenship. For respect generally varies directly with power.

The cult of the ministering angel

The loss of our assumed superiority would, as I said, make us more agreeable. It would also, one hopes, save our characters from the invalid atmosphere of all that nursing, coddling, soothing, tending, and comforting, which we have regarded as the special function of women so long that their life is often a perpetually occupied hospital or madhouse. Dr. Johnson said a man should never put himself out to nurse, but that is exactly what almost all the male sex does. We live in a sanatorium with female attendants. We have whined, 'A ministering angel thou!' till we have secured for ourselves a continuous supply of amateur nurses, much as we have made women moral by killing them physically or socially if they were not, and then maundering over the charm of their purity. We shall have to give up some of our notions upon woman's self-sacrifice, self-abnegation, and self-devotion, in so far as they mean sacrifice, abnegation, and devotion for the benefit of our own precious selves. But consider how much we shall gain by deliverance from that languid and hospital air in which we rot at ease!

8 'Why I went to prison'

Victor Duval (1885–1945) is mainly remembered for founding in January 1910 the Men's Political Union for Woman's Suffrage, which became the national bastion of male militancy until 1918. Victor was born into a family of resolute suffragists: his father, Ernest, was one of the regular orators of the Men's League for Women's Suffrage, his mother and sisters were all members of the Pankhursts' Women's Social and Political Union, and regularly involved in the violent trouble-making of the association (his sister Elsie was thrown in prison at nineteen and went on several hunger strikes). An idealist and a progressivist, Victor rapidly turned into an indefatigable activist of the cause. He joined for a while the Clapham branch of the League of the Young Liberals,[26] a motley crew of ardent young men and women, intent on the 're-awakening' of the tradition of Liberalism. The League promoted 'progressive principles', and supported the right of women to suffrage 'not *qua* woman, but *qua* person, *qua* citizen'.[27] But Victor became bitterly disappointed by the resistance of the party to women's votes: 'I am ashamed of the men who call themselves Liberal. I am ashamed of them because they have insulted Women – they have dragged the flag of Liberalism in the gutter and have trampled upon it' ('Why I Went to Prison', Address of Victor Duval at Caxton Hall, 1 November 1910;[28] the shorter version below was published three days later in the columns of the Pethick-Lawrences' paper *Votes for Women*). Duval enlisted hundreds of men in the Men's Political Union: they attended women's suffrage pageants and mass demonstrations, heckled candidates at electoral meetings, and lobbied Parliament regularly, either by the side of the Women's Social and Political Union or on its behalf. By 1913 the Men's Political Union had opened branches throughout London, and in all the major cities of the country. Victor fell in love with Una Dugdale, the celebrated hostess of their weekly 'At-Homes' attended by the suffragist intelligentsia, among them many generous donors to the Union. In 1912, they became an iconic feminist couple by demanding that the word obedience be with-

---

26 It counted three hundred branches intensively training their members as political speakers and organizers (and many prominent figures like Joseph Aubrey Rees, Lewis Harcourt, C. F. G. Masterman, David Lloyd George, or Maude Gurney Tyler). On the League of Young Liberals see Monacelli (2011).
27 J. M. Robertson, 'The Mission of Liberalism' (1908) in *Young Liberal Pamphlets* (London: National League of Young Liberals, 1911), p. 10.
28 *Suffrage Pamphlets*, 5 (London: Women's Freedom League), p. 13.

drawn from their marriage vows (a critical attitude in vogue in Unitarian circles since the 1840s). When Asquith consented at last to a Conciliation Bill to remove women's political disabilities, Victor molested 'the traitor', Lloyd George, in person, in the hope that it would put pressure to bear on the Liberal government, and subsequently joined the list of men imprisoned for the cause.[29] The account of this episode gave him an opportunity to expose the cruel treatment of the suffragettes, and rally more male support.

Victor D. Duval, 'My Week in Prison', *Votes for Women* (4 November 1910), p. 66

On reaching Pentonville some four hours after sentence was pronounced I was taken to what is known as the Receiving Room. This room had the appearance of a schoolroom, there being rows of forms, a few shelves of books, and a desk at one end where a prison officer sat. My name was taken, and the official blue paper was handed over to the receiving officer by the 'Black Maria' guard. I was then escorted to the Reception Room, a long compartment furnished with rows of little boxes on either side with a table at the end, at which sat one of the warders. I was put into one of these boxes quite near to the table, and locked in. Presently the door was opened and I was able to follow everything that was taking place. Nearly all the boxes were occupied, and men were being brought one by one before the officer at the table. I listened carefully to what was said, and I soon discovered that each man had to give certain particulars as to age, place of abode, whether married or not, and so on. The faces of nearly all the men were haggard, and the great majority of the 110 prisoners who presented themselves on this evening had no fixed home.

Refusal to wear prison dress

My turn came at last, and, after having furnished the information required of me, I was told to go into a little ante-room and wait. Presently a warder came up to me and told me to take off my shoes and undo my waistcoat, from which I gathered I was to undress and put on prison clothing, so I said, 'Do you mean to say that I, a political prisoner, am

29 He chose to be imprisoned for seven days rather than pay the forty-shilling fine: men, he wrote, must 'show the Government that they also are prepared ... to make sacrifices in order that justice shall be done to the women of the country' (p. 66). Forty Men's Political Union members would also be jailed or force-fed like Hugh. A. Franklin, who was force-fed 114 times.

to wear prison clothing?' He replied 'Yes, certainly.' 'Well,' I replied, 'I refuse to wear prison clothing, and shall be obliged if you will carry my message to the governor.' I was then told that I could retain my own clothes until the morrow, when instructions as to my treatment would be forthcoming. I was then taken to a cell and asked if I wanted supper. 'What is the supper?' I ventured to ask. 'Bread and porridge,' was the reply. So I declined with thanks. After the cell door had been slammed and fastened I began to examine the interior. There was a plank bed, a mattress, blankets and sheets, a small wooden table, a wooden stool, a tin of fresh water, two tin buckets, and a bundle of rags and brushes for cleaning purposes. I soon decided to make up my plank bed and retire for the night, but it was some hours before I closed my eyes.

The next morning I was called at six o'clock, and told to put out my tins and fold up my bedding. This I did, and at seven o'clock my breakfast – a piece of brown bread and a tin of the very poor looking stuff called tea was brought to me. I looked at it and explained to the warder that being a political prisoner I must insist upon having decent food, that I would not touch the prison food, and that I should like to see the governor. A couple of hours later the governor appeared. Having put my case before him, I was informed that he had no power to do otherwise than treat me as an ordinary second division prisoner, but that he would communicate with the Home Office and ascertain whether I could wear my own clothes and buy my own food. At the same time he urged me to eat something, pointing out that he did not want to have any trouble and that I, being a young man, would feel the effects of going without nourishment in after-life. Several more visits were paid me during the day by the governor, doctor, and chief warder but to all their entreaties I said I would wait and hear the reply from the Home Office. This came into in the afternoon and it was to this effect: while the Secretary of State considered that I was not entitled to special treatment, in view of the fact that the magistrate had taken a lenient view of my offence, he would on this occasion allow me to wear my own clothes and purchase my food from outside. The governor then explained to me that there was nobody in the prison who could fetch the food for me and asked me what I was going to do about it. I said to him: 'Do you mean to say that you have no machinery for administering the laws that are made?' He then said he would try and arrange something. After this little incident the food that I ordered was brought to me at the scheduled feeding-hours, and all I had to do was to sign a declaration that I would pay the bill.

On the Tuesday evening I tried to sleep, but could not do so; there seemed to be no air in the cell, and I felt as if I were being stifled. I lay awake all through the night, and was thankful when the bell rang for me to get up. When the governor and a visiting magistrate came to see later in the day I told them that I should like more exercise (I had been having only one hour out of the twenty-four in the fresh air); my request was granted, and during the rest of my stay I was permitted to have one and a-half and sometimes two hours.

I was pressed many times to pay the fine, was told of the stigma that would rest with my children, if ever I had any, on account of their father having been in prison, and how the women were able to take care of themselves. In reply to these statements I just tried to convince the officials of the necessity for strong and determined action, and I hope that, if ever they should have other suffrage prisoners under their charge, they will not weary them with these petty remarks; but will try and understand the spirit which moves certain individuals to go to prison rather than submit to the tyranny of an illiberal Government.

9 Women's share in the Co-operative movement

Joseph Clayton (1868–1943) was a novelist, a prolific biographer (of activists such as Robert Owen), and a respected historian (*Leaders of the People: Studies in Democratic History*, 1910; *Co-operation and the Trade Unions*, 1912; *The Rise and Decline of Socialism in Great Britain 1884–1924*, 1926). A Catholic convert, he was a regular contributor to the *Tablet* which, from 1888, under the influence of its editor J. G. Snead-Cox, began to speak favourably of women's enfranchisement. Clayton got involved in the activities of the Men's League for Woman Suffrage, and the Women Writers' Suffrage League. His pamphlet 'Votes for Women' (1918) was published by the Catholic Women's Suffrage Society. When a student at Oxford, he had befriended F. D. Maurice and Charles Kingsley, but he gave the full measure of his political engagement on joining the Leeds ILP branch. Clayton edited the *Labour Chronicle* (1896–1898) and *The New Age* (1906–1907), contributed to *Liberty*, an anarchist-communist paper, which publicized his forceful essays on industrial conditions ('Before Sunrise and Other Pieces', 1896). Self-deluded by his belief that 'the doctrines of the old Manchester School' were 'as dead as Deism in the eighteenth century' (*Co-operation*, p. 8), he expected Britain to spearhead the industrial co-operative movement. Because it had been run since Owen's times on democratic lines, and (on principle at least) was committed to sexual equality,[30] Clayton viewed it as a blueprint for a future society. Clayton features amongst the few socialists who welcomed the enrolment of women in the Co-operative movement, regarded as 'the great accomplishment of the working-class in the nineteenth century' (*Co-operation*, p. 7). In that respect he stands out from male unionists who were hostile to skilled female work, and approved of Labour's negative policy on women's labour.[31] The first reappearance of female militancy since Chartism, the Women's Co-operative Guild, was originally a League of fifty members founded by the Christian Socialist and Green's disciple Alice Acland in 1883.[32] Acland never wished women to turn over the sexual hierarchy, but the Guild provided women with a series of practical workshops and educational courses. Under the leadership of the radical Margaret Llewelyn Davies it lobbied for minimum wage and equal pay.[33] In the 1910s, it counted thirty thousand members, mostly suffragists, who agitated for a minimum wage for all co-operative employees. It kept a core agenda of women's rights until the Second World War,[34] notably spreading information on contraception in the name of the right to control one's body. The Guild was the sign of a burgeoning working-class feminism in a movement whose nature had

30 In 1833 the Owenite James Morrison had initiated a Women's Page in the *Pioneer* (a widely read working-class newspaper), and encouraged women to create separate female unions (Taylor, 1983: 94–6).
31 On sexual segregation in trades and unions, see Taylor (1983: chap. 4). However the Irish rebel James Connolly was also supportive of equal status for women in trade unions, as was the Labour MP Sir David James Shackleton, who introduced the 1910 Conciliation Bill. Connolly was considered by the suffragist Louie Bennett as 'a thorough feminist in every respect'.
32 She was the wife of Sir Arthur Acland, Liberal MP and fervent Co-operator. Several women members were also related to Co-operative men. From 1883 Samuel Bamford, the editor of *Co-operative News*, and Leonard Woolf introduced a 'Women's Page' to the paper, in support of women's claims.
33 The question of equal pay was first articulated at Robert Owen's Labour exchange in 1832. It found supporters in the Liberal politician and suffragist W. H. Dickinson (Banks, 1990), Emile Burns, and Henry Brailsford (*Equal Pay and the Family: A Proposal for the National Endowment of Motherhood*, 1918, written with K. D. Courtney). Its male 'champions' were undeniably Joseph B. Tate, co-founder and first secretary of the unofficial Equal Pay League in Manchester in 1904, and the Conservative Major J. W. Hill, who defended equal pay throughout his thirty-year career in the Commons (see his obituary in *The Sunday Times*, 25 December 1938, p. 13).
34 It was active in the granting of maternity benefits in 1911.

primarily been middle-class.[35] It was important in the forging of female solidarity. By 1913 it had become 'a microcosm of women's democracy',[36] an answer to Clayton's prayer to see the Central Committee on Education (1886) infuse the co-operative faith in both sexes.

Joseph Clayton, *Co-operation* (London: T. C. & E. C. Jack, and Edinburgh, New York: Dodge Publishing, [1912?]), pp. 80–3

'The concert, the library and news-room, the meeting, with a speech endured in the middle of it, have had a long innings. ... Ought we not to concentrate on the development of co-operative opinion among ourselves, our children, and our employees?'[37]

In the meantime local societies continue to hold their lectures, and concerts, and social gatherings – with the inevitable speech 'endured in the middle.'

And District Conferences are held by the different sections for the discussion of the internal questions of 'High Dividends,' 'The Minimum Wage,' and 'The Training of Employees.'

Mr. Rae, and there are many who agree with him, would have the Co-operative Union[38] and its Central Education Committee the recognised agencies for some unification of the educational work, the District Conference Associations working to supply material for a common economic policy.

As loyalty on the business side of co-operation is determined in each society by the measure of custom with the Wholesale, so loyalty on the educational side, it is maintained, is determined not only by the local expenditure on education, but also by the measure of support given to the Co-operative Union.

That prominent co-operators are anxiously concerned with the educational work of the societies and can find much that calls for improvement

35 On the emulating influence of the Guild on the emancipation movement see Scott (1998).
36 *New Statesman* (21 June 1913), p. 328.
37 Clayton quotes W. R. Rae, the chairman of the Sunderland Society's Committee on Education.
38 The Co-operative movement combined fair business practice with an ethos of mutuality. In the 1870s it developed into hundreds of self-governing societies grouped into two federations: the Co-operative Wholesale Society, a productive and distributive agency, with its own factories and depots, and the Co-operative Union, with a structure of districts for social services, education and propaganda purposes, which held an annual Congress.

in this work, is a sign of healthy life in the co-operative movement. There is no danger of co-operative principles being forgotten in the success of business, or the ideals of co-operators becoming despised, as long as men and women are ready at congresses and conferences to call attention to weakness in the movement, and to insist that all is not as well as it might be.

It is only when co-operators begin to assure themselves that all is entirely well with the movement, and to resent the suggestion that reform is needed, or that faith is cold, that danger can be scented. For the spirit of self-satisfaction is as fatal to co-operators as to others; while the receptive intelligence, the consciousness that being human and mortal occasional failure and mistakes are to be expected, the willingness to do battle with foes within no less stoutly than with foes without, are the things that make for strength in every good cause. And no assurance of success can make up for the absence of these things; for they are at the very root of all progress in the affairs of mankind.

Reference has already been made to the work of the Women's Co-operative Guild, and no account of the co-operative movement would be complete which left this work unmentioned. The Guild, in its own words, is 'a self-governing organisation of women, who work through Co-operation for the welfare of the people, seeking freedom for their own progress, and the equal fellowship of men and women in the home, the store, the workshop, and the State.' In the main the mission of the Guild has been to stir up women to an active interest in the co-operative store, and in the social questions that affect women no less than men. Women are the housekeepers and the purchasers. It is for them to understand the difference between pure goods made under fair conditions and cheap and nasty articles produced under quite other conditions. If the local store is stocked with, let us say, the soaps, cocoas, and jams of private firms instead of the soaps, cocoas, and jams produced by the Wholesale, it is chiefly because customers will have it so.

Women are not only customers, they are also shareholders in co-operative societies. They sit on educational and management committees, and on the Central Educational Committee. They have an equal responsibility with men for the wages paid to and the hours worked by co-operative employees.

That women, coming much later than men into public work in this country, and often discouraged by the foolish jealousy of men from taking a larger part in co-operative affairs, have in so many places proved their capacity as good co-operators, must be placed to the credit of the

Women's Guild. So valuable indeed has been the educational work of the Guild that in the last few years co-operative guilds for men have sprung up, and are now federated in a National Co-operative Men's Guild.

To-day when women are engaged so widely in commercial, professional, and political work, when they are chosen to sit on city councils and public education committees, and are, in fact, becoming as important in public life as they were in Anglo-Saxon times and in the later Middle Ages, their place in the co-operative movement must affect enormously the future of that movement.

Any lingering taint of male jealousy or survival of sex dominance that would exclude women from the fullest share in co-operative management is bound to damage the co-operative cause. On the other hand, the cordial welcoming of women to the various committees and boards within the co-operative movement gives an assurance of confidence in the future. And as, on the whole, co-operators have hitherto, in the matter of justice to women as in other matters, kept well in advance of public opinion, often leaving Parliament far behind – as in the case of the property of married women[39] – there is every reason to anticipate that in the immediate future women will share far more fully with men than they have yet done the management of co-operative stores and the direction of cooperative enterprise.

The future has its own secrets, but it is hardly to be supposed that with non-co-operative commerce engaging more and more the services of women, the vast businesses distributive and productive – of co-operators will not require the aid of women as co-directors with men. As these days approach, the educational work of the Women's Co-operative Guild begins to be discerned at its true value.

---

39 The Rochdale Pioneers Society (1844) engaged in the campaigning for the property rights of married women.

IV

Towards a new sexual culture

> I say this with no disrespect to women. Evolution has made them what they are, and evolution will remake them.
> G. W. Foote

1 'The most important discovery made upon mankind'

Richard Carlile (1790–1843), originally an itinerant tinsmith, grew up amidst the political agitation for a free press. In 1817, galvanized by Henry 'Orator' Hunt's speeches in London, the reading of Cobbett's twopenny sheets, and William Hone's *Reformists' Register*, both of which he hawked himself, he had started contributing 'scraps of his own' to the *News* when William Sherwin asked him to take over his *Register* and his shop in Fleet Street. Carlile turned into the champion of press freedom and freethought by courageously republishing Thomas Paine's *Rights of Man* and *The Age of Reason*, and Elihu Palmer's *Principles of Nature*, previously condemned as blasphemous. He was fined and thrown into jail many times for blasphemy and seditious libel. His incarcerations were for him an opportunity to dedicate time to omnivorous reading and profuse inflammatory writing (his *Address to Men of Science*, 1821, denounced scientists like Newton and Bacon as having succumbed to despotism). Heartened by the support of friends like G. Holyoake and W. J. Fox, and stimulated rather than impaired by repeated indictments on charge of blasphemy or sedition, in 1830, he turned an old music-hall, the London Rotunda, into a 'Freethought Coliseum', and, in spite of his imprisonments (over nine years in total), and the risk of transportation, he continued to serve his battle for freedom of speech and thought by means of his vigorous and fearless pen (he frequently addressed himself to the King or to Cabinet ministers).[1] He edited succes-

---

1 His sister, his wife and his shop men and women faithfully carried on his

5 Richard Carlile

sive radical papers, amongst which the *Republican* (formerly *Register*), one of the first working-class journals, published from prison (an amazing concession!); the *Deist*; the *Gorgon*; the *Lion* (in which he first developed his sexual theory); the *Prompter*, and the *Gauntlet*. He attracted the attention of Eliza Sharples, a freethinker and self-styled 'infidel', enemy of kings and priests, who became his 'moral wife' (Carlile having separated from his spouse). In 1825, perhaps because of his natural inclination to champion unpopular causes, but more probably as part of his crusade against priestcraft, Carlile pioneered a book on contraception. Converted by Francis Place's own pleas for 'the preventive check' (*Illustrations and Proofs of the Principles of Population*, 1822, and *To the Married of Both Sexes*, also known as the *Diabolical Handbills*, 1823), he ventured a first article on the subject in the *Republican*, 'What Is Love?' (May 1825). In February 1826, it became *Every Woman's Book*, and was published as an eighteen-penny pamphlet, with a frontispiece showing a naked Adam and Eve. The first advocacy of birth control ever published in Britain sold fifteen hundred copies in a week, creating a sensation and a lively debate in the *Republican*.[2] By May it was in its third edition. In 1828, a revised version appeared under the pseudonym of Dr Waters, entitled 'The Philosophy of the Sexes: or, Every Woman's Book' and sold ten thousand copies. Its acknowledgement of women's sexual desires and assertion of the need and right to satisfy them anticipated *The Fruits of Philosophy* (1832) by Charles Knowlton (who acknowledged Carlile's influence), and Robert Dale Owen's *Moral Physiology* (1831). Well before Drysdale [IV, 4] Carlile praised the healthiness of sexual commerce, and warned of the consequences of sexual frustration. The whole book resonates with a passion for sex equality, 'the source of virtue' (p. 19), and freedom of choice. Carlile condemned marriage laws as artificial shackles, and advised men not to blame women who 'chose to have a lover' (p. 31). He encouraged women to 'state their passion to the male', 'assume an equality', and plead their desires whenever they feel them (p. 8). Like many birth controllers Carlile considered contraception as part of the utilitarian calculus, as it is clear from the extract below. Fertility control, it would seem, was not central to his personal concerns: he had seven children with his first wife, and Eliza bore him another four children (incidentally

---

fight: 150 of them were sent to prison. In 1822, a female committee was organized in support of Carlile in Manchester.
2 Cobbett described the book as 'obscene and beastly'. See the series of articles which ensued, *Republican*, 13 (6 January – 7 July 1826).

he let her manage entirely on her own when she had her first baby). However, the propaganda conducted by Carlile released forces which set the birth control movement in motion: the book's views were influential on female Zetetics,[3] and the public scandal it created helped extend the boundaries of public discussion and debate on the issue of 'free trade in love'. From 1835, he turned messianic, preached a 'New Christianity', and lost most of his radical supporters. He remains however one of the first reformers to have made infidelity a popular issue, and one of the major contributors to the challenging of gender norms.

Richard Carlile, *Every Woman's Book; or, What Is Love?* (London: Richard Carlile, fourth edition, 1826), pp. 43–8

We would encourage genuine love, wherever it can be made conducive to the happiness of either sex. We would not call upon the females of this day to join in a procession with a Phallus at their head; nor upon Christian ladies to preserve the cross as the standard of their faith, since that cross is but the mathematical emblem of that Phallus, and that Phallus, the male organ of generation, the emblem of the vivifying power of animal and vegetable matter, an emblem on which the deified principle of reason always was and always will be periodically crucified, have a temporary death, and rise to life again. While we would preserve the moral spirit of love, we would have it to be the only religion of the State, as it admits of no sectarianism. We would purify whatever in it is gross and remove every gross idea from it, every idea that is not most refined and alike wise and moral.

It is the tact of those who are wedded to customs, to treat, as immoral, all theories and all practices which are opposed to them; but we, who introduce new theories and new practices, or revive old ones which we think should not have been put aside, would beg a truce with you and ask you to examine before you condemn, to think, consider, and deliberate well before you decide; and where you cannot show the contrary, pray give us credit for good motives.

3 In the 1820s, Zetetic societies (i.e., 'seeking after truth') sprang up in the wake of Carlile's fight for press freedom (McCalman, 1980). The first society was founded in 1821 in Edinburgh; mixed Zetetic clubs flourished rapidly throughout Britain. In the 1880s, the small Zetetical society that met in Conduit Street, London, to discuss agnosticism, evolution, and women's emancipation (with members such as Helen Taylor, the Shakespeare scholar Emma Phipson, Bernard Shaw, and Sidney Webb) was regarded as a centre of sedition.

It is known to all who have anything like an extensive knowledge of mankind, that all sorts of schemes and even outrages upon the body of the female have been used, to render conceptions abortive; but here is the grand preventive which may be used by the one party without being discovered by the other.

The great end is, not to let the semen of the male remain in the genital vessels of the female. Such is the only clean and safe means of preventing conceptions. A variety of herbs and leaves has been used as draughts; but, however powerful as poisons, they are not to be depended on; and must, in every case, injure the health of the female; besides this, every woman who resorts to these means feels degraded in her own opinion, from the consciousness that she has destroyed life. Here it is clear, that there is no life destroyed, nothing injurious to health, nothing but what must promote health, by removing all dread from the necessary practice of intercourse between the sexes. Nor is it to be called an indecent matter. The men, who have been instrumental in making the matter known in this country, are all elderly men, fathers of families of children grown up to be men or women, and men of first-rate moral characters, of first-rate learning, and some of the first politicians and philosophers that ever lived in this or any other country:[4] men, who are known, as above described, in almost every country in Europe and America, and who look upon this as the most important discovery that has yet been made upon mankind: important in every relation of popular morals, popular politics, domestic happiness, and social economy.

The great utility and importance of this measure may be summed up under the following heads:

1st. That no married couple shall have more children than they wish to have, and can maintain.

2nd. That no unhealthy woman shall bear children, that cannot be reared, and which endanger her own life in the parturition: that ineffectual pregnancy shall never be suffered.

3rd. That there be no illegitimate children, where they are not desired by the mother.

4th, and finally. That sexual commerce, where useful and desired, may be made a pleasure, independent of the dread of a conception that

---

4 The Methodist Rev. Joseph Townsend (1739–1816), author of *A Dissertation on the Poor Laws* (1786), brought the vaginal sponge to England in 1769. The device was alluded to by Bentham as a means of limiting births in order to reduce the poor rates ('Situation and Relief of the Poor', 1797).

blasts the prospects and happiness of the female.

If these reasons be not sufficient to satisfy the most fastidious mind, then the ignorance, the unfeeling ignorance under which that mind labours is to be pitied. We are all apt to be shocked at having long-established notions controverted. We value such notions as parts of our existence. We dislike the first examination of all controverting doctrines. But it is consistent with the current character of the things about us, that we are exposed to incessant change of habits and of doctrines: and all that is necessary to make us wise, is, that we freely examine every system, opinion, and thing that comes in our way, so as to interest or to shock us. 'Prejudices', says Lequinio, an elegant French writer, in his work entitled *Les Préjugés détruits*, 'arise out of ignorance and the want of reflection; these are the bases on which the system of despotism is erected, and it is the master-piece of art in a tyrant, to perpetuate the stupidity of a nation, in order to perpetuate its slavery and his own dominion.'

Boulanger has said most truly, 'Every man is proud of having discovered a new truth.' We are proud of this discovery. All men and all women will yet be proud of it. The prejudices of many may be offended by this book; but we trust to time and assuredly good intentions to wear away both offence and prejudice.

This book is not like one of those vile, mischievous, misleading, and fraudulent books commonly on sale for the gratification of ignorantly-diseased appetites. It is not like the lascivious books which are secretly though extensively sold by almost every bookseller. Those books are printed solely for a corrupt and corrupting money-getting purpose, and exhibit nothing but bad examples; while this book, recommended to every woman, and most properly called 'EVERY WOMAN'S BOOK', is a book of instruction on one of the most interesting subjects, not only to the female, but to the male, to families and friends individually, and to society at large. It is a book of physical, philosophical, and moral instruction, and not only deserves the appellation of *every woman's book*, but that *of a book for every man, woman, and child at the age of puberty.*

---

2 A man's devotion to his children

Advice to Young Men, a series of letters establishing rules of conduct to (middle- and upper-class) youths, bachelors, lovers, husbands, fathers, and citizens, ranks amongst the books that are useful to explore men's intimate experiences of domesticity – a part and parcel of 'the total fabric of men's worlds and the construction of masculinity' (Lewis, 1986: 4).[5] Described by G. K. Chesterton as 'the work of a happy man', the book encapsulates Cobbett's personal philosophy of life, and provides an interesting personal description of the joys of fatherhood and view of man's place in the private sphere. William Cobbett (1763–1835) was originally a farmer; he educated himself while in the army, where he wrote his first pamphlet (*The Soldier's Friend*, 1792). From France and America, where he had fled to avoid court martial, he launched his career as an anti-Jacobin polemicist. On his return to Britain he founded his own paper, the weekly *Political Register* (1802), to which he gave an increasingly radical editorial line in contrast with his earlier Conservative period. When the government imposed a tax on newspapers in 1815, he printed an additional 2d version (the *Register*) specifically for the working class, and circulation jumped to fifty thousand. His virulent articles against persecutions, injustice, government corruption, the borough-mongers, and discrimination against Catholics led to eight trials for libel, a two-year imprisonment in 1810, and a short exile in America. On his return in 1819, he carried on his strident publications against the government (he denounced the Peterloo massacre, and approved of the Captain Swing riots in the 1830s). Among his best-known works are a chronicle of agricultural England, *Rural Rides* (1822–1826), and *The Poor Man's Friend; or, Essays on the Rights and Duties of the Poor* (1829), written as part of his relentless campaign against poverty. Cobbett rejected what he called the 'damnable' Malthusian theories, arguing on the contrary that labourers should not be deprived of the right to early marriages and large families, a vindication he repeated in *Advice to Young Men*. The book can help grasp some of the emotional turmoil experienced by Victorian males when facing women's emancipation. In spite of its rather conservative admonitions (Cobbett was a Tory radical, a eulogist of traditional rural England),[6] the *Advice* reveals a set of complex attitudes regarding patriarchal authority in times of changing domestic ideals. Cobbett disapproved of 'the evils

---

5 *Advice to the Teens* (1818) by the engraver Isaac Taylor (1730–1807) also offers a valuable description of domestic bliss. His son, Isaac Taylor, also shared his view of fatherhood as friendship, and advertised the benefits of happiness and family love in *Home Education* (1838).
6 In reaction against the cold materialism of the age, Tory Radicals hankered for pre-industrial England, and defended a paternalist approach to secure the social welfare of the lowly.

of divided authority', and underlined that the husband must remain *the master* of his own house.[7] Yet, he reminded the husband of his *duty* to adhere to his marriage vows, and recommended that *the wife should be heard*. Cobbett proved indeed a constant, most considerate husband and father, always willing to do his 'share' of domestic work: 'Whenever I could spare a minute from business, the child was in my arms' (p. 157). With his wife, Anne Reid, he raised five children. Cobbett supervised their education closely. He established such a long and strong bond with them that when he was imprisoned in Newgate three of his children took turns to stay with him. His daughter Ann, fifteen, took dictation of the *Political Register*, and remained the strongest supporter of her father's campaigns; she was particularly proud of his public letter of protest to the King in defence of Queen Caroline [III, 3]. Remarkably also, the book promoted the pursuit of personal happiness as a virtue. G. D. H. Cole, one of Cobbett's biographers, wrote: 'His whole emphasis is on "selfhood", not because he preaches selfishness, but because he wants each man, and each woman, to find happiness in the successful exercise of his own will, the successful development of his own powers, the expression to the last drop of all the goodness he can squeeze out of himself',[8] or of his defiance of gender stereotypes.

William Cobbett, 'Letter to a Husband', *Advice to Young Men, and (Incidentally) to Young Women, in the Middle and Higher Ranks of Life* (London: W. Cobbett, 1829), letter IV, [paras 178–81]

178. When we consider what a young woman gives up on her wedding day; she makes a surrender, an absolute surrender, of her liberty, for the joint lives of the parties; she gives the husband the absolute right of causing her to live in what place, and in what manner and what society, he pleases; she gives him the power to take from her, and to use, for his own purposes, all her goods, unless reserved by some legal instrument; and, above all, she surrenders to him *her person*. Then, when we consider the pains which they endure for us, and the large share of all the anxious parental cares that fall to their lot; when we consider their devotion to us, and how unshaken their affection remains in our ailments, even

---

7 George Bainton's *The Wife as Lover and Friend*, for instance, insisted on woman's ability to 'agree in disagreement' (London: J. Clarke & Co., 1895), p. 42. Even in redefinitions of marital relationship the view of femininity as self-sacrificing was not easily shed.

8 *The Life of Cobbett* (London: W. Collins, Sons & Co., 1924), p. 213.

though the most tedious and disgusting; when we consider the offices that they perform, and cheerfully perform, for us, when, were we left to one another, we should perish from neglect; when we consider their devotion to their children, how evidently they love them better, in numerous instances, than their own lives; when we consider these things, how can a just man think any thing a trifle that affects their happiness? I was once going, in my gig, up the hill, in the village of FRANKFORD, near Philadelphia, when a little girl, about two years old, who had toddled away from a small house, was lying basking in the sun, in the middle of the road. About two hundred yards before I got to the child, the teams, five big horses in each, of three wagons, the drivers of which had stopped to drink at a tavern on the brow of the hill, started off, and came, nearly abreast, galloping down the road. I got my gig off the road as speedily as I could; but expected to see the poor child crushed to pieces. A young man, a journeyman carpenter, who was shingling a shed by the side of the road, seeing the child, and seeing the danger, though a stranger to the parents, jumped from the top of the shed, ran into the road, and snatched up the child, from scarcely an inch before the hoof of the leading horse. The horse's leg knocked him down; but he, catching the child by its clothes, flung it back, out of the way of the other horses, and saved himself by rolling back with surprising agility. The mother of the child, who had, apparently, been washing, seeing the teams coming, and seeing the situation of the child, rushed out, and catching up the child, just as the carpenter had flung it back, and hugging it in her arms, uttered *a shriek* such as I never heard before, never heard since, and, I hope, shall never hear again; and then she dropped down, as if perfectly dead! By the application of the usual means, she was restored, however, in a little while; and I, being about to depart, asked the carpenter if he were a married man, and whether he were a relation of the parents of the child. He said he was neither: 'Well, then,' said I, 'you merit the gratitude of every father and mother in the world, and I will show mine, by giving you what I have,' pulling out the nine or ten dollars that I had in my pocket. 'No; I thank you, Sir,' said he: 'I have only done what it was my duty to do.'

179. Bravery, disinterestedness, and maternal affection surpassing these, it is impossible to imagine. The *mother* was going right in amongst the feet of these powerful and wild horses, and amongst the wheels of the wagons. She had no thought for herself; no feeling of fear for her own life; her *shriek* was the sound of inexpressible joy; joy too great for her to support herself under. Perhaps ninety-nine mothers out of every hundred would have acted the same part, under similar circumstances.

There are, comparatively, very few women not replete with maternal love; and, by-the-by, take you care, if you meet with a girl who '*is not fond of children,*' not to marry her *by any means*. Some few there are who even make a boast that they 'cannot bear children,' that is, cannot *endure* them. I never knew a man that was good for *much* who had a dislike to little children; and I never knew a woman of that taste who was good for any thing at all. I have seen a few such in the course of my life, and I have never wished to see one of them a second time.

180. Being fond of little children argues no *effeminacy* in a man, but, as far as my observation has gone, the contrary. A regiment of soldiers presents no bad school wherein to study character. Soldiers have leisure, too, to play with children, as well as with 'women and dogs,' for which the proverb has made them famed. And I have never observed that effeminacy was at all the marked companion of fondness for little children. This fondness manifestly arises from a compassionate feeling towards creatures that are helpless, and that must be innocent. For my own part, how many days, how many months, all put together, have I spent with babies in my arms! My time, when at home, and when babies were going on, was chiefly divided between the pen and the baby. I have fed them and put them to sleep hundreds of times, though there were servants to whom the task might have been transferred. Yet, I have not been effeminate; I have not been idle; I have not been a waster of time; but I should have been all these if I had disliked babies, and had liked the porter pot and the grog glass.

181. It is an old saying, 'Praise the child, and you make love to the mother;' and it is surprising how far this will go. To a fond mother you can do nothing so pleasing as to praise the baby, and, the younger it is, the more she values the compliment. Say fine things to her, and take no notice of her baby, and she will despise you. I have often beheld this, in many women, with great admiration; and it is a thing that no husband ought to overlook; for if the wife wish her child to be admired by others, what must be the ardour of her wishes with regard to *his* admiration. There was a drunken dog of a Norfolk man in our regiment, who came from Thetford, I recollect, who used to say, that his wife would forgive him for spending all the pay, and the washing money into the bargain, 'if he would but kiss her ugly brat, and say it was pretty.' Now, though this was a very profligate fellow, he had *philosophy* in him; and certain it is, that there is nothing worthy of the name of conjugal happiness, unless the husband clearly evince that he is fond of his children, and that, too, from their very birth.

3 United only by nature's laws

Robert Owen (1771–1858) has received acknowledgment in feminist history for his 'theoretical and practical commitment to women's liberation' (Taylor, 1983: xiii).[9] Owen was a Welsh entrepreneurial mill manager who, from 1810 to 1828, implemented enlightened principles of management in New Lanark, a Scottish cotton mill,[10] after marrying Caroline Dale, the owner's daughter. A self-made man, keenly alive to the misery and destitution of the workers, he moved away from the utilitarian philosophy of Jeremy Bentham to embrace an ideal of mutual aid and universal charity. One of Owen's fundamental theories was that the character is formed *for* and not *by* the individual. He believed that man was a creature of circumstances and that, given the right environment and education,[11] social distress and unrest would come to an end. Owen defined his new science of society as 'the science of the influence of circumstances over the whole conduct character and proceedings of the human race' (*A New View of Society; or, Essays on the Principle of the Formation of the Human Character*, 1813).[12] He strove to create a 'New Moral World',[13] made up of self-governing and self-supporting co-operative colonies on the basis of communism in land (the project was to involve two thousand people living on two thousand acres).[14] He set up several communities to that aim (the first one in 1821 in London; there were more than 250 of

---

9   His son, Robert Dale Owen, who became an American citizen, is credited in feminist scholarship with being a supporter of women's rights regarding contraception (*Moral Physiology*, 1831).
10 Owen's efficient and innovative management of 'the human capital' of Lanark gained international acclaim. His enterprise was a triumph of social engineering, and Owen was consulted by government factory reformers.
11 His educational theories were largely inspired by Pestalozzi.
12 It drew upon Joseph Priestley's necessarianism (the recognition that everything has a cause and the universe is ruled by scientific laws that can be discovered). Developed by Charles Bray in his widely read *Philosophy of Necessity* (1841), it made a profound impression on nineteenth-century thought, becoming in particular the basis of Holyoake's gospel of Rationalism ('Science is the Providence of Man'), a justification for self-help, educational reforms, and a secular system of ethics.
13 Owen presented its fundamental principles in *The Book of the New Moral World* published in seven parts (1836–44).
14 Owen coined the word 'co-operative' in his short-lived paper the *Economist* (1821); it gave rise to the eponymous movement which developed after the foundation of the Rochdale Society of Equitable Pioneers (1844).

them in the 1830s). However his attempt to establish another community in Indiana, New Harmony, in 1825, floundered on financial difficulties. In the early 1830s, Owen's ideas, developed by William Thompson, provided the basis of Socialism in Britain (although they were lambasted by Marx as utopian and anti-revolutionary). Co-operatives, labour exchange and trades unions gathered momentum. Confident that the word of competitive industrial capitalism was reaching a crisis, Owen trusted that the advent of the millennium was close, and that it would revolutionize personal relationships. His articles on the need to free women from bondage first appeared in penny newspapers, the *Crisis* and the *New Moral World: or Gazette of the Universal Community Society of Rational Religionists*. The *Crisis*'s debates on the injustice of women's legal status stirred Owenite women into forming a short-lived venture in order to fight for equality – the trans-class 'Practical Moral Union of the Women of Great Britain and Ireland'. Owen's attacks on the bulwarks of contemporary society were never as scathing as his dismissal of its most sacred institution: *Lectures on the Marriages of the Priesthood in the Old Immoral World* (1835) depicted matrimony as 'a Satanic device of the Priesthood', and pleaded for cheap, easy divorce. The belief that to achieve physical and moral well-being human feelings should be given free rein led him to repudiate the entire system of the marital family. In Owen's Rational Society, as explained below, unions would be based on mutual affection and dissolvable at will, undoubtedly a liberating conception in the rethinking of gender relations.[15]

Robert Owen, *The Book of the New Moral World on Government and Laws* (London: J. Watson, 1844), Part 6, pp. 35–8

As soon, therefore, as man shall be enlightened respecting the laws of his nature, and thus made rational, and all shall be well educated and rightly placed, then will men and women unite according to their strongest affection, and union will never take place without mutual affection, nor will sexual crime be known, or any of its evils be experienced.

In a state of society thus made rational, there will be no human laws to counteract nature's all-wise laws. Man and woman, not united by nature's laws, will never be compelled, required, or expected, to asso-

---

15 Public lectures on the subject attracted large audiences and caused considerable controversy in the late 1830s. The issue was taken up by Frances Morrison's tract *The Influence of the Present Marriage System Upon the Character and Interests of Females, etc.* (1838).

ciate contrary to their feelings.[16] All human laws made with a view to force affection, have produced disease, crime, and misery continually, and, while persevered in, will always produce crime and misery. When society can be made rational, no attempt so insane as to endeavor to force affection by human laws, in opposition to nature's laws, will ever be made or thought of, much less introduced into the practice of any country. As all will be well educated, physically, mentally, morally, and practically, and equal in condition; as all will know the feelings, through the language of truth, which each is compelled to have for all others, there will be no disguise or deception regarding affection between any parties. Those having the strongest affection for each other will naturally unite; there will be no artificial obstacle in their way, and all will speak of their affections with as much simplicity and truth as they now express themselves respecting their likes and dislikes of any object of their senses, whether in seeing, hearing, tasting, smelling, or feeling. And why should they not, except from their total ignorance of their nature, and of the laws which govern their senses? The affections of the human race, which, through the most gross ignorance, are now, by human laws, made to produce more dreadful crime and misery than any other single cause, are capable of being made the source of the greatest happiness to all. The crimes and misery thus inflicted upon the human race, and especially upon often the most deserving of the female sex, are clouded in the shades of night, hidden from the public eye and sympathy, by the darkness of impenetrable secrecy from those who, could they but see such misery, and know the cause whence arising, would never suffer it to exist. These human laws attempting to regulate affection in opposition to nature, produce now, in addition to the enormous crime and misery which they hourly inflict upon all, the most absurd and inconsistent language and conduct between the sexes, keeping up a system of deception destructive of virtue, truth, common sense, and happiness. Trained from their cradle to believe that they have the power to love or hate at their will, they often say or swear to each other, that they will most affectionately love one another through life to death; being at the time so totally ignorant of the laws of their own nature, that they may not have the power to love each other even for a week, or perhaps not for twenty-four hours longer; for a look, word, or action, may destroy it

---

16 A legacy of the Miltonic tradition which considered that marrying without love was a sin. In radical circles loveless marriages were equated with prostitution [III, 1].

even in less than an hour. In a rational state of society, this blindness of the human intellect will be removed, and no such absurdities will exist.

Now, in this new state of society, the condition of the two sexes will be greatly changed. They will be trained, educated, employed, and placed to become through life, superior companions to each other. Women will be no longer made the slaves of or dependent upon men, more than men will be made slaves of and dependent upon women.

In a society in which the business will be to produce wealth, to distribute it, to form character, and to govern locally and generally, women may be trained and educated to be equally useful and valuable as the men, and in all these operations to give their assistance with equal beneficial effect as the men.

The progress of the world in various sciences, but especially in mechanism and chemistry, has been such within the last century as to equalize, to a great extent, the physical powers of men, women, and children, above a certain age; for now a single child of ten years of age, aided by machinery and chemistry, can effect as much as many men could do for a few years previous to these inventions.

The position, therefore, of men and women will be altogether different in the new from what it has been in the old state of society. They will be equal in education, rights, privileges, and personal liberty; they will be made to become the enlightened and delightful companions of each other, each being, upon all convenient occasions, with those who, by their nature, they are the most compelled to love; the affections will be thus freed from the often unbearable influence of disappointment or jealousy; and the horrid overwhelming crimes and sufferings arising, under the present irrational and insane system, from unavoidable prostitution, will be entirely unknown.

Could the respectable and influential members of society be made conscious of the causes and consequences of prostitution – of the misery which it inflicts upon millions of the finest naturally organized and finest dispositions among the human race, they would never rest until the *causes* of this gross injustice and male cruelty were entirely removed from the earth.

But it never can be removed, so long as society shall continue to be based on the supposition that individuals can love or hate at their pleasure, and that man shall attempt, by his puny efforts, when opposed to nature, to bind in affection those whom nature disjoins. Vain, foolish, irrational man has made this attempt, under one form or another, for many thousand years, and to-day he is as far from success as the day he made the first insane effort to accomplish that which is impossible for man to perform.

Therefore the eleventh law will be, that
'Both sexes shall have equal education, rights, privileges, and personal liberty; their marriages will arise from the general sympathies of their nature, uninfluenced by artificial distinctions, and be maintained as long as rational-formed individuals can maintain them, when placed under the most favorable circumstances to foster and encourage their continuance; but no such parties, in the rational-made society, shall be forced to cohabit and live together, when it shall be ascertained, under properly devised proceedings, necessary and useful for all, that they have been compelled to lose their affections to each other, – it being an essential condition of human happiness that individuals should have the power to associate with those for whom they are compelled to feel the greatest regard and affection. And as the Rational System has been introduced solely to ensure the most permanent happiness of the human race, no attempt shall be made by man's inhuman laws to force the affection of man or woman against nature.

4 'The return of powerful sexual feelings'

Born in Edinburgh into a family of eight children (his father had five children from two previous marriages), George Robert Drysdale (1824–1904) made himself a reputation at Glasgow University as a brilliant student, until he suddenly collapsed psychologically, and mysteriously disappeared abroad. On his return he studied medicine at Trinity, Dublin, and Edinburgh. George's reading diet (Adam Smith, Ricardo, the two Mills, Malthus), and the influence of the Secularist tradition, led him to argue for a complete overhaul of sexual morality in a major (but underexplored) opus, *Physical, Sexual, and Natural Religion* (1854). Drysdale however refused the moral restraint advocated by Malthus to keep the population growth in check (i.e., sexual abstinence),[17] preferring the use of contraceptive devices, because he considered regular sexual relations essential to mental and physical health. Several contraceptive methods were propounded and examined critically in the book. Well ahead of Freud,

17 The *Malthusian* (1879–1921) persistently targeted the working classes: 'We want the poor to be taught to limit their families by the same contraceptive methods which most married couples in the richer classes are employing', 27:10 (15 October 1913), p. 73.

George realized the importance of the sexual instinct and rejected the conventional stifling morality that suppressed sexual desires; he believed in a 'Natural Religion' that favoured the physical over the spiritual world: he advocated free love (from puberty), divorce on demand, and the abolition of marriage considered as the acme of women's oppression. The book gave a full description of female and male sexual organs, as well as of the mechanisms of pleasure, and underlined the evils of abstinence. Most contentiously, it denied Dr Acton's theory that women have little sexual desire, asserting on the contrary that their sexual instincts were as powerful as men's. The book not only shattered the idea of female natural purity and chastity but also culminated in the argument that the practice of prostitution was in that respect preferable to abstinence.[18] Drysale managed to get the work published by Edward Truelove, a freethinker and former Owenite.[19] He signed it anonymously,[20] and had it translated into most European languages at his own expense. Drysdale diagnosed poverty as a consequence of overpopulation, prostitution, and venereal diseases, and was obsessed with its eradication. In order to propagate his theories among the working classes, he sold the book's section on birth control in penny pamphlets (under a variety of titles such as *Poverty: Its Causes and Cure*), and convinced his younger brother Charles to revive the Malthusian League (1877–1927). The book was reprinted thirty-five times in enlarged editions (under the title *The Elements of Social Science; Or Physical, Sexual, and Natural Religion. An Exposition of the True Cause and Only Cure of the Primary Evils: Poverty, Prostitution and Celibacy*). It became an international best seller, selling ninety thousand copies by 1914. Although not devoid of a moral code, the book was denounced as 'the Bible of the brothel'; unsurprisingly it created both great sensation and furore, including in freethinking milieux.[21] Drysdale pioneered a new

18 The Unitarian writings in the 1840s represented fallen women as seduced innocents and put the blame for the existence of prostitution on the denial of women's sexual passions. George showed great compassion for prostitutes in the book.
19 Truelove was later imprisoned for publishing in 1870 Robert Dale Owen's *Moral Physiology*, which advocated birth control.
20 The book was for long believed to have been written by George's brother, Charles. George's articles to Bradlaugh's *National Reformer* in the 1860s were written under a pseudonym (G. R.).
21 The book provoked considerable division in Secularist ranks: Harriet Law, Sophia Dobson Collet, Joseph Barker, and Francis Newman repudiated it. Annie Besant did not endorse it fully.

theory of morals based on the belief that a healthy sex life was essential to happiness, a testimony of his desire to improve society and promote harmonious relations between the sexes.

George R. Drysdale, *Physical, Sexual, and Natural Religion* (London: E. Truelove, 1855), pp. 171–3

I know the host of prejudices that will oppose the recognition of sexual intercourse, as the great remedy in sexual enfeeblement in woman, but I am absolutely certain too that it will be recognised. It is in vain that we strive against the decrees of nature; we may exhaust ourselves in forming unnatural theories, and in forbidding any attempt to compare them with the natural laws; we may be content that the subject should continue shrouded in mystery, and that our young women should be racked and tortured by innumerable diseases, rather than allow the least departure from our prejudiced schemes; we may persecute and anathematise all those poets, philosophers and physicians, who, horror-struck at the amount of sexual misery, endeavour to find a new path out of the labyrinth; but not one jot, not one iota, does nature move for all our vehemence, and she will force us at last, exhausted by our sufferings, to confess our errors and recognise her infallibility. I do not see how any man of common sense, far less a scientific physician, can fail to see, that nature intended that the sexual organs should be used, as soon as they are fully developed. The sexual passions are strongest at that time; and we might foresee with certainty, that if the natural intentions be defeated, disease and misery must result. It is clear too, that for diseases arising from such a cause, the natural and obvious remedy is to supply the normal exercise, the want of which occasions the disorder. In the case of genital enfeeblement in man, M. Lallemand[22] has shown clearly by the results of his treatment, as well as by his general reasoning, that sexual exercise is the true natural and efficient remedy; and his views have been adopted by a great many of the most enlightened medical men in this country, and must eventually be accepted by all, however much they are opposed by Christian prejudices.

Now, I ask, how is it possible that a similar reasoning should not apply to woman? In her, too, the sexual organs are early developed, and powerful sexual appetites roused; she is liable to analogous states of sexual enfeeblement and derangement, consequent on the non-exercise of her

---

22 Dr François Lallemand advocated frequent intercourse as beneficial to sexual health (*Des pertes séminales involontaires*, 3 vols, Paris, 1836–1842).

sexual organs; and can any philosophical mind infer otherwise, than that a proper exercise is the treatment required for her cure? Nay, we find that in the chance cases in which marriage has come to the succour of these unfortunates, it has generally proved curative; and we may be satisfied that if the sexual means were duly used (which is frequently by no means the case in marriage, over-indulgence producing exhaustion and satiety instead of reinvigoration), along with other means of bracing the health, very few cases of chlorosis, or the allied affections, could resist it. But the fact is, that there are few men, who, on calmly considering the subject, would fail to see that a due amount of sexual intercourse is one great thing needed to preserve and restore the health in the youth of both sexes; and it is a common remark among men on seeing a girl languid and sickly, that what she needs is venereal gratification. It is impossible to avoid the conclusion that the natural exercise is the great means, without which it is absolutely impossible to prevent or cure an immense amount of disease and misery. When once we have clearly recognised this grand truth, – certainly one of the most important which the physician, or the moral philosopher, can apprehend at the present day – we will be in a fitter position for reasoning upon the possibility of procuring for every human being this great essential of health, happiness, or virtue: but upon this question I shall speak hereafter.

There is a great deal of erroneous feeling attaching to the subject of the sexual desires in woman. To have strong sexual passions is held to be rather a disgrace for a woman, and they are looked down upon as animal, sensual, coarse, and deserving of reprobation. The moral emotions of love are indeed thought beautiful in her; but the physical ones are rather held unwomanly and debasing. This is a great error. In woman, exactly as in man, strong sexual appetites are a very great virtue; as they are the signs of a vigorous frame, healthy sexual organs, and a naturally-developed sexual disposition. The more intense the venereal appetites, and the keener the sense of the normal sexual gratifications, provided it do not hold a diseased proportion to the other parts of the constitution, the higher is the sexual virtue of the individual. It is exactly the same with the venereal appetite as with the appetite for food. If a woman be healthy, and have a frame braced by exercise and a natural life, she will have a strong appetite and a keen relish for food, and it is exactly the same with the sexual desires. The strongest appetites, and the greatest enjoyment in their gratification, have been fixed by nature as the reward of obedience to her laws, and the preservation of health by a due exercise of all the functions, neither excessive nor deficient. The man or woman who is borne down by a weakened and diseased digestion, will recognise strength of stomach and vigour of appetite to be the greatest of all desirable virtues for them, that which lies at the root of every other advantage; and in the same way he who is wallowing in spermatorrhoea, impotence, and sexual disgust, or the morbid and chlorotic girl, may recognise sexual power and strong sexual appetites, as the highest and most important of all virtues for them in their position. Other virtues are in such cases a dream and a delusion to the sufferers – unattainable, or even if apparently attainable, of little real and permanent advantage. Instead of a girl being looked down upon for having strong sexual passions, it is one of her highest virtues; while feeble or morbid desires are the sign of a diseased or deteriorated frame. Those who have the most healthy desires are the chosen children of nature, whom she thus deems worthiest to continue our race. In sexual diseases, the venereal desires are generally deadened or rendered morbid; and one of the best signs of restoration to health is the return of powerful sexual feelings.

5 A father's role in the education of his children

Sir John Robert Seeley's writings appeared in major periodicals and played a great role in the socio-political debates of the late Victorian era. Before becoming a renowned ideologue, Seeley (1834–1895) had made himself a reputation as a pedagogue, particularly while Regius Professor of Modern History at Cambridge, a post which he held from 1869. A great lover of literature and poetry, a passionate lecturer, he believed in the practical value of history and treated it as 'a school of statesmanship'.[23] In his best-selling *Ecce Homo: A Survey of the Life and Work of Jesus Christ* (1865), published anonymously, Seeley saw himself as the educator of the national mind, and argued that man's sense of social obligation was stronger than individual self-interest. Seeley was born into a family of Evangelical intellectuals, but when a student he was much taken with the Christian Socialists' idea of a socially responsible Christianity. In the 1860s he mixed with the Positivists, who helped him articulate the need for a specifically English religion of humanity. He

---

23 Like Thomas Arnold at Oxford (1841–1842), Seeley contributed to giving the discipline its academic credentials. He considered the University to be a 'great seminary of politicians' training men for leadership, not scholarship ('The Teaching of Politics', *Lectures and Essays*).

therefore strongly believed that Church and State should join forces in the re-organizing of society and the improvement of its moral values. *Ecce Homo*, seemingly another interpretation of the meaning of Christ's life, was in fact an attempt to define the social role of the elites, a reflection of Maurice's influence (his comparison of the Church to a state and the priest to a statesman is reminiscent of the Coleridgean clerisy). Seeley has been rightly celebrated for his defence of British imperialism (*The Expansion of England*, 1883). He is remembered as the first thinker of 'the United States of Europe' (the title of one of his lectures in 1871), but he has remained 'one of the unsung heroes in the history of women's emancipation' (Wormwell, 1977: 60). Seeley was an inspiring persona in the reform of university education, which he viewed as the key to social progress ('Liberal Education in Universities', *Lectures and Essays*, 1870), and from the 1860s promoted women's access to Cambridge. He taught at Maurice's Working Men's College, associated with Emily Davies's campaigns (he was a close friend of her brother, John Llewelyn Davies [II, 7]), supported Ann Clough's North of England Council, lectured girls at Hitchin Girls' School (1873–1881), and involved himself in the creation of Newnham College in 1875, with Henry Sidgwick and John Peile, a former fellow-student at Christ's. Although unhappy in marriage, Seeley displayed a particular attachment to the family, which he regarded as an institution primarily responsible for social stability (and as a form of political organization). His devotion from her birth to his only child Frances[24] testifies to his adherence to a type of manliness embodied by Jesus, 'a creature of almost feminine tenderness and humanity' (*Ecce Homo*).[25] In the exhortation below Seeley reminded fathers of the critical importance of forging a strong moral character in their children.[26] While reasserting the prerogative of the paterfamilias (a

---

24 He watched her progress with great tenderness, but strangely gave her an unsystematic and leisurely education. She never went to school or college and was exclusively taught by him in the arts and literature.
25 The Evangelicals' idea of a manliness of self-sacrifice and emotion was close to what they regarded as feminine qualities. Seeley is here influenced by F. D. Maurice, who saw in Christ 'a Spirit which makes men feminine, if feminine means courteous, deferential, free from brutal and insolent pretensions but which also gives women manliness, if manliness means the vigour to live for the cause of Humanity and die for it', Lecture 20, *Social Morality* (London: Macmillan, 1869), p. 461. See [III, 5].
26 'The cultivation of a perfect character in each and all' was one of the ethical bedrocks of British Liberalism' (Leighton, 2004: 293). Developing a religious

fact which interfered with the growing recognition of mothers' rights, and complicated the passing of reforms), the emphasis placed on the role of fathers can also be read as a refusal to put maleness and domesticity at odds. Like Cobbett's [IV, 2], Seeley's text illustrates how integral to respectable manliness the domestic sphere had become, and his incitement to replace old ideals of paternal nurturance by softer ones[27] attests to the 'shift in gender identity as well as in family dynamics' that took place in men's relationships to the home during the nineteenth century (Tosh, 1999: 2).[28] Similarly, *The Nemesis of Faith* (1849), by another public moralist and imperialist, James Anthony Froude, offers valuable insights into the phenomenon that Andrew Halliday, a popular Scottish journalist, described as a 'great metamorphosis'.[29]

J. R. Seeley, 'The Church as a Teacher of Morality', *Lectures and Essays* (London: Macmillan & Co., 1870), pp. 268–71

My own profession constantly brings before me instances of an immorality – so I think it should be called – which proceeds simply from want of instruction in morals, which has most disastrous consequences, and which, I believe, the Church could cure. I mean the habit which fathers have of delegating altogether to others the education of their children. Not from any indifference to the welfare of their children, not from any deliberate contempt for moral obligation, but simply from never having had this particular duty pointed out to them, they become guilty of a neglect the immediate consequences of which are sometimes startling, and the less direct and obvious consequences beyond calculation. I have

---

sense of moral duty and of personal calling in both sexes was an imperious social need. Such factors force more nuanced views of nineteenth-century gender relations. 'Viewed in this light', therefore, 'the emphasis on character training in girls' didactic fiction becomes more socially significant than a mere patriarchally inspired plot to restrict women to a limited sphere. Estimation of character for both sexes is established as one of the fundamental elements of the spirit of the age' (Rowbotham, 1989: 103).
27 Also advocated by Herbert Spencer, 'The Moral Discipline of Children', *British Quarterly Review* (1858), 364–90.
28 See also Delap et al. (2009). Men's increasing pleasure in their fatherly roles is also attested to by writings on the enjoyment of fatherhood (Davidoff and Hall, 2002: 329–35). William Shaen's correspondence is another testimony of the male enjoyment of domesticity and the development of new ideas of parenthood.
29 Andrew Halliday, 'Fathers', *All the Year Round* 14 (2 September 1865), 133–35.

met with young men who have been suffered to grow up in an incredible intellectual barbarism, the father working conscientiously for them all the time, but delegating altogether the particular work of education. I do not suppose such extreme cases are common; the majority of parents are not so unfortunate in their choice of delegates; they find teachers for their sons who are tolerably competent to teach, and they persuade themselves, no doubt, that it is really best not to interfere with those who have made a special study for the art of education. The principle of division of labour is adopted. The father has not time to do all that is necessary to be done for his children; part he will do himself, but part must be entrusted to others. He hands over to others the child's education, his mind, his soul. He reserves to himself the finance department. It is not easy to estimate the mischief produced by this division of labour. I know scarcely any cause from which the community suffers so much. In the first place, consider the effect produced upon the parent himself. It is open to him to give so much time and thought to educating his children, or the same amount of both to making the money to pay for their education; and he elects the latter. In other words, he chooses an occupation which is in many cases the most sordid and illiberal drudgery, and in very few cases can be highly improving, instead of the most improving occupation in which he can be engaged. Surely there is no task which life brings with it, at least to the average man, calculated to raise him so much as the task of educating his children. It is by far the greatest and most delicate problem which he ever has to solve. It demands all his powers of thought and contrivance, and by making so constant a demand upon them forms and disciplines them: at the same time it disciplines the affections. In short, a man cannot educate his children without at the same time in a much greater degree educating himself. What trade or profession does as much for the man who follows it? Not perhaps the most intellectual of all; and assuredly a good many of the occupations by which men make money are for all other purposes a mere waste of time. What then are we to think of the division of labour by which a father devolves upon others all that is valuable and dignified in fatherhood, and retains only its burdens and anxieties? What an impoverishment of character must be the effect of such an abdication of the paternal dignity! It must lead inevitably to those low views of the actual prevalence of which we are always complaining, that money-worship, that morbid industry, that insensibility to the highest interests and enjoyments.

But what is the effect upon the children themselves? I am not of course maintaining that the father should take the place of the schoolmaster, but that he should actively co-operate with the schoolmaster and supplement his work. Now his neglect of this duty to a great extent paralyses the schoolmaster. We have recently been told on good authority that the high average culture of the Scotch is due mainly to parental influence in education. It is to find an equivalent for this in England that we are always hopelessly labouring. That division of labour by which the parent loses so much is, even for its special purpose, a mistake. The teaching of special subjects may be delegated, but there is much in education which cannot be delegated, very much which can only be done at home, and a good deal which can be done only by the father. But if the child's intellectual loss is great, his moral loss is perhaps still greater. When the father elects to perform his parental duties entirely in the counting-house, he practically surrenders his claim to filial affection. Instead of sympathy, personal care, and intimate friendship, such a father only gives his son money, a gift which will not inspire any enthusiastic gratitude. Distant respect is all that he can look for, and in the want of filial feelings the son loses more than the father loses by not inspiring them.

Here, then is an example, as it seems to me, of an abuse which the Church might remove. It is an abuse which springs from no inveterate vice of human nature, but from a moral rudeness, an ignorance which a little instruction might cure. Without much eloquence, preachers might make men ashamed of a negligence like this. And if a better way of thinking on such a point were introduced, the effects would be incalculable. The standard of national cultivation might be permanently raised and a kind of self-denial introduced which Englishmen seldom practice, the self-denial not of giving money but of refraining from earning it.

My profession, as I have said, brings this matter particularly before my notice. The teacher can do little for the pupil for whom his parents have done nothing, and to show parents their duty is evidently in the province of the teachers of morality. It is therefore at this particular point that it becomes most clearly visible to me how little teaching of morality there is in England, and in how unenlightened a condition is the moral sense of a great proportion of the nation.

---

6 A Malthusian view of married life

Montague Hugues Crackanthorpe (1832–1913), né Cookson – he changed his name to inherit a large family estate in Westmorland – started his education at Merchant Taylors' School, where he showed promising academic gifts. His years in Oxford, where he graduated as a DCL in 1859, confirmed him as an outstanding scholar, particularly in mathematics. Cookson, appointed QC in 1875, was a prominent and respected figure in the Chancery Division, and occupied prestigious judicial positions throughout his life. A Liberal Unionist, he took a great interest in the political affairs and social problems of his time (particularly the Home Rule question, but also crime, unemployment, and the 'immigration of destitute aliens'), and reached a large public through his numerous contributions to leading progressive journals. Cookson was eugenically minded and active in the Malthusian League, without ever adhering to either movement. Under the influence of Henry Fawcett's *Essays and Lectures on Social and Political Subjects* (1872), he never doubted that population should be restrained ('The Morality of Married Life', 1872; *Population and Progress*, 1907). Contraception was for him the 'D. E.' (determining element) in the falling birthrate among the affluent. His allusion to the fact 'that the conditions of our existence are far more elastic than is commonly believed' ('The Morality of Married Life', p. 412) is a veiled reference to the 'safe' period. However, his advocacy of the limitation of births was not strictly utilitarian. It stemmed from a 'devotion to the welfare of Humanity', as much as from a preoccupation with women's welfare. Cookson's article goes well beyond the recommendation of birth control in pursuit of a stable political economy. It deplores the physical and psychological damage that uncontrolled childbearing had on women. His indictment of numerous families as injurious to personal development was quite remarkable; so was his praise of marriage as 'the sweet companionship of matched minds' (perhaps a reference to his own marriage to Blanche, a writer on women's issues). The article read as an exhortation to women 'to escape ... bondage', in keeping with Cookson's campaign for their civic rights (he signed the Declaration of Men in support of Women's Suffrage in *The Times*, 23 March 1909). His views earned him a reputation as a Malthusian, but he neither fully embraced the ideas of Malthus nor did he see eye to eye with the eugenicist Francis Galton, although, on his offer, in 1909 he accepted the chair of the Eugenics Education Society. His work undoubtedly placed him amongst the reformers of 'the Social Evil', but his political ambition to create a National Party, and to win a Parliamentary seat, failed – perhaps because of his cross-bench mentality, but more probably as a consequence of his support of 'the preventive check'.[30]

30 Cookson was reviled for it by the *Daily News* in 1879. In 1868 Viscount

Montague Cookson, 'The Morality of Married Life', *Fortnightly Review*, new series, 12 (1872), 398–400

It seems to be taken for granted that marriage once entered upon, all control over ourselves not only ceases but ought to cease; and that, instead of the conjugal relations being subject to regulative laws, husbands and wives have no standard of morality corresponding to that which is set up for the government of other folk.

The time has arrived when it has become necessary to use plain speech on this matter, and I for one can no longer hesitate to avow my belief that this last view of marriage is not only vicious in principle, but often fraught with the most mischievous consequences. For what does it amount to? First, it involves a break in the education of humanity which is incompatible with the continuity of moral growth, and has no parallel in the processes of development of the physical world. Secondly, as held by the middle and upper classes, it means that man is free up to a certain point in his career, free, that is, to choose his own vocation, to work out the best part of himself, to enlarge his experience by travel, to recreate his strength by leisure, to store his mind with varied knowledge; but that when he marries he surrenders this freedom utterly, embarks on an unknown sea, exposes his fair hopes to shipwreck, here and there has to exhaust all his energies in the toil and stress of life – in a word becomes a victim to new circumstances, against which it is vain for him to struggle. Is there one of us who cannot call to mind a dozen instances of this kind amongst our acquaintance? Look at the poor married curates and incumbents, whose large families have passed into a proverb. Twenty-five years ago the man whose hair is now silvering with premature age, had a reputation in his university, was enthusiastic in the cause of science, conspicuous for general culture, promised many brilliant things; since then he has had ten children, for whose education (all he had to give them) he has overtaxed his powers till he has sunk to the level of his own drudgery, and his mind has become the mind of a pedagogue. His friends are at a loss whether to pity or to praise him most. 'Excellent fellow,' they exclaim, 'but he has been sorely weighted in the race of life. To put out so many boys in the world is too much for any man.' So is walking thirty miles a day up a hill for ten successive days, or any other similar self-imposed task; and if we do survive the achievement, where is the glory, if it leaves us at the finish but the wreck of our proper selves? We may perhaps have learnt

---

Amberley's political career had also been ruined because of his support of contraception and woman suffrage.

some virtues in the process, such as patience, resignation, the habit of sustained effort; but these we could have made our own equally well in other paths of life, gladdened by grander glimpses of God's universe as helps to lift our hearts to him. What right has any one of us deliberately to narrow his own intellectual horizon, any more than to cut off his right hand or put out one of his eyes?

If we turn from the husband to the wife the prospect is often still more melancholy, and this from the very fact that it is not considered either by herself or those around her to call for any particular sympathy. I pass by the recurrence of her physical suffering, the months of dreary out-look, uncrowned by any adequate reward when they only result in adding a fresh term to a series already too long. I pass by the heedless risking of the matured and more valuable life for one whose approach was no signal for joy, and whose chance of foothold now that he has come is openly acknowledged, by those who love him best, to be too faint for speculation. The unnecessary multiplication of children causes greater disasters than these, although not so patent to the superficial observer. It tends to arrest the education of the married woman at its most critical stage, and, by absorbing her whole attention, renders her incapable of fulfilling duties for which she might be otherwise fit, or might easily fit herself. Society, it is true, does not require a wife to be much more than the head-domestic of her establishment, and if her nursery is full it commonly permits her head to be empty. Where this is the case, the germ of the mischief may be dormant for a time, but the day inevitably comes when it springs into life, and the children have forced upon them the painful consciousness that they have outgrown at least one of their parents. Who shall say whether the maternal influence has not in that awakening received its death-blow? 'A foolish son,' says Solomon, 'is a heaviness to his mother.' It is equally true that a foolish mother is lightly esteemed by her son.

It cannot but be that both sexes should suffer when either transgresses the due limits which it is in the power of each to observe; but the deterioration which the woman undergoes in the process is far greater than that of the man. Everybody admits that this is true of the single state, but it is not less true of the married, and indeed has a wider application there; for whereas the enlarged sense of responsibility which an increasing family creates may act on the father as a spur to greater exertion, the concentration of the mother's whole being on the details of the domestic drama grows and must grow with each new birth, until at last her daily life becomes one theatre of trivialities, the curtain of which is never allowed to drop. Nor usually would she have it otherwise. Sufficient for her if the teething is not abnormally troublesome, or the pleasing variation of the measles and whooping-cough does not recur too frequently. Life for her has only two practical sides, maternity and the management of her household. The higher education of women, she remarks, may be a capital theme for learned spinsters to descant upon, but, she adds with a complacent sneer these advanced females will soon sober down when they have had half-a-dozen babies. Inquire her views on any of the topics of the day, her mind is either a blank, or, if intelligent, she catches up the last expression of her husband's opinion upon them, sometimes echoing his own words; ask her if she keeps up any of these interests which had so great a charm for her girlhood, she tells you she has never had a moment to spare since her marriage; will she play you that air of Beethoven which still, at the end of six years, lingers in your memory? she never touches the piano now.

7 'A new code of manners between the sexes'

From an early age, looking at the case of his own mother and sisters, Edward Carpenter (1844–1929) had felt concerned by the 'misery' and 'tragic emptiness' of the self-sacrificing life led by most middle-class women. Carpenter was himself a very sensitive man, inhabited by an 'insuperable *feeling* of falsity and dislocation'. He found it hard to fit in in Victorian society, whether as deacon or lecturer in Cambridge, even as a peripatetic teacher in the University Extension Movement (aimed at developing the education of women and the newly enfranchised working class). Carpenter's dislike of industrial capitalism (*Civilization: Its Cause and Cure*, 1889) led him, with John Ruskin and William Morris, to become one of the key figures of the 'Back to the Land' movement in England in the 1880s. Once settled at Millthorpe, he awakened to a new spiritual life and practised a simpler, self-sufficient alternative style of life in the company of his lover George Merrill, entertaining a wide array of writers, bohemian intellectuals and social reformers. For some he was the iconic sandal wearer, vegetarian, nudist and spiritual prophet, for others an embarrassing crank. Carpenter's own brand of mystic, Hindu-inspired, ethical socialism, verging on anarchism (he was a friend of Kropotkin), marginalized him within the various socialist circles to which he belonged, including the Independent Labour Party. But he was close and inspirational to many female activists (such as Katherine Glasier, who converted to socialism after reading him, Olive Schreiner,

Edith Lees, Annie Besant, or Charlotte Despard, whom he campaigned with). His awareness that his masculinity did not conform to the social expectations of Victorian society led him to write on homosexuality, reject marriage as a form of oppression, and plead for contraception, as well as economic and sexual freedom.[31] Carpenter continued however to regard the division of labour as the result of intrinsic biological differences between the sexes. But his sharp analyses of gender relations – his denunciation of the 'serfdom' of woman, his exhortation to put an end to her 'enslavement' and 'to dispose of herself and of her sex perfectly freely', his craving for 'a new code of manners between the sexes' – fed into the emancipation movement and prepared the advent of a 'new Modern Woman'. *Love's Coming-of-Age* (1896), originally a series of four talks,[32] was translated into several languages and went through eleven editions. *The Intermediate Sex* (1908) developed the idea of an androgynous, higher type of humanity. Carpenter's view of a democracy of free men and women, in free and equal association, was particularly popular in Sylvia Pankhurst's Workers' Suffrage Federation (he was himself involved in the movement). If his socialism was more personal than institutional, his work remained influential in the general discussion of sexual politics well into the twentieth century.

Edward Carpenter, 'Woman in Freedom', *Love's Coming-of-Age. A Series of Papers on the Relations of the Sexes* (Manchester: Labour Press, 1896), pp. 58–63

I say the signs of revolt on the part of the lady class – revolt long delayed but now spreading all along the line – are evident enough. When, however, we come to the second type of woman mentioned in the preceding pages, the working-wife, we – naturally enough – do not find much conscious movement. The life of the household drudge is too like that of a slave, too much consumed in mere toil, too little illuminated by any knowledge, for her to rise of herself to any other conception of existence. Nevertheless it is not difficult to see that general and social changes are working to bring about her liberation also. Improved house-construction, public bakeries and laundries, and so forth, and, what is much more important,

31 Carpenter deplored the view of women as machines for perpetual reproduction; he nevertheless opposed artificial checks and recommended relying on the monthly cycle instead.
32 *Homogenic Love, and Its Place in a Free Society*; *Sex-Love, and Its Place in a Free Society*; *Woman, and Her Place in a Free Society*; *Marriage in Free Society* (1894).

a more rational and simple and healthful notion of food and furniture, are tending very largely to reduce the labors of Housework and Cookery; and conservative though women are in their habits, when these changes are brought to their doors they cannot but see the advantage of them. Public institutions too are more and more taking over the responsibilities and the cost of educating and rearing children; and even here and there we may discern a drift towards the amalgamation of households, which by introducing a common life and division of labor among the women-folk will probably do much to cheer and lighten their lot. None of these changes, however, will be of great use unless or until they wake the overworked woman herself to see and insist on her rights to a better life, and until they force from the man a frank acknowledgment of her claim. And surely here and there the man himself will do something to educate his mate to this point. We see no reason indeed why he should not assist in some part of the domestic work, and thus contribute his share of labor and intelligence to the conduct of the house; nor why the woman – being thus relieved – should not occasionally, and when desirable, find salaried work outside, and so contribute to the maintenance of the family, and to her own security and sense of independence. The over-differentiation of the labors of the sexes to-day is at once a perpetuation of the servitude of women and a cause of misunderstanding between her and man, and of lack of interest in each other's doings.

The third type of woman, the prostitute, provides us with that question which – according to Bebel – is the sphinx-riddle that modern society cannot solve, and yet which unsolved threatens society's destruction. The commercial prostitution of love is the last outcome of our whole social system, and its most clear condemnation. It flaunts in our streets, it hides itself in the garment of respectability under the name of matrimony, it eats in actual physical disease and death right through our midst; it is fed by the oppression and the ignorance of women, by their poverty and denied means of livelihood, and by the hypocritical puritanism which forbids them by millions not only to gratify but even to speak of their natural desires; and it is encouraged by the callousness of an age which has accustomed men to buy and sell for money every most precious thing – even the life-long labor of their brothers, therefore why not also the very bodies of their sisters?

Here there is no solution *except* the freedom of woman – which means of course also the freedom of the masses of the people, men and women, and the ceasing altogether of economic slavery. There is no solution which will not include the redemption of the terms 'free woman' and 'free love' to their *true* and rightful significance. Let every woman whose heart bleeds for the sufferings of her sex, hasten to declare herself and to constitute herself, as far as she possibly can, a free woman. Let her accept the term with all the odium that belongs to it; let her insist on her right to speak, dress, think, act, and above all to use her sex, as she deems best; let her face the scorn and the ridicule; let her 'lose her own life' if she likes assured that only so can come deliverance, and that only when the free woman is honored will the prostitute cease to exist. And let every man who really would respect his counterpart, entreat her also to act so; let him never by word or deed tempt her to grant as a bargain what can only be precious as a gift; let him see her with pleasure stand a little aloof; let him help her to gain her feet; so at last, by what slight sacrifices on his part such a course may involve, will it dawn upon him that he has gained a real companion and helpmate on life's journey.

The whole evil of commercial prostitution arises out of the domination of Man in matters of sex. Better indeed were a Saturnalia of *free* men and women than the spectacle which as it is our great cities present at night. Here in Sex, the women's instincts are, as a rule, so clean, so direct, so well-rooted in the needs of the race, that except for man's domination they would scarcely have suffered this perversion. Sex in man is an unorganised passion, an individual need or impetus; but in woman it may more properly be termed a constructive instinct, with the larger signification that that involves. Even more than man should woman be 'free' to work out the problem of her sex-relations as may commend itself best to her – hampered as little as possible by legal, conventional, or economic considerations, and relying chiefly on her own native sense of tact in the matter. Once thus free – free from the mere cash-nexus to a husband, from the money-slavery of the streets, from the nameless terrors of social opinion, and from the threats of the choice of perpetual virginity or perpetual bondage – would she not indeed choose her career (whether that of wife and mother, or that of free companion, or one of single blessedness) far better for herself than it is chosen *for* her to-day – regarding really in some degree the needs of society, and the welfare of children, and the sincerity and durability of her relations to her lovers, and less the petty motives of profit and fear?

The point is that the whole conception of a nobler Womanhood for the future has to proceed candidly from this basis of her complete freedom as to the disposal of her sex, and from the healthy conviction that, with whatever individual aberrations, she will on the whole use that freedom rationally and well. And surely this – in view too of some decent education of the young on sexual matters – is not too great a demand to make on our faith in women. If it is, then indeed we are undone – for short of this we can only retain them in servitude, and society in its form of the hell on earth which it largely is to-day.

8 A new age about to commence

The Rev. Frederick Augustus Morland Spencer (1878–1962) graduated in Divinity at Oxford and became a preacher of distinction. Deeply involved in Biblical scholarship and exegetical issues, he authored several theological essays: *Human Ideals* (1917), *The Ethics of the Gospel* (1925), *Civilisation Remade by Christ* (1928), *The Theory of Christ's Ethics* (1929), and *The Future Life: A New Interpretation of the Christian Doctrine* (1935). As much concerned by pastoral matters as he was by temporal duties, he intended to address the moral problems of his times 'in the light of the Gospel', and contributed several articles on the topic to the prestigious *Expository Times*. Spencer, who had developed a particular interest in the question of women's vote, served as secretary of the Oxford branch of the Church League for Women's Suffrage, and was much valued for the support he brought to the Cause [I, 8]. In June 1913, he married Gertrude Burke, an Australian activist who had been the Commonwealth Government delegate to the International Women Suffrage Alliance in 1912.[33] Their marriage ceremony, celebrated at the Chapel Royal (the Savoy, London) by the suffragist Rev. Hugh Chapman, made the headlines when the couple refused the ritual of the giving away of the bride, and had the word 'obey' omitted from the traditional vows (following the example set by Victor Duval and Una Dugdale the year before). The columns of the *Monthly Magazine* (1912–1917) in which Spencer developed his argument testify to the growing assimilation of the new exegesis into the Anglican mainstream. 'Truth is indeed immutable but humanity is progressive; and thus the form in which the truth is presented must be examined in relation to the age in which the revelation was made.'[34] His interpretation

33 Between 1914 and 1918 Spencer served as a chaplain in the Australian Imperial Forces.
34 Brooke Foss Westcott, *An Introduction to the Study of the Gospels* (Cambridge and London: Macmillan, sixth edition, 1881), p. 16. St Paul's insistence on the subjection of women was increasingly interpreted as the product of rabbinical teaching, not of the divine will. Westcott's unorthodox views were first aired in *Essays and Reviews* (1860).

of the figure of Jesus as the epiphany of sex equality – the male and female sex being but 'two aspects of one essentially indivisible perfection' (p. 14), and of Christ's humility, unselfishness, and kindness as the essence of manliness – was endorsed by a whole generation of reformers in the 1870s and 1880s [III, 5; IV, 5].[35] With most of the contributors to the League's paper, he inveighed against the Church's 'sins', particularly its past indifference to moral issues, and its unjust treatment of women. Spencer considered discrimination against women as a legitimate cause for revolt in society (the League publicly condoned the violent methods of the Women's Social and Political Union). Undoubtedly influenced by Charles Gore's Lux Mundi group, Spencer harnessed the principle of evolution to his demonstration to assert that women's emancipation was part of God's mysterious ways,[36] and that it would bring about the redemption of the world. Unsurprisingly, he cherished a conservative view of women's mission as 'lovers of children', but his positive evaluation of their healing and purifying social role was empowering for many.[37] Welcoming women's 'large part in the transformation of society', he anticipated that it would 'develop their own personalities' (p. 14), and help them achieve personal fufilment.

The Rev. Frederick A. M. Spencer, 'The Evolution of Woman' (A Sermon preached in the Chancel of St. Mary-the-Virgin's, Oxford, January 25, 1912), *Church League for Women's Suffrage* (March 1912), pp. 12–13

The movement of women for obtaining political power is part of a general growth of womanhood. And this growth of womanhood is one among several changes going on now in humanity.

35 The view was consequential in the development, in late century, of more companionate marital relationships, resting on love, and with equal duties of submission between spouses.
36 As he explained in the sermon, 'some species that has long been insignificant and comparatively undistinguished is mysteriously quickened to rapid evolution, at last surpassing the previously dominant species. So it is with woman. This I put forward as a philosophical and theological justification of the women's movement' (p. 13).
37 From the 1890s, millions of women were part of the Church's 'army of philanthropy', and gained their first experience of activity outside the home in the name of Christianity (Geddes Poole, 2014). The social purity crusader Ellis Hopkins was responsible for the mobilization of thousands of churchwomen in moral reform.

In the evolution of mankind there are periods of slow growth and apparent stagnation, and even of decadence, and there are relatively short periods of rapid growth and transition. We are now in one of the periods of rapid growth and transition. Humanity appears to be altering in its very fundamentals – religion is changing. As an instance, consider that fifty years ago the central ideas of Christianity seemed to be sin against God and forgiveness by God and the salvation of souls. The place of these in current religious thought has been largely taken by the ideas of self-sacrifice and love and the evolution of humanity into the Kingdom of God. Without here attempting to estimate the gain and loss in this change, I would suggest that these contrasted ideas are probably not exclusive, but rather inclusive of one another. Forgiveness and love are in part at least the same. The salvation of souls and the evolution of humanity are perhaps two aspects of one process. Still, men do think differently on religion from what they did a generation or two back. And human society is changing. There is widespread dissatisfaction with the present conduct of industry, and efforts are being made to secure good conditions of life for the mass of the people by co-operation and organization. And sex is changing. Women feel within them growing powers which demand scope for exercise; and they are revolting against their traditional position as instruments in the hands of men for their use and pleasure. And in other ways mankind is changing. People are hankering after modes of living in food and dress and the conveniences and comforts of existence that will be less wasteful, less troublesome, more conducive to health, simpler, more beautiful, less cruel to their fellow-creatures, than these at present in vogue.

So much by way of preliminary. Now I want to bring into relation religion and the evolution of humanity and the women's movement.

First, how does the idea of evolution affect Christianity? I want you to consider what Christianity meant for its early adherents. It meant the Kingdom of God which was to come before the present generation had passed. It meant faith in Jesus as the Christ, involving dying with Him and raising with Him even in this mortal existence. It carried with it the obligation to witness for Jesus Christ and to preach the Gospel.

Now the power of Christianity and the divine life and inspiration to which Christianity was the means showed themselves in martyrdoms and, more widely, in the social ostracism and voluntary hardship with allegiance to Christ involved. Now it is significant that, although Christianity produced such extraordinary fortitude and renunciation, yet it failed to save the Græco-Roman civilization. But if we look closer, we perceive that it never set itself to do this. Early Christianity never undertook the task of reforming the conditions of society, as is evidenced by the fact that it condoned slavery. Christianity aimed at producing that faith in virtue of which souls would attain eternal life; it did not aim at any radical reformation of ordinary human existence. Now why? Because the end of the age was at hand, and a new age was about to commence. It would have seemed lost labour to improve the present age just before its conclusion. But was the Church mistaken in believing in the approaching end of the age? The answer is that the Church grasped truth symbolically. The age did come to an end for the Jews in the breakup of their community and the destruction of their temple; the age did come to an end for the European civilization of that era when the barbarians destroyed the Roman Empire and brought in the Dark Ages. Now, on the one hand, we may believe it was ordained by Providence that religion and civilization should run the course they have. On the other hand, we see that both civilization and religion suffered through not being more closely connected. Civilization decayed and perished; and religion lost its vitality.

Yes: Christianity, from the day when the persecutions ceased, began to decline. Faith, which formerly involved facing ignominy and torture for the sake of the Gospel, became assent to theological formulas – a matter of the intellect, and not of the heart. So soon as Christianity became generally accepted, it lost the greater part of its content. The Christian was still required to live a decently moral life, to be generous and merciful, to assent to certain dogmas, and to take part in worship. But there was little else he was required to do. The cessation of persecution took the force out of religion.

Now the idea of evolution is restoring to Christianity its pristine vigour. For the conception of humanity as evolving and organic constitutes a call to every human being to take part in promoting the right evolution. It demands that each life should be devoted wholly to the realization of the ideal of mankind. And since humanity is a complex of physical and mental and spiritual, and involves social organization for the maintenance and furtherance of human life in its various sides and elements, no department of human activity is unrelated to the supreme end for all.

Faith and hope and charity, which have been languishing for want of sufficient objects, are stimulated to manifold growth. The idea of the growing Kingdom of God calls for self-sacrifice and endurance and love, and for the absolute permeation of the life by the will of God. Religion, which formerly has been an appendage to life and a refining influence on life, becomes the dominant principle of all the life, both individual and social. All human life is to be through and through determined by the will of God, for the evolution of humanity into the Kingdom of God. The development of Christianity that is now taking place constitutes the most important moment of its history since its beginning, since for the first time Christianity is being brought into relation to the whole life of man evolving into the ideal ordained by God.

So much for the influence of the idea of evolution on Christianity. What is the influence of Christianity on evolution? The influence of Christianity on evolution consists in providing the determining principles of evolution. Christianity makes us see evolution as the working-out of the will of God. Christianity calls for loving self-sacrifice on behalf of evolution. Christianity shows this loving self-sacrifice to be the means to spiritual life, and holds out the hope of the final supremacy of the spiritual life, even to the overcoming of mortality and physical limitations.

There is now commencing the rational, moral, social, loving, religious, spiritual, self-evolution of humanity to be the Kingdom of God.

---

9 'A new avatar of love'

After a brief and unsuccessful educational career in Australia (1875–1879), Henry Havelock Ellis (1859–1939), the son of a sea captain, returned to England and set out to study medicine, prompted by acute personal, sexual, and intellectual preoccupations. He obtained an MD, and dedicated himself to the scientific study of human sexuality. At the time of Oscar Wilde's trial, he co-authored the first medical textbook on homosexuality (*Sexual Inversion*, 1897), which was immediately banned.[38] His ground-breaking views, published in prominent Victorian journals and periodicals, and psychoanalytical descriptions of transitional and intermediate cases (*Studies in the Psychology of Sex*, 7 vols, 1897–1928),[39] made him a major figure of sexology in the 1920s and 1930s. Ellis was convinced that sex was 'the central problem of life', and that the sexual impulse should not be repressed but, on the contrary, fulfilled if one was to lead a healthy, spiritually happy life. He wished to bring to

38 The publisher, Dr Villiers, associated with the Legitimation League (suspected of anarchism), was subsequently tried. In 1902 several thousand copies were destroyed by the police.
39 Which Freud drew upon and expanded from in *The World of Dreams* (1911).

light its physiological and psychological as well as sociological aspects. Imbibed with the philosophy of James Hinton's *Life in Nature* (1862) describing the benefits of a life in harmony with nature, Ellis helped found in 1883 the Fellowship of the New Life[40] (from which the Fabian Society emerged), where he met his wife, and progressive intellectuals and socialist reformers like Edward Carpenter, the Webbs, and George Bernard Shaw. In his time Ellis was most renowned, particularly in America, as the 'greatest exponent of the woman question' (according to his friend the anarchist publisher Joseph Ishill). But although Ellis was one of the first advocates of sexual freedom, he has remained a controversial figure in modern feminism, because his concern for woman's pleasure was treated as a new form of male domination. Ellis enthusiastically endorsed the new science of eugenics as the 'ultimate movement for social reform', and linked women's liberation and pleasure to social stability. As he explained in his eponymous book, in which he retraces and analyses the history of women's emancipation (1912), the task of social hygiene was to a great extent a woman's task. His call upon women to claim their erotic rights (*The Erotic Rights of Women, And The Objects of Marriage*, 1918) was indeed part of a wider concern for 'national efficiency' which confirmed women's roles as Empire builders, and smacked of social control. Ellis may have believed in deep biological differences between the sexes, he nevertheless contributed to the acceptation of sexuality as a powerful, positive, and healthy lifeforce (*Task of Social Hygiene*, chap. 8), and definitely asserted women's 'autonomous authority' over their bodies: 'A training in sexual hygiene has no meaning if it is not a training, for men and women alike, in personal and social responsibility, in the right to know and to discriminate, and in so doing to attain self-conquest' (*Task of Social Hygiene*, pp. 309–10). From his *Today* article in October 1884 ('Women and Socialism') to *The Philosophy of Conflict* (1919), he supported suffrage as 'an act of social justice', urged equal pay for equal work, and state maintenance for unmarried mothers. Ellis proved the ally, and even the mentor, of several women's rights activists. He contributed to the *Birth Control Review* launched by the Malthusian League lecturer Stella Browne, co-founder of the British Society for the Study of Sex Psychology, and one of the few women

---

40 A circle of Hinton's followers, founded in London in 1883 by Thomas Davidson, stressing personal development and reformation, educational change, as the basis for the social renovation of the world. Several of its members became involved in the socialist movement.

who defended artificial birth control; he introduced Margaret Sanger to Malthus and to eugenics, convincing her to lead the birth control movement in America; he heartily supported Ellen Key's plea for marriage reform, and was the long-lasting intellectual soulmate and admirer of the Victorian rebel Olive Schreiner. Discredited both for alleged love affairs and sexual impotence, Ellis led a life as unconventional as his writings. Deliberately flouting established moral conventions, he married the lesbian feminist writer Edith Lees in an attempt to experiment with a new, more egalitarian type of partnership between the sexes.

Havelock Ellis, *The Task of Social Hygiene* (London: Constable, 1912), pp. 129–33

It would be premature to attempt to define the exact outline of the new forms of romantic love, or the precise lineaments of the beings who will most ardently evoke that love. In literature, indeed, the ideals of life cast their shadow before, and we may surely trace a change in the erotic ideals mirrored in literature. The woman whom Dickens idealized in David Copperfield is unlike indeed to the series of women of a new type introduced by George Meredith, and the modern heroine generally exhibits more of the robust, open-eyed and spontaneous qualities of that later type than the blind and clinging nature of the amiable simpletons of the older type. That the changed conditions of civilization should produce new types of womanhood and of love is not surprising, if we realize that, even within the ancient chivalrous forms it was possible to produce similar robust types when the qualities of a race were favourable to them. Spain furnishes a notable illustration. Spanish literature from Cervantes and Tirso to Valera and Blasco Ibañez reflects a type of woman who stands on the same ground as man and is his equal and often his superior on that ground, alike in vigour of body and of spirit, acquiring all that she cares to of virility, while losing nothing feminine that is of worth. [*Footnote*: Havelock Ellis, *The Soul of Spain*, chap. III, 'The Women of Spain'.] In more than one respect the ideal woman of Spain is the ideal woman our civilization now renders necessary. The women of the future, Grete Meisel-Hess[41] declares in her femininely clever and frank discussion of present-day conditions, *Die Sexuelle Krise*, will be full, strong, elementary natures, devoid alike of the impulse to destroy or the aptitude to be destroyed. She considers, moreover, that

---

41 The Jewish feminist Grete Meisel-Hess (1879–1922).

so far from romantic love being a thing of the past, 'love as a form of worship is reserved for the future.' [*Footnote*: Grete Meisel-Hess, *Die Sexuelle Krise*, 1909, pp. 148, 168.] In the past it has only been found among a few rare souls; in the future world, fostered by the finer selection of a conscious eugenics, and a new reverence and care for motherhood, we may reasonably hope for a truly efficient humanity, the bearers and conservers of the highest human emotions. It is in this sense, indeed, that the voices of the greatest and most typical leaders of the woman's movement of emancipation to-day are heard. Ellen Key, in her *Love and Marriage*, seeks to conciliate the cultivation of a free and sacred sexual relationship with the worship of the child, as the embodiment of the future race, while Olive Schreiner proclaims in her *Woman and Labour* that the woman of the future will walk side by side with man in a higher and deeper relationship than has ever been possible before because it will involve a new community in activity and insight.

Nor is it alone from the feminine side that these forecasts are made. Certainly for the most part love has been cultivated more by women than by men. Primacy in the genius of intellect belongs incontestably to men, but in the genius of love it has doubtless oftener been achieved by women. They have usually understood better than men that in this matter, as Goethe insisted, it is the lover and not the beloved who reaps the chief fruits of love. 'It is better to love, even violently,' wrote the forsaken Portuguese nun, in her immortal *Letters*, 'than merely to be loved.' He who loses his life here saves it, for it is only in so far as he becomes a crucified god that Love wins the sacrifice of human hearts. Of late years, by an inevitable reaction, women have sometimes forgotten this eternal verity. The women of the twentieth century in their anxiety for self-possession and their rightful eagerness to gain positions they feel they have been too long excluded from, have perhaps yet failed to realize that the women of the eighteenth century, who exerted a sway over life that the women of no age before or since have possessed, were, above all women, great and heroic lovers, and that those two fundamental facts cannot be cut asunder. But this failure, temporary as it is doubtless destined to be, will work for good if it is the point of departure for a revival among men of the art of love.

Men indeed have here fallen behind women. The old saying, so tediously often quoted, concerning love as a 'thing apart' in the lives of men would scarcely have occurred to a medieval poet of Provence or Florence. It is not enough for women to proclaim a new avatar of love if men are not ready and eager to learn its art and to practise its discipline. In a profoundly suggestive fragment on love left incomplete at his death by the distinguished sociologist Tarde,[42] [*Footnote*: 'La Morale Sexuelle', *Archives d'Anthropologie Criminelle*, January 1907.] he suggests that when masculine energy dies down in the fields of political ambition and commercial gain, as it already has in the field of warfare, the energy liberated by greater social organization and cohesion may find scope once more in love. For too long a period love, like war and politics and commerce, has been chiefly monopolized by the predatory type of man, in this field symbolized by the figure of Don Juan. In the future, Tarde suggests, the Don Juan type of lover may fall into disrepute, giving place to the Virgilian type, for whom love is not a thing apart but a form of life embodying its best and highest activities.

When we come upon utterances of this kind we are tempted to think that they represent merely the poetic dreams of individuals, standing too far ahead of their fellows to possess any significance for men and women in general. But it is probable that Ovid, and certain that Dante, set forth erotic conceptions that were unintelligible to most of their contemporaries, yet they have been immensely influential over the ideas and emotions of men in later ages. The poets and prophets of one generation are engaged in moulding ideals which will be realized in the lives of a subsequent generation; in repressing their own most intimate emotions, as it has been truly said, they become the leaders in a long file of men and women. Whatever may yet be uncertain and undefined, we may assuredly believe that the emotion of love is far too deeply rooted in the depth of man's organism and woman's organism ever to be torn out or ever to be thrust into a subordinate place. And we may also believe that there is no measurable limit to its power of putting forth ever new and miraculous flowers.

---

42 The French criminologist Gabriel Tarde (1843–1904).

References

Anderson, Olive (1991) 'The Feminism of T. H. Green: A Late-Victorian Success Story?', *History of Political Thought*, 12:4 (Winter), 671–93.

Andrews, Robert, M. (2015) *Lay Activism and the High Church Movement of the Late Eighteenth Century* (Leiden: Brill).

Auchterlonie, Mitzi (2007) *Conservative Suffragists: The Women's Vote and the Tory Party* (London: Tauris Academic Studies).

Banks, Olive (1990) *The Biographical Dictionary of British Feminists, vol. 2, A Supplement, 1900–1945* (New York: New York University Press).

Bebbington, David (1982) *The Nonconformist Conscience: Chapel and Politics, 1870–1914* (London: G. Allen & Unwin).

Bland, Lucy (1995) *Banishing the Beast: English Feminism and Sexual Morality, 1885–1914* (Harmondsworth: Penguin).

Brent, Richard (1987) *Liberal Anglican Politics: Whiggery, Religion, and Reform, 1830–1841* (Oxford: Clarendon Press).

Broughton, T. L., and Helen Rogers (2007) *Gender and Fatherhood in the Nineteenth Century* (New York: Palgrave Macmillan).

Brown, Elsa Barkley (1991) 'Polyrhythms and Improvization: Lessons for Women's History', *History Workshop Journal*, 31, 85–90.

Bryant, Margaret (1979) *The Unexpected Revolution: A Study in the History of the Education of Women and Girls in the Nineteenth Century* (University of London Institute of Education, Studies in Education, new series, 10).

Bush, Julia (2007) *Women Against the Vote: Female Anti-Suffragism in Britain* (Oxford: Oxford University Press).

Chernock, Ariane (2010) *Men and the Making of Modern Feminism* (Stanford: Stanford University Press).

Collini, Stefan (1991) *Public Moralists: Political Thought and Intellectual Life in Britain 1850–1930* (Oxford: Clarendon Press).

Crawford, Elisabeth (2006) *The Women's Suffrage Movement in Britain and Ireland* (London: Routledge).

Davidoff, Leonore, and Catherine Hall (2002) *Family Fortunes: Men and Women of the English Middle Class, 1780–1850* (Abingdon: Routledge).

Delap, Lucy (2005) 'Feminist and Anti-feminist Encounters in Edwardian Britain', *Historical Research*, 78:201, 377–99.
Delap, Lucy, Ben Griffin and Abigail Wills (eds) (2009) *The Politics of Domestic Authority in Britain since 1800* (London: Palgrave).
Dyhouse, Carol (1981) *Girls Growing Up in Late Victorian and Edwardian England* (London: Routlege & Kegan Paul).
Fletcher, Sheila (1980) *Feminists and Bureaucrats: A Study in the Development of Girls' Education in the Nineteenth Century* (Cambridge: Cambridge University Press).
— (1982) 'Co-education and the Victorian Grammar School', *History of Education*, 1:2, 87–98.
Frost, G. (2008) *Living in Sin: Cohabiting as Husband and Wife in Nineteenth-century England* (Manchester: Manchester University Press).
Fryer, Peter (1965) *The Birth Controllers* (London: Secker & Warburg).
Geddes Poole, Andrea (2014) *Philanthropy and the Construction of Victorian Women's Citizenship* (Toronto: University of Toronto Press).
Gill, Sean (1994) *Women and the Church of England from the Eighteenth Century to the Present* (London: SPCK).
Gleadle, Kathryn (1995) *The Early Feminists: Radical Unitarians and the Emergence of the Women's Rights Movements, 1831–51* (Basingstoke: Palgrave Macmillan).
— (2002) *Radical Writing on Women, 1800–1850* (Basingstoke: Palgrave).
Goldman, Lawrence (ed.) (1989) *The Blind Victorian: Henry Fawcett and British Liberalism* (Cambridge: Cambridge University Press).
— (2004) *Science, Reform, and Politics in Victorian Britain: The Social Science Association. 1857–1886* (Cambridge: Cambridge University Press).
Griffin, Ben (2014) *The Politics of Gender in Victorian Britain: Masculinity, Political Culture and the Struggle for Women's Rights* (Cambridge: Cambridge University Press).
Hammerton, A. J. (1992) *Cruelty and Companionship: Conflict in Nineteenth-century Married Life* (London: Routledge).
John, Angela V. and Clare Eustance (eds) (1997) *The Men's Share? Masculinities, Male Support and Women's Suffrage in Britain, 1890–1920* (London: Routledge).
Kamm, Josephine (2010) *Hope Deferred: Girls' Education in English History* (London: Routledge Revivals).
Kent, Christopher (1978) *Brains and Numbers: Elitism, Comtism, and Democracy in Mid-Victorian England* (Toronto: University of Toronto Press).
Kimmel, Michael S., and Peter F. Murphy (2004) *Feminism and Masculinities* (Oxford: Oxford University Press).
Kitson Clark, G. (1973) *Churchmen and the Condition of England, 1832–1885* (London: Methuen).
Leighton, Denys, P. (2004) *The Greenian Moment: T. H. Green, Religion and Political Argument in Victorian Britain* (Exeter: Imprint Academic).

Lewis, Jane (ed.) (1986) *Labour and Love* (Oxford: Blackwell).
Lloyd, Jennifer M. (2009) *Women and the Shaping of British Methodism: Persistent Preachers, 1807–1907* (Manchester: Manchester University Press).
McCalman, Iain (1980) 'Females, Feminism and Free Love in an Early Nineteenth-Century Radical Movement', *Labour History*, 38 (May), 1–25.
McCormack, Matthew (2007) *Public Men: Masculinity and Politics in Modern Britain* (Basingstoke: Palgrave Macmillan).
McLaren, Angus (1978) *Birth Control in Nineteenth-century England* (London: Croom Helm).
Monacelli, Martine (2005) 'A Guru for British Eugenicists? Auguste Forel and the *New Age*', *Franco-British Studies*, Journal of the University of London Institute in Paris, 36, 47–62.
— (2010) 'Effacer la faute d'Eve: tentatives des militantes anglaises au dix-neuvième siècle pour (re) penser l'origine', *Résonances*, 11 (June), 11–25.
— (2011) 'Le nouveau libéralisme entre réforme et utopie: le cas des *Young Liberals* (1903–1914)', *Revue française de civilisation britannique*, 16:2, 61–74.
Monacelli, Martine, and Michel Prum (dir.) (2010) *Ces hommes qui épousèrent la cause des femmes* (Paris: Editions de l'Atelier).
Nelson, Claudia (1995) *Invisible Men: Fatherhood in Victorian Periodicals, 1850–1910* (London: The University of Georgia Press).
Norman, Edward (1987) *The Victorian Christian Socialists* (Cambridge: Cambridge University Press).
Pankhurst, Richard K. (1954) *William Thompson, 1775–1833. Britain's Pioneer Socialist, Feminist, and Co-operator* (London: Watts & Co).
Parry, Jonathan (2006) *The Politics of Patriotism: English Liberalism, National Identity and Europe, 1830–1886* (Cambridge: Cambridge University Press).
Pugh, Martin (2000) *The March of the Women: A Revisionist Analysis of the Campaign for Women's Suffrage, 1866–1914* (Oxford: Oxford University Press).
Richards, N. J. (1977) 'British Nonconformity and the Liberal Party, 1868–1906', *Journal of Religious History*, 9:4, 387–401.
Richter, Melvin (1964) *The Politics of Conscience: T. H. Green and His Age* (Cambridge, MA: Harvard University Press).
Rover, Constance (1967) *Women's Suffrage and Party Politics in Britain* (London: Routledge & Kegan Paul).
Rowbotham, Judith (1989) *Good Girls Make Good Wives: Guidance for Girls in Victorian Fiction* (Oxford: Blackwell).
Royle, Edward (1974) *Victorian Infidels: The Origins of the British Secularist Movement 1791–1866* (Manchester: Manchester University Press).
— (1980) *Radicals, Secularists and Republicans: Popular Freethought in Britain, 1866–1915* (Manchester: Manchester University Press).
Schwartz, Laura (2013) *Infidel Feminism: Secularism, Religion and Women's Emancipation, 1830–1914* (Manchester: Manchester University Press).
Schwarzkopf, Jutta (1991) *Women in the Chartist Movement* (London: Macmillan).

Scotland, Nigel (2007) *Squires in the Slums: Settlements and Missions in Late Victorian Britain* (London: Tauris).

Scott, Gillian (1998) *Feminism and the Politics of Working Women: The Women's Co-operative Guild, 1880s to the Second World War* (London: Routledge).

Shanley, Mary Lyndon (1989) *Feminism, Marriage, and the Law in Victorian England* (Princeton: Princeton University Press).

Shoemaker, Robert B. (1998) *Gender in English Society, 1650–1850: The Emergence of Separate Spheres?* (London: Longman).

Skinner, Quentin (1969) 'Meaning and Understanding in the History of Ideas', *History and Theory*, 8, 3–53.

Strange, Julie-Marie (2015) *Fatherhood and the British Working Class, 1865–1914* (Cambridge: Cambridge University Press).

Strauss, Sylvia (1982) *Traitors to the Masculine Cause: The Men's Campaigns for Women's Rights* (Westport, CT, and London: Greenwood Press).

Taylor, Barbara (1983) *Eve and the New Jerusalem* (London; Virago Press).

Thompson, Lawrence (1971), *The Enthusiasts: A Biography of John & Katharine Bruce Glasier* (London: Victor Gollancz).

Tosh, John (1999) *A Man's Place: Masculinity and the Middle-class Home in Victorian England* (London: Yale University Press).

— (2005) *Manliness and Masculinities in Nineteenth-century Britain: Essays on Gender, Family and Empire* (New York, Pearson Education).

Vicinus, Martha (1985) *Independent Women: Work and Community for Single Women, 1850–1920* (Chicago: University of Chicago Press).

Vickery, Amanda (ed.) (2001) *Women, Privilege and Power: British Politics 1750 to the Present* (Stanford: Stanford University Press).

Watts, Ruth (1998) *Gender, Power and the Unitarians in England, 1760–1860* (London: Longman).

Wormwell, D. (1977) *Sir J. R. Seeley and the Uses of History* (Cambridge: Cambridge University Press).

Index

Acland, Alice 151
Acland, Arthur 151n.32
Acland, Thomas Dyke (11th Baronet) 32, 89, 151n.32
Acton, William 170
Adams, J. C. 22
Adams, William 119
Adams, William Bridges (Junius Redivivus) 10, 119–20, 121n.3
Agg-Gardner, James Tynte 38n.177
Aitkin, John 10, 10n.47
Aldred, Guy Alfred 14, 60n.15
Allbutt, Henry Arthur 35
Allinson, T. R. 35, 35n.167
Amberley, John Russell (Viscount) 178n.30
Amos, Sheldon 30
Applegarth, Robert 31, 31n.146
Arnold, Matthew 32n.151, 33
Arnold, Thomas 16, 16n.82, 32n.151, 117, 173n.23
Ashley-Cooper, Anthony (7th Earl of Shaftesbury) 5, 92
Ashurst, W. H. 8, 8n.39, 10n.50, 11n.53, 31n.148, 64
Aspland, Robert 24, 123
Asquith, Herbert 17n.88, 39, 145, 148
Astell, Mary 5n.22
Aveling, Edward Bibens 13n.62, 60–1

Bacon, Francis 155
Badley, J. H. 115
Bailey, Samuel 11
Bainton, George 20, 162n.7
Balfour, Clara Lucas 67
Ball, W. P. 25
Bamford, Samuel 151n.32
Bamford-Slack, John 38n.177
Barbauld, Anna Laetitia 2n.7
Baring, Evelyn (1st Earl of Cromer) 41n.194
Barker, Joseph 25, 170n.21
Barmby, Catherine 6, 7n.33
Barmby, John Goodwyn 6, 6n.27, 8, 8n.38, 44, 49
Barnett, Samuel 17n.88
Bax, Belfort 60
Beach, Michael Hicks 83
Beale, Dorothy 88, 89
Beard, John Relly 10n.47
Bebel, August 61, 183
Becker, Lydia 41n.193
Beesly, Emily 15
Bennett, Louie 151n.31
Bentham, Jeremy 9n.44, 34, 45, 53, 135, 59n.4, 165
Besant, Annie 3n.14, 13n.64–5, 14n.71, 19n.94, 20, 26n.119, 36n.168, 36n.170, 37, 57n.11, 60–1, 64, 170n.21, 182
Bethell (Beauclerc), Marie 22n.103
biblical criticism 23–5, 74, 185

women's biblical criticism 26n.119
Biggs, William 8n.35, 49, 55
Billington-Greig, Teresa 40
birth control 14, 14n.72–3, 33–8, 33n.157, 35n.163–7, 36n.168, 37n.171, 38n.174–5, 44, 52, 52n.4, 61, 64, 111, 151, 157–60, 159n.4, 165n.9, 169, 170, 170n.19, 178–82, 182n.31
  and eugenics 37, 190–1
  and Fabians 37, 37n.173
  and Malthusian League 36–7, 61n.20, 170, 178, 190
  and physicians 35, 35n.165
  and Socialists 61, 61n.20, 111
Blackwell, Elisabeth 19, 35n.165, 97, 106
Blair, W. T. 20
Blatchford, Robert 60n.17
Bodichon, Barbara *see* Leigh Smith (Bodichon), Barbara
Bondfield, Margaret 41n.191
Bone, Florence 71
Booth, Charles 143
Boucherette, Jessie 29n.137
Boulanger, Nicolas-Antoine 160
Bourne, Hugh 69
Bouverie *see* Pleydell-Bouverie, Edward
Bowring, née Castle, Lady Deborah 6n.24
Boyd-Kinnear, John 124
Bradlaugh, Alice 61
Bradlaugh (Bonner), Hypatia 13n.65
Bradlaugh, Charles 11n.54, 12, 12n.59, 13, 25, 25n.112, 36, 36n.168, 36n.170, 60–1, 64, 170n.20
Brailsford, Henry 144n.25, 151n.33
Brassey, Thomas 31
Bray, Charles 3n.14, 14, 165n.12

Bray, John Francis 7n.34
Bridges, Mary Alice 15
Bright, Jacob 30, 30n.141, 32n.150, 38n.177, 41, 104, 117n.27
Broad Church movement 14n.75, 15–16, 16n.79, 25, 107–8
  and evolution 77, 187, 189
Broadhurst, Thomas 85
Brooke, Emma 139
Brougham, H. P. (1st Baron Brougham and Vaux) 30–2, 56, 104, 126–7, 127n.10, 129n.15, 132
Browne, Stella 190
Brunswick, Caroline of 126–7
Bryant, Sophie 21n.100
Bryce, James 22, 32, 32n.152
Buckingham, James Silk 10
Burke, Gertrude 185
Burns, Emile 151n.33
Burrows, Herbert 61
Bushnell, Katherine 25n.115
Busk, Alice 19
Buss, Frances Mary 21n.100, 22n.104, 23, 60, 88, 108
Butler, George 22, 30n.139
Butler, Josephine 2n.4, 5n.23, 17, 30, 56, 96, 124n.7, 132n.18
Butler, William 23

Cady Stanton, Elisabeth 74
Caird, Mona 13n.65, 139n.22
Campion, William 35n.162
Carlile, Richard 3n.8, 4n.17, 35, 35n.163, 64, 123n.5, 155–8, 155n.1
Carlisle, George Howard (7th Earl of) 127n.10
Carlyle, Thomas 4n.18, 96n.8
Carpenter, Edward 40n.186, 143, 181–2, 182n.31
Carpenter, J. Estlin 9n.45
Carr, George Shoobridge 37

Carus-Wilson, William 6n.25
Case, William 10n.50
Cattell, Christopher Charles 13n.67
Cave-Brown-Cave, Frances and Beatrice Mabel 140
Cayley, Arthur 22
Cecil, Lord Robert (Viscount Cecil of Chelwood) 41
Chadwick, Edwin 29n.133
Chapman, Cecil 41
Chapman, Elisabeth Rachel 20, 24
Chapman, Hugh 185
Chappellsmith, Margaret 7n.33, 13n.61, 67
Chartism 3n.11, 3n.14, 4n.18, 6–9, 8n.35–40, 9n.41, 9n.43, 11n.54, 17n.56, 18, 33n.156, 48–9, 48n.2, 64, 96, 119n.1, 123
    Female Chartist Associations 8, 9n.41, 48n.2, 69n.26
    women's suffrage 7–8, 8n.40
Chatterton, Daniel 61n.20
Chesterton, G. K. 161
Chichester, née Ford, Sophia 3n.8
Christian Socialism 18–21, 18n.91, 19n.93–4, 20, 27n.125, 88–9, 173
    muscular Christianity 89, 96, 135n.21
    women's education 21–3
Clapperton, Jane Hume 139n.22
Clarke, Adam 69
Clayton, Godwin 41
Clayton, Joseph 40n.183, 150–2
Cleave, John 35n.164
Clough, Ann 21n.101, 22, 174
Cobb, Elisabeth 139
Cobbe, Frances Power 13n.65, 14n.71, 26n.119, 72
Cobbett, William 155, 157n.2, 159–62, 162n.8, 175

Coit, Stanton 14n.74
Colenso, J. W. 25
Coleridge, S. T. 16, 18
    national clerisy 16n.81
Coley, Samuel 69
Collet, Collet Dobson 8
Collet, Sophia Dobson 13n.65, 26n.119, 57n.11, 170n.21
Collins, John 9n.43
Comte, Auguste 14, 15, 28n.131, 64
    Positivism 75
    Religion of Humanity 14n.75, 64, 173
Condorcet, Nicolas (marquis de) 4n.17
Congreve, Richard 14n.75
Connolly, James 151n.31
Contagious Diseases Acts see prostitution
Cookson see Crackanthorpe, né Cookson, Montague Hughes
Cooper, Robert 24
Co-operatism 18n.91, 44–6, 44n.1, 64, 88, 150–3, 151n.32, 152n.38, 165, 165n.14, 166
    Women's Co-operative Guild 36n.168, 108, 151, 153–4
Copley, John Singleton (1st Baron Lyndhurst) 127n.13
Corben, Louisa 18
Cosmo Gordon Lang, William 18, 74
Courtney, K. D. 151n.33
Courtney, Leonard Henry 38n.177, 41, 41n.195
Cowper-Temple, William Francis 10n.14
Cowrie, John 66, 66n.23
Cox, Francis A. 24
Crackanthorpe, Blanche 178
Crackanthorpe, né Cookson, Montague Hughes 35n.166, 177–9, 178n.30

Index

Craig, Isa 30
Creighton, Louise 18, 18n.89
Cromer, Lord *see* Baring, Evelyn (1st Earl of Cromer)
Crompton, Mary 108
Crosskey, H. W. 24, 24n.110
Curzon, George Nathaniel (Marquess Curzon of Kedleston) 41n.194

Dale, Caroline 165
Dale, Thomas 22
Darwin, Charles 28n.131, 60, 96, 111, 113
Davidson, Thomas 19n.40
Davies, Emily 4n.20, 5n.23, 20, 29n.137, 32, 92, 108, 174
Davies, John Llewelyn 14n.75, 22, 32, 107–8, 174
Davies, Margaret C. Llewelyn 108, 151
Dawson, George 10, 10n.51, 119
Dawson, Julia 36n.168
Denison, Edward 17n.84
Denman, Thomas (3rd Baron) 38n.177
Despard, Charlotte 40, 182
Dickens, Charles 123, 191
Dickinson, W. H. 38n.177, 151n.33
Dilke, Sir Charles (2nd Baronet) 38n.177
Dimsdale, Robert (Baron) 38n.177
Disraeli, Benjamin 26n.120, 104
Dissenters 3n.10
  Baptists 69
  Methodism 5n.22, 20n.98, 69, 69n.26
  Nonconformist conscience 27, 27n.125, 56
  Quakers 7n.29, 69
  Unitarians 3n.12, 9–11, 9n.44–5, 11n.54, 23n.108, 56n.7, 120, 121n.3, 122–3, 123n.14, 170n.18
divorce, views on 66, 79, 120–2, 129n.15, 132, 166, 170
divorce acts 26n.120, 127, 127n.13, 133
Dixie, Florence 14n.68, 66
Doherty, Hugh 52n.5
Downes, Robert Percival 69–71
Drysdale, Charles Robert 36, 60n.15, 170, 170n.20
Drysdale, Charles Vickery 38n.174
Drysdale, George Robert 4n.17, 14, 36n.170, 66, 157, 169–71
Dugdale (Duval), Una 147, 185
Dunstan, Walter 35n.165
Duval, Elsie 147
Duval, Ernest 147
Duval, Victor 40, 40n.186, 40n.189, 143, 147–8, 185

Ede, Sarah Moore 74
Ede, William Moore 74
Edgeworth, Maria 90, 90n.5
Edwards-Heathcote, Justinian 42
Eliot, George 15, 19n.95, 60n.15, 141
Ellis, Henry Havelock 115n.24, 189–91
Elmy, Benjamin William 14, 30, 41, 60n.15
equal pay 151n.33, 190
Estlin, J. P. 10n. 46, 123n.4
Ethical movement 14, 14n.74, 21n.100
Eugenics 34, 37, 115, 115n.24, 139–40, 178, 190–2
Evangelicals 5–6, 5n.21–3, 174n.25

Faithfull, Emily 29n.137
Faithfull, Lilian Mary 2, 2n.5, 5n.23
Faithfull Begg, Ferdinand 38n.177, 42n.197
Farnworth, Richard 69
Farrar, F. W. 21n.102, 25, 25n.116

fatherhood, views on 85, 96, 104, 127n.9, 161, 161n.5, 162, 164, 174–6, 175n.28
Fawcett, Cicely 140
Fawcett, Henry 27n.123, 29n.133, 36n.168, 135–6, 178
Fawcett, née Garrett, Millicent 19, 39, 102, 135–6
Fenwick Miller, Florence 13n.65
Ferard, Elizabeth 17n.83
Finch, John 66
Fitch, Joshua 4n.20, 22, 32, 33n.155, 83, 89
Fleming, G. A. 7n.31
Fletcher Welch, née Ford, Georgiana 3n.8
Flower, Benjamin 119, 119n.2
Flower, Eliza 123
Flower, Sarah 119
Follen, Eliza Lee Cabot 11
Foote, G. W. 14, 14n.69, 155
Forel, Auguste 35n.165
Forster, John 11
Forsyth, William 104–5
Fourier, Charles 52, 52n.5
Fox, Eliza 123n.6
Fox, W. J. 9, 10, 64, 120, 121n.3, 122–4, 123n.5, 155
Francis, J. E. 41
Frankin, Laura and Leonard 40n.183
Franklin, Benjamin 137
Franklin, Hugh A. 148n.29
Freethought *see* Secularism
Fremantle, W. A. 17
Frend, William 10
Freud, Sigmund 170, 189n.39
Froebel, Friedrich 115
Froude, James Anthony 175
Fry, Elisabeth 96
Fuller, Margaret 68

Galsworthy, John 40n.186

Galton, Francis 37, 139, 178
Gardiner, A. G. 144n.25
Garrard, William 8
Garrett (Anderson), Elisabeth 106
Geddes, Alexander 23n.108
George, Walter Lionel 77–9
Gillespie, H. J. 41
Gladstone, Herbert 27, 135
Glasier, John B. 60n.16
Glasier, Katherine 60n.16, 181
Godwin, William 4n.17, 7n.32, 34, 141
Goethe, J. W., von 141, 192
Gonne, Thomas 40n.186
Gore, Charles 18, 19n.92, 24–5, 25n.117, 26n.120, 74, 186
Gott, J. W. 14n.72
Grant, Alexander (10th Baronet) 100–1
Grant, Cecil 115–16
Green, Charlotte 21n.100
Green, T. H. 17n.88, 18, 20n.98, 21, 21n.100, 22n.103, 25, 25n.114, 27, 27n.126, 28n.129, 32, 42, 42n.200, 52n.6, 57n.11, 111, 151
Greenhough, J. G. 20
Grey, Charles (2nd Earl) 67
Grey, Maria 4n.20
Grimstone, Mary Leman 7n.3
Gurney, Russell 32n.150, 101n.14, 132n.18

Halliday, Andrew 175, 175n.29
Hammond, J. L. 130n.16
Hansard, Septimus 19
Harben, H. D. 37n.173
Harcourt, Lewis Vernon (1st Viscount) 147n.26
Hardie, Keir 41, 41n.196, 60
Hardy, E. J. 20
Hardy, Thomas 40n.186
Hare, Thomas 32n.150

Harrison, Ethel 15
Harte, Richard 35n.166
Hartley, David 9n.44
Haslam, Thomas J. 35n.166
Hassell, Richard 35n.162
Hasting, G. W. 30–1, 66n.24, 89, 127n.12
Hastings, Beatrice 37n.173
Haughton, James 8, 49
Hawkes, Sidney 10n.50
Headlam, Stewart D. 19n.94, 61n.20
Henderson, Arthur 41n.191
Hennell, Charles 24
Hennell, Sara 3n.14, 5n.21, 13n.65, 26n.119, 57n.11
Henry, Agnes 13n.63
Herbert, Auberon 31
Hetherington, Henry 35n.164
Heyrick, Elizabeth 2n.7
Higgins, Geoffrey 24
Hill, Frederic 10n.48
Hill, J. W., Major 15n.33
Hill, James and Caroline 49
Hill, Matthew Davenport 10, 31
Hill, Octavia 17, 88
Hincks, T. D. 10n.47
Hinscliff, Claude 74
Hinton, James 190, 190n.40
Hitchman, William 35n.165
Hobhouse, Arthur (1st Baron Hobhouse of Hadspen) 32n.154, 97, 127n.12, 130–2,
Hobhouse, L. T. 28n.129, 130n.16
Hobson, J. A. 37
Hodgson, Norman 116
Hodgson, W. B. 89n.4
Holland, Henry Richard Vassall-Fox (3rd Baron) 83n.1
Holland, Henry Scott 18, 19n.92, 25, 26n.120, 27n.125, 74
Holt, George 10n.46, 22n.104
Holyoake, Austin 35n.164, 35n.166

Holyoake, George 11n.54, 12, 12n.57–9, 14–15, 18n.91, 24n.111, 26n.119, 29n.133, 31n.149, 64–6, 92, 155, 165n.12
Hone, William 155
Hopkins, Ellis 17, 186n.37
Hopkins, Joshua 60n.15
Horner, Francis 83
Horsley, Victor 41
Hort, F. J. A. 20
Hoskyns, Edwyn 18
Howard, Geoffrey 38n.177
Howard, George *see* Carlisle, George Howard (7th Earl of)
Hughes, Hugh Price 20, 20n.98, 27n.125–6
Hughes, Thomas 16n.82, 32, 135, 135n.21
Hume, David 144n.24
Hunt, Henry (Orator) 39n.178, 155
Hyndman, Henry 60

Independent Labour Party (ILP) 150, 181,
Inge, Susanna 8n.40
Ironside, Isaac 8
Ishill, Joseph 190

Jackson, Henry 22
Jacobinism 7n.32
Jacobs, Herbert 40n.186
James, John Angell 70n.28
Jamrach, A. W. G. 40n.186
Jarrett, Rebecca 56
Jebb, Ann 2n.7
Jebb, R. C. 22
Jeffrey, Francis 83
Jerrold, D. W. 11n.53, 66
Jewsbury, Geraldine 66, 66n.22
Jex-Blake, Sophia 101
Johnson, Samuel ('Dr') 146
Jones, Margaret Wynne 143

Jowett, Benjamin 16n.82, 21–2, 25, 25n.113
Joyce, Jeremiah 10n.47, 10n.48

Kaye-Smith, Sheila 78
Kemp, George 38n.177
Kenney, Annie 40n.190
Ker, W. P. 10 1n.15
Keswick, J. B. 35n.166
Key, Ellen 191, 192
Kingsley, Charles 22, 29n.133, 96–7, 150
Knight, Anne 7, 8, 8n.40
Knowlton, Charles 36n.170, 157
Kropotkin (Lebedeff), Sasha 78
Kropotkin, P. A. 143, 181
Kyllmann, Max 41

Laing, David 22, 22n.105, 23
Lallemand, François 171, 171n.22
LaMont, John 8
Lansbury, George 41, 41n.196
Lansdowne, Henry Charles Keith Petty-Fitzmaurice (5th Marquess of) 129
Lant Carpenter, Russell 10, 10n.48, 123
Law, Harriet 13n.64, 13n.66, 64, 170n.21
Lawrence (Pethick-Lawrence), Frederick 40, 41
Lee, Alice 140
Lee, Rachel F. A. ('Baroness Despenser') 2n.7
Lees, Edith 182, 191
Leigh Smith (Bodichon), Barbara 31, 52, 66, 136
Leman, Mary Grimstone 66
Lequinio, Joseph-Marie 160
Levy, J. H. 31
Lewes, George Henry 60n.15, 141
Lewis, Sarah 5n.21
Lewis-Faning, E. 38n.175

Liberal Anglicans *see* Broad Church movement
Liberal reforms 26–8
and Fabians 28n.131, 111
New Liberalism 28, 28n.130, 111, 143
social gospel 42
Young Liberals 147
Lidgett, J. S. 19
Linton, W. J. 10, 10n.51, 49
Lloyd George, David 143, 147n.26, 148
Locke, John 9n.44
Lovett, William 8–9, 9n.43, 44n.1, 64, 70n.28
Ludlow, J. M. 20
Lyndhurst *see* Copley, John Singleton (1st Baron Lyndhurst)
Lyttelton, Edward 24, 58n.14
Lyttelton, G. W. (4th Baron) 4n.20, 32n.154
Lytton, Victor Alexander George Robert Bulwer-Lytton (2nd Earl of) 41

Macarthur, Mary 41n.191
Macauley, Eliza 7n.33, 13n.61
MacLaren, Duncan 31n.148
Malleson, Elisabeth 21
Malthus, T. R. 4n.17, 34, 34n.159, 35, 36n.169, 44, 61n.20, 96, 169, 178, 191
see also birth control
Mansfield, Katherine 88
Marcet, Jane 10n.46, 86
Margoliouth, D. S. 15n.78
Markby, Thomas 22
marriage, views on 7n.32, 10n.50–1, 11, 13n.66, 14, 19–20, 24n.110, 31, 34, 35n.166, 38n.175, 44–5, 49, 52n.6, 53, 60n.15–16, 61, 64, 66, 79, 120–3, 121n.3, 126–7, 127n.13, 132n.18, 134,

139, 140–2, 148, 157, 161,
162, 162n.7, 166–70, 166n.15,
167n.16, 172, 178–85, 186n.35,
190–1
domestic abuse 19, 24, 27, 52,
129n.15, 132n.18
married women's property rights
10, 10n.50, 13n.67, 19, 26,
30n.141, 31, 31n.144, 41n.193,
65, 89, 108, 123–4, 126–30,
128n.14, 132, 132n.17–18,
133–5, 154, 154n.39
Marsh, Catherine 96
Marshall, Alfred 22
Martin, Emma 7, 7n.33, 13n.61,
26n.119, 60n.15, 67
Martin, T. Carlaw 28n.128
Martineau, Harriet 10n.46, 13n.65,
15, 15n.76, 26n.119, 66, 86,
120
Martineau, James 9n.44, 23n.108
Marx, Eleanor 60–1, 139
Marx, Karl 60, 61n.20, 166
Mason, Charlotte 115
Mason, Hugh 38n.177
Massey, Gerald 8, 8n.36
Massingham, Henry 143
Masterman, C. F. G. 37, 147n.26
Maudsley, Henry 112
Maurice, Frederik Denis 16n.82, 18,
18n.90–1, 19, 19n.94, 20–2,
29n.133, 88–9, 96–7, 107–9,
150, 174, 174n.25
Mayer, H. V. 13n.67
McCabe, Joseph 25
McCullough, J. R. 35
McLaren, Charles 38n.177
McLaren, W. S. B. 38n.177
Mechanics' Institutes 3n.12, 11
Meisel-Hess, Grete 191, 191n.41,
192
Meredith, George, 191
Merrill, George 181

Meteyard, Eliza 11
Meynell, Francis 40n.183
Mill, James 4n.17, 52n.4
Mill, John Stuart 4n.15, 29n.133, 31,
34, 52–3, 52n.4, 104–5, 135–6,
143, 144
Miller, J. R. 20
Mitchell, Kate 35n.165
Mond, Alfred 39n.182
Montessori, Maria 115
More, Hannah 6n.25
Morell, John 10
Morley, Henry 10n.15
Morley, Samuel 57
Morris, William 181
Morrison, Frances 7n.33, 166n.15
Morrison, James 151
Mozley, Herbert Newman 28n.128,
132n.18
Mundella, A. J. 30
Myers, F. W. H. 127n.12

Nash, Henry 22n.104
National Association for the
    Promotion of Social Science
    (SSA) 28–32, 28n.104,
    28n.132, 29n.135, 38, 127–8
    and Contagious Diseases
        Acts 30, 30n.138, 30n.143,
        31n.145–6
    and Married Women Property
        Act 31
    and women's education 32–3
    and women's suffrage 38
    and women's work 31
Neesom, Charles. H. 8, 8n.37
Nevinson, Henry 41, 143–4
New Woman, 70, 79
Newman, Francis W. 25, 30, 170n.21
Newton, Isaac, 28n.131, 102, 155
Nightingale, Florence 96, 139
Norgate, Thomas Starling 39n.178
Norris, J. P. 89

Northcroft, George J. H. 70
Norton, Caroline 123

O'Connor, Feargus 49
Ogden, C. K. (Adelyne More, pseudo) 34n.158
Oliphant, Margaret 53
Ossoli, née Fuller, Margaret 99, 99n.12
Owen, Robert 3n.8, 6, 6n.26, 6n.28, 7, 7n.32, 11, 11n.52, 12, 18n.91, 28n.131, 44, 52, 64, 88, 92, 150, 151n.33, 165–6, 165n.10, 165n.13–14, 166
  Rational Society 6n.26, 166
  science of society 165
  social missionaries 7n.23, 12, 13n.61
  Socialist movement 6–7
Owen, Robert Dale 157, 165n.9, 170n.19

Paine, Thomas 4n.16, 155
Palmer, Elihu 155, 158
Palmer, John Henry 35n.166
Palmer, Susanna 132n.18
Pankhurst, Christabel 40
Pankhurst, Emmeline 40
Pankhurst, Richard Marsden 41, 41n.193
Pankhurst, Sylvia 40n.186, 40n.188, 40n.190, 182
Parkes (Belloc), Bessie Rayner 2n.5, 29n.137, 56, 66
Parry, J. H. 8, 10n.50
Paterson, Emma 15, 15n.77, 31
Paterson, Thomas 15n.77
Pattison, Francis 15
Pattison, Mark 21
Pearson, Charles Henry 132n.18
Pearson, Karl 138–40
Pease (Nichol), Elisabeth 29n.137
Peel, Sir Robert (2nd Baronet) 68

Peile, John 174
Percival, John 22
Perry, Sir Thomas Erskine 127n.11, 127n.13
Pestalozzi, J. H. 10, 115, 165n.11
Pethick (Pethick-Lawrence), Emmeline 17n.85, 20n.98, 40n.190
Phipson, Emma 158n.3
Place (Adams), Elisabeth 119
Place, Francis 34–5, 52, 52n.4, 119, 119n.1, 157
Playfair, Lyon (1st Baron) 106
Pleydell-Bouverie, Edward 137
Portal, Ethel 19
Potter (Webb), Beatrix 15, 17, 41n.195
Pratt, Hodgson 31, 31n.149
Priestley, Joseph 9n.44, 23n.108, 88, 123, 165n.12
Primrose League 42
Procter, Adelaide 29n.137
prostitution 10n.50, 14, 55–6, 56n.7, 57n.11, 121n.3, 123, 140, 168, 170, 170n.18, 183–4
  Contagious Diseases Acts 8n.39, 17n.87, 20n.98, 26, 30, 30n.138, 30n.143, 31n.145–6, 56, 56n.9, 61–2, 140
Prout, Victor 40n.186
public halls 3n.11

radicalism 2, 2n.6, 3, 4n.15, 11, 34, 34n.160, 56, 69
radical circles 2n.7, 3, 3n.9, 4, 4n.15, 8n.35, 13–14, 14n.75, 16, 18, 19, 22, 29n.133, 34n.160, 56n.7, 119, 119n.1–2, 123, 139, 155, 157, 158n.3, 161n.6, 167n.16, 190
Ratcliff, Dorothy Una 71
Rathbone, Eleanor 21n.100
Redalls, George 14
Rees, Joseph Aubrey 147n.26

Reid, Anne 162
Reid, Marion 8n.40
Reid, R. T. 57
Renan, Ernest 19n.95
Renwick, George 42n.197
Reynolds, W. H. 37
Ricardo, David 28n.131, 169
Richardson, Benjamin Ward 73
Richardson, Mary 40n.190
Richardson, Reginald John 8, 48–9
Rigg, J. R. 70
Ritchie, D. G. 37, 111–12
Roalfe, Matilda 13n.63
Robertson, J. M. 13n.67, 14n.72, 24, 6In.20, 147n.27
Robins, E. 40n.190
Robinson, Hugh 23n.106, 32n.154
Roby, Henry 32, 32n.152
Roebuck, J. A. 8
Rogers, John 69
Rollitt, Sir Albert Kaye 38n.177
Ross, W. S. 14n.68
Roundell, Charles S. 22
Royden, Agnes Maude 18, 75
Ruskin, John 29n.133, 70, 94, 105, 181
Russell, John (1st Earl Russell) 27n.122, 39

Saint Simonians 7n.29, 52, 52n.5
Saleeby, C. W. 115
Salisbury, Robert Arthur Talbot Gascoyne-Cecil (3rd Marquess of) 41
Salt, T. C. 8
Sanger, Margaret 33n.157, 191
Scharlieb, Mary 35n.165
Schreiner, Olive 139, 181, 191–2
Scott, Benjamin 56n.9
Scott, Thomas 3n.14
Scott, Walter 107
Secularism 3n.14, 5n.21, 11–15, 35, 64, 155

Secularist papers 13–14
Seeley, Frances 174
Seeley, John Robert 16n.80, 19n.95, 21n.102, 173–5, 173n.23, 174n.25
Selborne, William Waldegrave Palmer (2nd Earl of) 27n.127, 41
Shackleton, David James 38n.177, 151n.31
Shaen, William 10n.50, 11, 11n.53, 31, 31n.145, 55, 175n.28
Shaftesbury, Lord see Ashley-Cooper, Anthony (7th Earl of Shaftesbury)
Sharp, Evelyn 143
Sharpe, Maria 139n.22
Sharples, Eliza 6n.28, 13n.61, 66n.24, 157
Shaw, George Bernard 40n.186, 158n.3, 190
Shaw-Lefevre, G. J. 32n.150
Shepherd, William 10n.48
Sherwin, William 155
Sherwood, Richard 41
Sidgwick, Henry 21, 21n.101, 22, 174
Simpson, David 69n.26
Slack, Ada 36n.168
Smiles, Samuel 28, 70
Smith, Adam 169
Smith, James Elishama 6, 6n.28
Smith, Mary 39n.178
Smith, Saba, Lady Holland 85, 85n.2
Smith, Sheila Kaye 78
Smith, Sydney 83–5, 101
Smith, William 10n.50
Snead-Cox, J. G. 150
Snowden, Philip 41, 41n.196
Social Darwinism 112n.19
Socialism 60, 60n.16, 111, 123, 166, 190n.40
see also Owen, Robert

Solly, Henry 31, 31n.149
Somerville, Mary 86, 109
Southcott, Joanna 7n.29
Southwell, Charles 13, 13n.66
Southwood Smith, Thomas 10, 10n.49, 11n.53
Sowden, Mary 13n.65
Spence, Thomas 119n.1
Spencer, Frederick Augustus Morland 185–6, 185n.33
Spencer, Herbert 112, 112n.19, 115, 175n.27
Squier, J. O. 24
Staël, Germaine de 66
Standring, George 37, 61n.20
Stanger, Henry York 38n.177
Stansfeld, James 10n.50, 15, 31, 31n.148, 55
Stead, Estelle Wilson 57n.12
Stead, W. T. 56–7, 61
Steinthal, S. A. 41
Stephen, Leslie 96
Steuart, James 34n.159
Stewart, Dugal 83
Stopes, Mary 33n.157, 78
Strachey, Ray 2n.5
Strauss, D. F. 19n.95
Stuart, James 22
Symes, Joseph 37

Tait, A. C. 17n.83
Tait, William 56n.7
Talfourd, Thomas 10n.50, 127
Tarde, Gabriel 193, 193n.42
Tate, Joseph B. 15In.33
Tayler, J. J. 23n.108
Taylor, Charles Bell 30
Taylor, Harriet 7n.33, 52, 65, 93, 120
Taylor, Helen 158n.3
Taylor, Isaac (father and son) 161n.5
Taylor, Richard Whately Cooke 92–3, 117n.27

Taylor, Robert 24
Taylor, William Cooke 92
Temple, William 15n.78
Templetown, Henry Edward Montagu (4th Viscount) 38n.177, 42
Tennyson, Alfred 71, 100
Thom, J. H. 23n.108
Thompson, William 4n.17, 44–5, 52, 166
Thornton Smith, Miss 13n.65
Tomkinson, H. R. 89
Townsend, Joseph 34n.159, 159n.4
Toynbee, Arnold 17n.88, 111
Trevelyan, Charles 100
Truelove, Edward 35n.164, 170
Tuckwell, Gertrude 19n.94
Tuckwell, William 19
Turner, William 123
Tyler, Maude Gurney 147n.26

university settlements 17, 17n.84, 18–19, 143

Vance, Edith 13n.65
Vassal, Elisabeth 83n.1
Venturi, née Ashurst, Emilie
Vickery (Drysdale), Alice 38n.174, 60n.15
Villiers, Roland de 189n.38
Vincent, Henry 9n.42
Vogt, A. C. Carl 113–14, 113n.21
Voysey, Charles 14

Wakefield, Edward 34
Wallace, Robert 34n.159
Ward, née Arnold, Mary Augusta 42n.200
Watkins, John 8
Watson, James 35n.164
Watts, Charles 14n.68, 36n.170
Watts, Kate 13n.65, 64
Webb, Sidney 37n.173, 158n.3

Wesley, John 5n.22, 69
Westcott, Brooke Foss 19n.92, 25, 185n.34
Westlake, John 21, 21n.99, 32n.150
Wheeler, Anna 6n.28, 7, 7n.33, 44, 52n.5
Wheelwright, Edith Gray 71
Wilberforce, William 5
Wilde, Oscar 189
Wilderspin, Samuel 10
Williams, Charles Fleming 40n.183
Wilson, Charlotte 139, 139n.22
Wilson, Henry J. 30, 30n.140
Wilson, James Maurice 22n.103
Winterbotham, Henry 32n.154, 117n.27
Witcop, Rose 60n.15
Wollstonecraft, Mary 2n.7, 66, 115, 141
Wolstenholme (Elmy), Elisabeth 2n.4, 14n.73, 32n.150, 36n.168, 60n.15
woman's employment 17, 19, 19n.92, 19n.94, 31, 89n.4, 93–5, 123–6, 124n.7, 132n.18, 136, 139, 151
unions 18n.89, 31, 136, 151n.30–1

women's higher education 20n.98, 21n.101, 31n.145, 32–3, 89n.3, 92–3, 100–1, 101n.15, 105, 108–10, 132, 174, 181
biological effects of 102, 112–15
medical degrees 97, 101, 101n.14, 106–8, 110
women's suffrage 8, 8n.35–40, 10, 13n.67, 14, 20, 21n.101, 24, 30n.108, 38–43, 41n.196, 42n.197, 42n.199, 48, 52, 66, 104, 127n.10, 136–8, 141, 150, 178, 182, 185
and Church 15n.78, 17–18, 40n.183, 74, 185–9
leagues 15n.78, 40n.183, 40n.183–6
suffrage bills 38n.177, 39, 41n.193, 52, 104, 148
women Antis 1n.2, 42n.200
Woodall, William 38n.177, 41n.195
Wooler, T. J. 52n.4
Woolf, Leonard 15n.32
Worcester, Dean of *see* Ede, William Moore
Wright, Frances 7n.33

Zetetic societies 158n.3